双语名著无障碍阅读丛书

经典集锦

福尔摩斯探案经典之

血字的研究

A Study in Scarlet

[英国] 柯南·道尔 著
潘华凌 译

中国出版集团
中译出版社

图书在版编目（CIP）数据

福尔摩斯探案经典．血字的研究：汉英对照/（英）柯南道尔著；潘华凌译．—北京：中译出版社，2014.8（2023.2 重印）
（双语名著无障碍阅读丛书）
ISBN 978-7-5001-3275-2

Ⅰ.①福… Ⅱ.①柯… ②潘… Ⅲ.①英语—汉语—对照读物 ②侦探小说—英国—现代 Ⅳ.①H319.4：Ⅰ

中国版本图书馆 CIP 数据核字（2014）第 151407 号

出版发行/中译出版社
地　　址/北京市西城区新街口外大街 28 号普天德胜主楼四层
电　　话/(010) 68359827；68359303（发行部）；68359725（编辑部）
邮　　编/100044
传　　真/(010) 68357870
电子邮箱/book@ctph.com.cn
网　　址/http://www.ctph.com.cn

责任编辑/范祥镇　王诗同　杨佳特
封面设计/潘　峰

排　　版/杰瑞腾达科技发展有限公司
印　　刷/永清县晔盛亚胶印有限公司
经　　销/新华书店

规　　格/710 毫米 ×1000 毫米　1/16
印　　张/17
字　　数/218 千字
版　　次/2014 年 8 月第一版
印　　次/2023 年 2 月第五次

ISBN 978-7-5001-3275-2　　　　**定价：**57.00 元

出版前言

多年以来，中国对外翻译出版有限公司凭借国内一流的翻译和出版实力及资源，精心策划、出版了大批双语读物，在海内外读者中和业界内产生了良好、深远的影响，形成了自己鲜明的出版特色。

二十世纪八九十年代出版的英汉（汉英）对照“一百丛书”，声名远扬，成为一套最权威、最有特色且又实用的双语读物，影响了一代又一代英语学习者和中华传统文化研究者、爱好者；还有“英若诚名剧译丛”、“中华传统文化精粹丛书”、“美丽英文书系”，这些优秀的双语读物，有的畅销，有的常销不衰反复再版，有的被选为大学英语阅读教材，受到广大读者的喜爱，获得了良好的社会效益和经济效益。

“双语名著无障碍阅读丛书”是中译专门为中学生和英语学习者精心打造的又一品牌，是一个新的双语读物系列，具有以下特点：

选题创新——该系列图书是国内第一套为中小学生量身打造的双语名著读物，所选篇目均为教育部颁布的语文新课标必读书目，或为中学生以及同等文化水平的社会读者喜闻乐见的世界名著，重新编译为英汉（汉英）

对照的双语读本。这些书既给青少年读者提供了成长过程中不可或缺的精神食粮，又让他们领略到原著的精髓和魅力，对他们更好地学习英文大有裨益；同时，丛书中入选的《论语》、《茶馆》、《家》等汉英对照读物，亦是热爱中国传统文化的中外读者所共知的经典名篇，能使读者充分享受阅读经典的无限乐趣。

无障碍阅读——中学生阅读世界文学名著的原著会遇到很多生词和文化难点。针对这一情况，我们给每一本读物原文中的较难词汇和不易理解之处都加上了注释，在内文的版式设计上也采取英汉（或汉英）对照方式，扫清了学生阅读时的障碍。

优良品质——中译双语读物多年来在读者中享有良好口碑，这得益于作者和出版者对于图书质量的不懈追求。"双语名著无障碍阅读丛书"继承了中译双语读物的优良传统——精选的篇目、优秀的译文、方便实用的注解，秉承着对每一个读者负责的精神，竭力打造精品图书。

愿这套丛书成为广大读者的良师益友，愿读者在英语学习和传统文化学习两方面都取得新的突破。

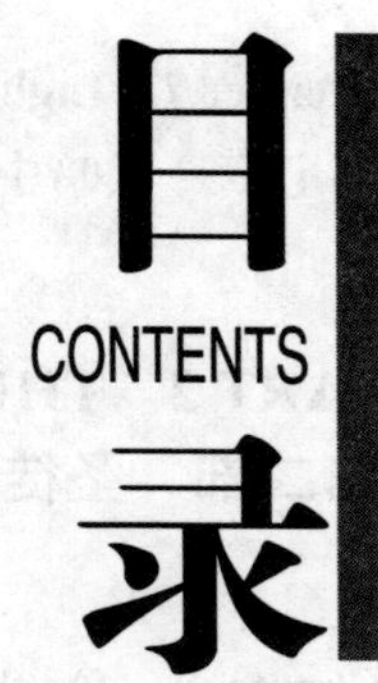

PART 2　THE COUNTRY OF THE SAINTS
第二部　圣徒的区域

PART 1

BEING A REPRINT FROM THE REMINISCENCES OF JOHN H. WATSON, M.D., LATE OF THE ARMY MEDICAL DEPARTMENT

第一部

医学博士、前陆军军医约翰·H.华生回忆录

Chapter 1 Mr. Sherlock Holmes

In the year 1878 I took my degree of Doctor of Medicine of the University of London, and **proceeded**① to Netley to go through the course prescribed for **surgeons**② in the Army. Having completed my studies there, I was duly attached to the Fifth Northumberland **Fusiliers**③ as assistant surgeon. The **regiment**④ was stationed in India at the time, and before I could join it, the second Afghan war had broken out. On landing at Bombay, I learned that my corps had advanced through the passes, and was already deep in the enemy's country. I followed, however, with many other officers who were in the same situation as myself, and succeeded in reaching Candahar in safety, where I found my regiment, and at once entered upon my new duties.

The campaign brought honours and promotion to many, but for me it had nothing but misfortune and disaster. I was removed from my **brigade**⑤ and attached to the Berkshires, with whom I served at the **fatal**⑥ battle of Maiwand. There I was struck on the shoulder by a Jezail bullet, which shattered the bone and grazed the **subclavian**⑦ **artery**⑧. I should have fallen into the hands of the murderous Ghazis had it not been for the devotion and courage shown by Murray, my **orderly**⑨, who threw me across a pack-horse, and succeeded in bringing me safely to the British lines.

Worn with pain, and weak from the prolonged hardships which I had undergone, I was removed, with a great train of wounded sufferers, to the base

第一章　夏洛克·福尔摩斯先生

① proceed [prə'si:d] *v.* 继续做，接着做
② surgeon ['sə:dʒən] *n.* 外科医生
③ fusilier [fju:zə'liə] *n.* 燧发枪手
④ regiment ['redʒimənt] *n.* （军队的）团
⑤ brigade [bri'geid] *n.* （军队的）旅
⑥ fatal ['feitəl] *a.* 重大的
⑦ subclavian [sʌb'kleiviən] *a.* 锁骨下的
⑧ artery ['ɑ:təri] *n.* 动脉
⑨ orderly ['ɔ:dəli] *n.* 传令兵；勤务兵

1878年，我获得了伦敦大学的医学博士学位，接着又到内特雷进修了为军队外科医生开设的课程。完成了在内特雷的进修之后，我立刻就被派往诺森伯兰第五燧发枪团担任助理军医。该燧发枪团当时驻扎在印度，我还没有到达部队的驻地，第二次阿富汗战争就爆发了。我刚在孟买上岸，便就得知，自己所属的那个团已经向前推进，跨过了重重关口，深入到了敌人的腹地。然而，我和许多别的军官一道跟随了上去，因为他们的处境也和我一样。最后我安全抵达了坎大哈，找到了自己所属的团，于是立刻开始履行自己的职责。

此次战争给许多人带来了荣誉和升迁，但给我带来的却是灾难和不幸。我被调离了所属部队，转到了伯克郡步兵旅，跟随该旅参加了迈万德那场惨烈的战役。战斗中，我的肩膀被一颗阿富汗长滑膛枪子弹击中，击碎了肩胛骨，擦破了锁骨下动脉。我的勤务兵默里忠诚热心，勇气可嘉，把我抬到驮马的背上，安全地送到了英军阵地。要不是有他相救，我恐怕已经落入那些凶残狠毒的伊斯兰圣战者手里了。

我因伤痛而面容憔悴，因经受长时间的艰难困苦而体质虚弱，于是，随同一大批伤病员，转移到了位于

hospital at Peshawar. Here I **rallied**①, and had already improved so far as to be able to walk about the **wards**②, and even to bask a little upon the **verandah**③, when I was struck down by **enteric fever**④, that curse of our Indian possessions. For months my life was despaired of, and when at last I came to myself and became **convalescent**⑤, I was so weak and **emaciated**⑥ that a medical board determined that not a day should be lost in sending me back to England. I was dispatched, accordingly, in the troopship *Orontes*, and landed a month later on Portsmouth jetty, with my health irretrievably ruined, but with permission from a **paternal**⑦ government to spend the next nine months in attempting to improve it.

I had neither kith nor kin in England, and was therefore as free as air—or as free as an income of eleven shillings and sixpence a day will permit a man to be. Under such circumstances, I naturally **gravitated**⑧ to London, that great **cesspool**⑨ into which all the loungers and idlers of the Empire are irresistibly drained. There I stayed for some time at a private hotel in the Strand, leading a comfortless, meaningless existence, and spending such money as I had, considerably more freely than I ought. So alarming did the state of my finances become, that I soon realized that I must either leave the metropolis and **rusticate**⑩ somewhere in the country, or that I must make a complete alteration in my style of living. Choosing the latter alternative, I began by making up my mind to leave the hotel, and to take up my quarters in some less pretentious and less expensive **domicile**⑪.

On the very day that I had come to this conclusion, I was standing at the Criterion Bar, when some one tapped me on the shoulder, and turning round I recognized young Stamford, who had been a **dresser**⑫ under me at Barts. The sight of a friendly face in the great wilderness of London is a pleasant thing indeed to a lonely man. In old days Stamford had never been a particular **crony**⑬ of mine, but now I hailed him with enthusiasm, and he, in his turn, appeared to be delighted to see me. In the **exuberance**⑭ of my joy, I asked him to lunch with me at the Holborn, and we started off together in a **hansom**⑮.

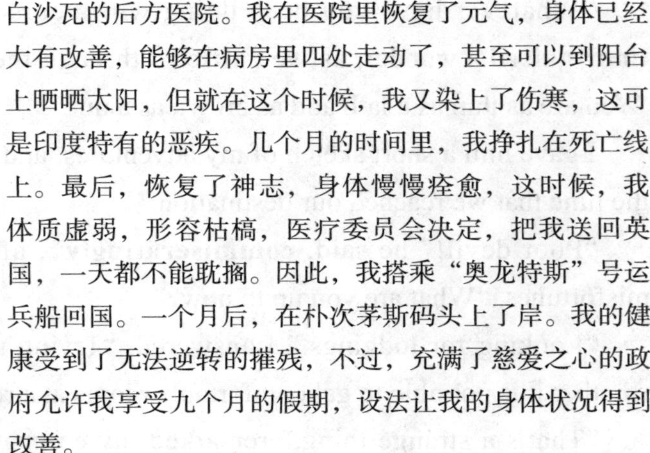

白沙瓦的后方医院。我在医院里恢复了元气，身体已经大有改善，能够在病房里四处走动了，甚至可以到阳台上晒晒太阳，但就在这个时候，我又染上了伤寒，这可是印度特有的恶疾。几个月的时间里，我挣扎在死亡线上。最后，恢复了神志，身体慢慢痊愈，这时候，我体质虚弱，形容枯槁，医疗委员会决定，把我送回英国，一天都不能耽搁。因此，我搭乘“奥龙特斯”号运兵船回国。一个月后，在朴次茅斯码头上了岸。我的健康受到了无法逆转的摧残，不过，充满了慈爱之心的政府允许我享受九个月的假期，设法让我的身体状况得到改善。

我在英格兰举目无亲，因此，就像空气一样自由自在——或者说，就像一个每天拥有十一先令六便士固定收入的人一样，活得逍遥自在。在这种状况下，我自然而然地选择了伦敦，因为这是个巨大的藏污纳垢之所，大英帝国的所有游手好闲之徒都对它趋之若鹜，蜂拥而至。我在伦敦斯特兰德大街的一家私人旅馆里待了一段时间，生活索然寡味，百无聊赖，花钱大手大脚，大大超出了自己承受能力。我在经济上变得很拮据了，于是，很快就意识到了，自己必须做出抉择，要么离开伦敦，搬到乡下的某个地方去，要么彻底改变生活方式。我选择了后者，决定搬离那家旅馆，寻找一个不那么奢华、不那么昂贵的住处。

我做出了决定的当天，伫立在克莱蒂伦酒吧门口，突然感觉有人轻轻地拍了拍我的肩膀。回头一看，原来是小斯坦福德，他是我在巴茨医院时的助手。偌大的伦敦城，人海茫茫，能够见到一张亲切的面孔，对一个孤独寂寞的人来说，确实是件倍感喜悦的事情。昔日，我和斯坦福德并没有什么特别的交情，但这时候，我却热情洋溢地同他寒暄了起来，而他似乎也很高兴见到我。兴奋之中，我邀请他和我一道到霍尔本餐厅共进午餐，

① rally ['ræli] *v.* 精神振作，身体恢复
② ward [wɔ:d] *n.* 病房
③ verandah [və'rændə] *n.* 阳台
④ enteric fever 伤寒
⑤ convalescent [ˌkɔnvə'lesənt] *a.* 渐愈的
⑥ emaciated [i'meisieitid] *a.* 憔悴的
⑦ paternal [pə'tə:nəl] *a.* 仁慈的
⑧ gravitate ['grævi,teit] *v.* 被吸引到
⑨ cesspool ['sespu:l] *n.* 污秽之所
⑩ rusticate ['rʌsti,keit] *v.* 在农村定居
⑪ domicile ['dɔmisail] *n.* 住处
⑫ dresser ['dresə] *n.* 外科手术助手
⑬ crony ['krəuni] *n.* 朋友
⑭ exuberance [ig'zju:bərəns] *n.* 热情洋溢
⑮ hansom ['hænsəm] *n.* 二轮双座小马车

"Whatever have you been doing with yourself, Watson?" he asked in **undisguised**[①] wonder, as we **rattled**[②] through the crowded London streets. "You are as thin as a lath and as brown as a nut."

I gave him a short sketch of my adventures, and had hardly concluded it by the time that we reached our destination.

"Poor devil!" he said, **commiseratingly**[③], after he had listened to my misfortunes. "What are you up to now?"

"Looking for lodgings." I answered. "Trying to solve the problem as to whether it is possible to get comfortable rooms at a reasonable price."

"That's a strange thing," remarked my companion; "you are the second man to-day that has used that expression to me."

"And who was the first?" I asked.

"A fellow who is working at the chemical laboratory up at the hospital. He was **bemoaning**[④] himself this morning because he could not get someone to go halves with him in some nice rooms which he had found, and which were too much for his purse."

"**By Jove**[⑤]!" I cried, "if he really wants someone to share the rooms and the expense, I am the very man for him. I should prefer having a partner to being alone."

Young Stamford looked rather strangely at me over his wine-glass. "You don't know Sherlock Holmes yet," he said; "perhaps you would not care for him as a **constant**[⑥] companion."

"Why, what is there against him?"

"Oh, I didn't say there was anything against him. He is a little queer in his ideas—an enthusiast in some branches of science. As far as I know he is a decent fellow enough."

"A medical student, I suppose?" said I.

"No—I have no idea what he intends to **go in for**[⑦]. I believe he **is well up in**[⑧]

① undisguised [ˌʌndis'gaizd] *a.* 不加掩饰的
② rattle ['rætl] *v.* 格嗒格嗒地行进
③ commiseratingly [kə'mizəˌreitiŋli] *ad.* 同情地
④ bemoan [bi'məun] *v.* 抱怨
⑤ by Jove 天哪
⑥ constant ['kɔnstənt] *a.* 不变的
⑦ go in for 从事，致力于
⑧ be well up in 对…很精通

于是我们便乘坐马车出发了。

“你一直在忙些什么呢，华生？”我们乘坐的马车辘辘驶过熙熙攘攘的伦敦街头时，他问了一声，惊异之情溢于言表，“看你骨瘦如柴、面黄肌瘦的样子。”

我简略地向他叙述自己的遭遇，还没有叙述完，目的地就到了。

“倒霉透顶啊！”他听了我的不幸遭遇之后，满怀同情地说，“你现在在干什么呢？”

“在寻找住处呢，”我回答说，“看看能不能找到价格合理同时又舒适的房子。”

“真是不可思议啊，”我的同伴说，“你是今天第二个对我说同样的话的人。”

“那第一个是什么人啊？”我问。

“是一个在医院实验室工作的人。他今天上午还在唉声叹气，说他找到了一处寓所，可惜自己的经济实力有限，付不起租金，正愁找不到合租的人呢。”

“天哪，”我大声说，“如果他真想要找个人合租寓所，分摊房租，我就是他最合适的人选。我正想要有个伴儿，不喜欢一个人独居。”

小斯坦福德手里端着酒杯，表情怪异地看着我。“你还不了解夏洛克·福尔摩斯那个人，”他说，“说不定，你不会乐意同他长期共处呢。”

“啊，他品行有什么问题吗？”

“噢，倒不是说他品行有问题。他只是想法有点怪异——热衷于某些科学领域。就我所知道的情况来看，他是个挺正派的人。”

“我看他是研究医学的吧？”我问

“不是——我不知道他具体研究什么的。我认为，他很熟悉解剖学，还是个一流的药剂师。但是，据我所知，他从未接受过系统的医学教育，研究涉及的领域很

anatomy[①], and he is a first-class chemist; but, as far as I know, he has never taken out any systematic medical classes. His studies are very **desultory**[②] and **eccentric**[③], but he has **amassed**[④] a lot of **out-of-the-way**[⑤] knowledge which would astonish his professors."

"Did you never ask him what he was going in for?" I asked.

"No; he is not a man that it is easy to **draw out**[⑥], though he can be communicative enough when the fancy seizes him."

"I should like to meet him," I said. "If I am to lodge with anyone, I should prefer a man of studious and quiet habits. I am not strong enough yet to stand much noise or excitement. I had enough of both in Afghanistan to last me for the remainder of my natural existence. How could I meet this friend of yours?"

"He is sure to be at the laboratory," returned my companion. "He either avoids the place for weeks, or else he works there from morning to night. If you like, we shall drive round together after luncheon."

"Certainly," I answered, and the conversation drifted away into other channels.

As we made our way to the hospital after leaving the Holborn, Stamford gave me a few more particulars about the gentleman whom I proposed to take as a fellow-lodger.

"You mustn't blame me if you don't get on with him," he said; "I know nothing more of him than I have learned from meeting him occasionally in the laboratory. You proposed this arrangement, so you must not hold me responsible."

"If we don't get on it will be easy to part company," I answered. "It seems to me, Stamford," I added, looking hard at my companion, "that you have some reason for washing your hands of the matter. Is this fellow's temper so **formidable**[⑦], or what is it? Don't be **mealy-mouthed**[⑧] about it."

"It is not easy to express the inexpressible," he answered with a laugh. "Holmes is a little too scientific for my tastes—it approaches to cold-

① anatomy [ə'nætəmi] *n.* 解剖学
② desultory ['desəl,tɔ:ri] *a.* 杂乱的
③ eccentric [ik'sentrik] *a.* 怪异的
④ amass [ə'mæs] *v.* 积累
⑤ out-of-the-way [autəv ðə'wei] *a.* 冷僻的，奇特的
⑥ draw out 引出；引…畅谈

庞杂怪异。不过，倒是积累了大量偏僻冷门的知识，令教授们都大为惊讶。”

“你就没有问过他，到底在研究什么东西吗？”我问。

“没有，他不是那种能轻易被人把心里话套出来的人，不过兴致上来了，也还是挺健谈的。”

“我想见见他，”我说，“如果要找个人合住的话，我倒是想找个勤奋刻苦、喜欢安静的人。我身体还不是很好，受不了太多的吵闹或者刺激。我在阿富汗时，这两种情形都受够了，一辈子都不想再受那个罪了。我怎样才能见到你那位朋友呢？”

“他肯定在实验室里，”我的同伴回答说，“他要么几个星期都不去那儿，要么一天到晚泡在那儿。如果你愿意，我们午餐后一道乘车过去。”

“没问题！”我回答说，然后话题就转到别的方面去了。

在我们离开霍尔本餐厅前往医院的途中，斯坦福德又向我介绍了一些关于我想要与其合租的那位先生的情况。

“如果你同他相处得不融洽，可不要责怪我啊，”他说，“我只是偶尔在实验室里碰到他，对他的情况略微知道一点点而已。合租寓所的事情是你自己提出来的，所以，有什么事情我可不负责任。”

“如果我们合不来，分开也很容易啊，”我回答说。“我觉得吧，斯坦福德，”我接着又说，眼睛盯着我的同伴，“你想要撇清自己与此事的关系，这其中一定有原因吧？那家伙是脾气暴躁呢，还是别的什么？你就别藏着掖着的啦。”

⑦ formidable ['fɔ:midəbl] *a.* 可怕的
⑧ mealy-mouthed ['mi:li,mauðd] *a.* 说话拐弯抹角的

“对于无法说得清楚的情况，当然不好怎么说啦，”他回答说，哈哈笑了起来，“按照我的标准来判断，福尔摩斯有点科学过了头——近乎于冷血。我可以想象得到，他会拿一小撮新配制的生物碱给他的某个朋友尝，

bloodedness. I could imagine his giving a friend a little pinch of the latest vegetable **alkaloid**[①], not out of **malevolence**[②], you understand, but simply out of a spirit of inquiry in order to have an accurate idea of the effects. To do him justice, I think that he would take it himself with the same readiness. He appears to have a passion for definite and exact knowledge."

"Very right too."

"Yes, but it may be pushed to **excess**[③]. When it comes to beating the **subjects**[④] in the **dissecting-rooms**[⑤] with a stick, it is certainly taking rather a **bizarre**[⑥] shape."

"Beating the subjects!"

"Yes, to verify how far **bruises**[⑦] may be produced after death. I saw him at it with my own eyes."

"And yet you say he is not a medical student?"

"No. Heaven knows what the objects of his studies are. But here we are, and you must form your own impressions about him." As he spoke, we turned down a narrow lane and passed through a small side-door, which opened into a wing of the great hospital. It was familiar ground to me, and I needed no guiding as we **ascended**[⑧] the bleak stone staircase and made our way down the long corridor with its vista of whitewashed wall and dun-coloured doors. Near the further end a low arched passage branched away from it and led to the chemical laboratory.

This was a lofty chamber, lined and littered with countless bottles. Broad, low tables were scattered about, which bristled with **retorts**[⑨], test-tubes, and little Bunsen lamps, with their blue flickering flames. There was only one student in the room, who was bending over a distant table absorbed in his work. At the sound of our steps he glanced round and sprang to his feet with a cry of pleasure. "I've found it! I've found it," he shouted to my companion, running towards us with a test-tube in his hand. "I have found a **re-agent**[⑩] which is **precipitated**[⑪] by **haemoglobin**[⑫], and by nothing else." Had he discovered a gold mine, greater delight could not have shone upon his features.

① alkaloid ['ælkəlɔid] *n.* 生物碱
② malevolence [mə'levələns] *n.* 恶意
③ excess ['ekses] *n.* 过分
④ subject ['sʌbdʒikt] *n.* 解剖的尸体
⑤ dissecting-room [di'sektiŋ,ruːm] *n.* 解剖室
⑥ bizarre [bi'zɑː] *a.* 怪诞的
⑦ bruise [bruːz] *n.* 伤痕
⑧ ascend [ə'send] *v.* 攀登
⑨ retort [ri'tɔːt] *n.* 曲颈瓶
⑩ re-agent [riː'eidʒənt] *n.* 试剂
⑪ precipitate [pri'sipiteit] *v.* 沉淀析出
⑫ haemoglobin ['hiːməu,gləubin] *n.* 血红蛋白

并不是怀有什么恶意，你知道的，纯粹是出于一种孜孜以求的精神，想要确切地知道其效果如何。替他说句公道话，我觉得，他自己也会随时去尝那个东西。他似乎很热衷于追求知识的精准性。”

“这也是很对的做法啊。”

“是啊，但可能过火了一点儿。如果那种热情表现在在解剖室里用棍子抽打尸体，这肯定就显得怪异了。”

“抽打尸体！”

“是啊，为了证实人死以后还会形成什么样的伤痕。我亲眼看见他这么做的。”

“但你不是说他不是研究医学的吗？”

“对啊，天知道他是研究些什么的。但我们已经到了，对他有什么看法，你自己做出判断吧。”他说这话时，我们拐进了一条狭窄的巷子，然后进入了一道小的边门，边门通向医院大楼的一翼。我很熟悉这个地方，不需要人引导，我们便上了冰冷的石头台阶，沿着长长的走廊向前行进，走廊两壁刷成了白色，上面开了几扇暗褐色的小门。走廊远处的尽头有一条低矮的拱形走廊，直通化学实验室。

实验室是个空间很高的房间，数不清的瓶瓶罐罐，有的排成一行行，有的乱摆乱放着。里面杂乱地摆放着几张又宽又矮的桌子，桌面上立着曲颈瓶、试管和一些闪烁着蓝光的小型本生灯。室内只有一名研究者，只见他坐在远处的一张桌子边，弓腰曲背，埋头工作着。听到我们进入的脚步声后，他回过头瞥了一眼，然后一跃站起身子，兴高采烈地喊了起来。“我找到了！我找到了！”他冲着我的同伴直嚷嚷，手里拿着一支试管，向我们跑了过来，“我找到了一种试剂，只能用血红蛋白质来沉淀析出，别的都不行。”他脸上洋溢着喜悦的神情，那样子胜过发现了一座金矿。

“这位是华生医生，这位是福尔摩斯先生，”斯坦福

"Dr. Watson, Mr. Sherlock Holmes," said Stamford, introducing us.

"How are you?" he said **cordially**[①], gripping my hand with a strength for which I should hardly have given him credit. "You have been in Afghanistan, I **perceive**[②]."

"How on earth did you know that?" I asked in astonishment.

"Never mind," said he, chuckling to himself. "The question now is about haemoglobin. No doubt you see the significance of this discovery of mine?"

"It is interesting, chemically, no doubt," I answered, "but practically——"

"Why, man, it is the most practical **medico-legal**[③] discovery for years. Don't you see that it gives us an **infallible**[④] test for blood stains. Come over here now!" He seized me by the coat-sleeve in his eagerness, and drew me over to the table at which he had been working. "Let us have some fresh blood," he said, digging a long **bodkin**[⑤] into his finger, and drawing off the resulting drop of blood in a chemical **pipette**[⑥]. "Now, I add this small quantity of blood to a litre of water. You perceive that the resulting mixture has the appearance of pure water. The **proportion**[⑦] of blood cannot be more than one in a million. I have no doubt, however, that we shall be able to obtain the characteristic reaction." As he spoke, he threw into the vessel a few white crystals, and then added some drops of a transparent fluid. In an instant the contents assumed a dull **mahogany**[⑧] colour, and a brownish dust was precipitated to the bottom of the glass jar.

"Ha! ha!" he cried, clapping his hands, and looking as delighted as a child with a new toy. "What do you think of that?"

"It seems to be a very delicate test," I remarked.

"Beautiful! beautiful! The old **guaiacum**[⑨] test was very clumsy and uncertain. So is the microscopic examination for blood **corpuscles**[⑩]. The latter is valueless if the stains are a few hours old. Now, this appears to act as well whether the blood is old or new. Had this test been invented, there are hundreds

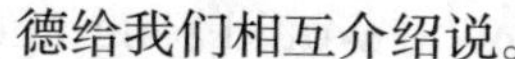

德给我们相互介绍说。

“您好，”福尔摩斯热情洋溢地说，一边使劲地握住我的一只手，力气大得令我简直难以置信，“我看得出来，您一直待在阿富汗那边。”

“您怎么知道的呢？”我惊讶地问。

“这就别管了，”他说着，咯咯地笑了起来，“还是谈谈血红蛋白吧。毫无疑问，您看得出我的这个发现的重大意义吧？”

“从化学研究上来看，这很有意思，毫无疑问，”我回答说，“但从实际运用的角度来看——”

“啊，先生，这可是多年来法医学上最实用的发现啊。您没发现这种试剂可以用来准确无误地鉴别血迹吗？到这边来吧！”他迫不及待地拉住我的袖口，把我拽到他先前工作着的那张桌子旁边。“我们先弄点鲜血，”他说着，把一根长针插入自己的手指，接着用一根吸管吸了流出的一滴血，“现在，把这一点点血放进一公升水里去。您看，这种混合液看起来就像清水一样，其中血液所占的比例还不到百万分之一。不过，我毫不怀疑，我们还是能够获得那种特别的化学反应。”他说着，就把几粒白色晶体扔进容器，然后又加入了几滴透明的液体。片刻之后，里面的溶液变成了暗红色，一些棕色浑浊物析出后沉淀到了瓶底。

“哈！哈！”他大声说着，拍着双手，就像孩子玩一件新玩具那样兴致勃勃，“您觉得怎么样？”

“这看来是个很灵敏的实验，”我说。

“妙极了！妙极了！昔日的愈创木脂检测法操作不方便，也不可靠。用显微镜检测血细胞的方法也同样如此。如果血迹是几个小时前留下的，显微镜检测法根本没有用。但现在，不论新鲜的，还是陈旧的血迹，这种方法都有效。有了这样的检测法，数以百计逍遥法外的罪犯早就受到法律的制裁了。”

① cordially [ˈkɔːdjəli] *ad.* 热诚地

② perceive [pəˈsiːv] *v.* 认为

③ medico-legal [ˌmedikəuˈliːgəl] *a.* 法医学的

④ infallible [inˈfæləbl] *a.* 准确无误的

⑤ bodkin [ˈbɔdkin] *n.* 粗针

⑥ pipette [piˈpet] *n.* 吸液管

⑦ proportion [prəˈpɔːʃən] *n.* 比例

⑧ mahogany [məˈhɔgəni] *n.* 红褐色

⑨ guaiacum [ˈgwaiəkəm] *n.* 愈创木

⑩ corpuscle [ˈkɔːpəsəl] *n.* 血球；细胞

of men now walking the earth who would long ago have paid the penalty of their crimes."

"Indeed!" I murmured.

"Criminal cases are continually **hinging upon**[1] that one point. A man is **suspected of**[2] a crime months perhaps after it has been **committed**[3]. His **linen**[4] or clothes are examined, and brownish stains discovered upon them. Are they blood stains, or mud stains, or rust stains, or fruit stains, or what are they? That is a question which has puzzled many an expert, and why? Because there was no reliable test. Now we have the Sherlock Holmes's test, and there will no longer be any difficulty."

His eyes fairly glittered as he spoke, and he put his hand over his heart and bowed as if to some applauding crowd **conjured**[5] up by his imagination.

"You are to be congratulated," I remarked, considerably surprised at his enthusiasm.

"There was the case of Von Bischoff at Frankfort last year. He would certainly have been hung had this test been in existence. Then there was Mason of Bradford, and the **notorious**[6] Muller, and Lefevre of Montpellier, and Samson of New Orleans. I could name a score of cases in which it would have been decisive."

"You seem to be a walking calendar of crime," said Stamford with a laugh. "You might start a paper on those lines. Call it the 'Police News of the Past.' "

"Very interesting reading it might be made, too," remarked Sherlock Holmes, sticking a small piece of **plaster**[7] over the **prick**[8] on his finger. "I have to be careful," he continued, turning to me with a smile, "for I **dabble**[9] with poisons a good deal." He held out his hand as he spoke, and I noticed that it was all **mottled**[10] over with similar pieces of plaster, and discoloured with strong acids.

"We came here on business," said Stamford, sitting down on a high three-legged stool, and pushing another one in my direction with his foot. "My friend here wants to take **diggings**[11], and as you were complaining

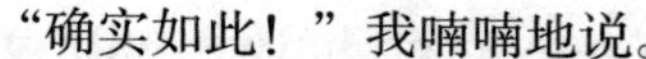

“确实如此！”我喃喃地说。

“各种刑事案件一直是根据这一点来侦破的。一桩案件可能发生了几个月之后，才能确定嫌疑犯。警方仔细查看其内衣裤或者其他衣物，发现了粘在上面的棕褐色污迹。污迹究竟是血迹，或是泥迹，或是锈迹，或是果汁残迹，还是别的什么东西呢？这个问题令众多专家困惑不已。为什么呢？因为没有可靠的检测方法。现在我们有了夏洛克·福尔摩斯的检测法，不再会有什么困难了。”

① hinge upon 取决于
② be suspected of 被怀疑
③ commit [kə'mit] *v.* 犯罪
④ linen ['linin] *n.* 内衣裤

他说这话时，眼睛闪着亮光。一只手按在胸口，鞠了一躬，仿佛是在对想象中喝彩的观众鞠躬。

“值得恭喜您啊！”我说，他欣喜激动的样子令我很吃惊。

⑤ conjure ['kʌndʒə] *v.* 使呈现于脑际；想象

“去年，法兰克福发生了冯·比朔夫案件，如果当时有这种检测法，他肯定被送上了绞刑架。后来又有布拉德福德的梅森、臭名昭著的马勒、蒙彼利埃的勒非弗和新奥尔良的萨姆森。这种检测法可以对案件侦破起决定性的作用，这样的案件我可以列举出二十桩。”

⑥ notorious [nəu'tɔːriəs] *a.* 臭名昭著的

“您可真是刑事案件的活目录啊，”斯坦福德说着，哈哈笑了起来，“您可以办一份这方面的报纸，就把它叫做《警界旧闻报》吧。”

“这种报纸阅读起来也会很有意思啊，”福尔摩斯说着，把一小块橡皮膏贴在手指的伤口上，“我得小心点儿，”他接着说，一边转过身对着我，露出了微笑，“因为我接触很多有毒的东西。”他说着把手伸了出来，我注意到，上面贴满了大小差不多的橡皮膏，它们由于强酸的腐蚀而变颜色了。

⑦ plaster ['plɑːstə] *n.* 橡皮膏
⑧ prick [prik] *n.* 刺孔
⑨ dabble ['dæbl] *v.* 涉猎
⑩ mottle ['mɔtl] *v.* 使斑驳

“我们有事情到这儿来，”斯坦福德说着，在一个三脚高凳上坐了下来，并且用一只脚把另一个凳子向着我的方向推了过来，“我这位朋友想要找一处寓所，你不

⑪ diggings ['digiŋz] *n.* 住所

that you could get no one to go halves with you, I thought that I had better bring you together."

Sherlock Holmes seemed delighted at the idea of sharing his rooms with me. "I have my eye on a suite in Baker Street," he said, "which would **suit us down to the ground**[①]. You don't mind the smell of strong tobacco, I hope?"

"I always smoke 'ship's' myself," I answered.

"That's good enough. I generally have chemicals about, and occasionally do experiments. Would that annoy you?"

"By no means."

"Let me see—what are my other shortcomings. I get in the **dumps**[②] at times, and don't open my mouth for days on end. You must not think I am **sulky**[③] when I do that. Just let me alone, and I'll soon be right. What have you to **confess**[④] now? It's just as well for two fellows to know the worst of one another before they begin to live together."

I laughed at this cross-examination. "I keep a **bull pup**[⑤]," I said, "and I object to **rows**[⑥] because my nerves are shaken, and I get up at all sorts of ungodly hours, and I am extremely lazy. I have another set of **vices**[⑦] when I'm well, but those are the **principal**[⑧] ones at present."

"Do you include violin-playing in your **category**[⑨] of rows?" he asked, anxiously.

"It depends on the player," I answered. "A well-played violin is a treat for the gods—a badly-played one——"

"Oh, that's all right," he cried, with a merry laugh. "I think we may consider the thing as settled—that is, if the rooms are agreeable to you."

"When shall we see them?"

"Call for me here at noon to-morrow, and we'll go together and settle everything," he answered.

"All right—noon exactly," said I, shaking his hand.

We left him working among his chemicals, and we walked together towards

是抱怨找不到与您合租的人吗，所以我就想，最好把你们两个人撮合到一块儿。”

夏洛克·福尔摩斯得知能够同我合租寓所，显得很高兴。“我看中了贝克大街的一套公寓，”他说，“特别适合于我们两个人住。但愿您不会在意浓烈的烟草味吧？”

“我自己一直抽‘船’牌烟，”我回答说。

“那就好。我身边一般会有化学药品，时不时地会做些实验，您会反感吗？”

“绝对不会。”

“让我想想看——我还有什么其他缺点呢？我有时会阴郁沉闷，一连几天都不开口说话。如果遇上那样的情况，您可别以为是我生气了，您别在乎就是了，我很快就会恢复正常。您有什么要说明的吗？两个人合住到一块儿，事先最好知道彼此最坏的毛病。”

面对这种相互之间的审查，我不禁笑了起来。“我养了一只小斗牛犬，”我说，“我厌恶吵闹声，因为我会心烦意乱。还有就是，我起床毫无规律可言，而且懒惰得要命。身体健康的时候，还有另外一些毛病，但眼下主要的毛病就这些。”

“您把拉小提琴的声音也包含在您说的吵闹声当中吗？”他迫不及待地问。

“那要取决于拉琴的人，”我回答说，“如果拉得动听，连神都会认为是一种享受——但如果拉得糟糕——”

“噢，那就好，”福尔摩斯大声说，高兴地笑了起来，“我觉得，如果您对寓所满意的话，这事就算是定下来了。”

“那我们什么时间去看房呢？”

“明天中午，您到这儿来找我，我们到时一起去，把所有事都定下来，”他说回答。

“那好，明天中午准时见，”我一边说一边同他握手。

① suit sb down to the ground 完全适合

② dump [dʌmp] *n.* 忧郁

③ sulky ['sʌlki] *a.* 生闷气的

④ confess [kən'fes] *v.* 承认，坦白

⑤ bull pup 斗牛犬

⑥ row [rəu] *n.* 吵闹

⑦ vice [vais] *n.* 缺点

⑧ principal ['prinsəpəl] *a.* 主要的

⑨ category ['kætigəri] *n.* 种类

my hotel.

"By the way," I asked suddenly, stopping and turning upon Stamford, "how the **deuce**① did he know that I had come from Afghanistan?"

My companion smiled an **enigmatical**② smile. "That's just his little **peculiarity**③," he said. "A good many people have wanted to know how he finds things out."

"Oh! a mystery is it?" I cried, rubbing my hands. "This is very **piquant**④. I am much **obliged**⑤ to you for bringing us together. 'The proper study of mankind is man,' you know."

"You must study him, then," Stamford said, as he bade me good-bye. "You'll find him a **knotty**⑥ problem, though. I'll **wager**⑦ he learns more about you than you about him. Good-bye."

"Good-bye," I answered, and strolled on to my hotel, considerably interested in my new **acquaintance**⑧.

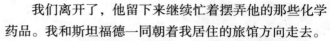

我们离开了，他留下来继续忙着摆弄他的那些化学药品。我和斯坦福德一同朝着我居住的旅馆方向走去。

“对啦，”我突然停住了脚步，转身问斯坦福德，“他是怎么知道我去过阿富汗的呢？”

我的同伴露出了诡异的笑容。“这正是他的一个小怪癖，”他说，“许多人都想知道他是如何揣摩事情的。”

“噢！是个谜，对吗？”我大声说，双手搓揉着，“太有意思啦。你把我们两个人撮合到一块儿，真是太感谢你啦。要知道，‘研究人类在于研究具体的人。’”

“那你必须要研究研究他，”我们分别时，斯坦福德对我说，“不过，你会发现，他是个不容易研究的对象啊。我敢说，他对你的了解定会胜过你对他的了解。再见吧。”

“再见，”我回答说，漫步走向我住的旅馆，心里面对我的那位新相识充满了好奇。

① the deuce （用以加强语气）究竟

② enigmatical [ˌenigˈmætikəl] *a.* 谜一般的

③ peculiarity [piˌkjuːliːˈæriti] *n.* 怪癖

④ piquant [ˈpikənt] *a.* 有趣的

⑤ obliged [əˈblaidʒd] *a.* 感谢的

⑥ knotty [ˈnɔti] *a.* 困难的，棘手的

⑦ wager [ˈweidʒə] *v.* 保证；打赌

⑧ acquaintance [əˈkweintəns] *n.* 相识的人

Chapter 2　The Science of Deduction

We met next day as he had arranged, and **inspected**[①] the rooms at No. 221B, Baker Street, of which he had spoken at our meeting. They consisted of a couple of comfortable bed-rooms and a single large airy sitting-room, cheerfully **furnished**[②], and **illuminated**[③] by two broad windows. So desirable in every way were the apartments, and so moderate did the terms seem when divided between us, that the bargain was concluded upon the spot, and we at once entered into **possession**[④]. That very evening I moved my things round from the hotel, and on the following morning Sherlock Holmes followed me with several boxes and **portmanteaus**[⑤]. For a day or two we were busily employed in unpacking and laying out our property to the best advantage. That done, we gradually began to settle down and to **accommodate**[⑥] ourselves to our new surroundings.

Holmes was certainly not a difficult man to live with. He was quiet in his ways, and his habits were regular. It was rare for him to be up after ten at night, and he had invariably breakfasted and gone out before I rose in the morning. Sometimes he spent his day at the chemical laboratory, sometimes in the dissecting-rooms, and occasionally in long walks, which appeared to take him into the lowest **portions**[⑦] of the City. Nothing could **exceed**[⑧] his energy when the working fit was upon him; but now and again a reaction would seize him, and for days on end he would lie upon the sofa in the sitting-room, hardly **uttering**[⑨] a word or moving a muscle from morning to night. On these occasions I have noticed

第二章 演绎推理

① inspect [in'spekt] *v.* 查看

② furnish ['fə:niʃ] *v.* 配备家具

③ illuminate [i'lu:mineit] *v.* 照亮

④ possession [pə'zeʃən] *n.* 财产，这里指房子

⑤ portmanteau [pɔ:t'mæntəu] *n.* 旅行箱

⑥ accommodate [ə'kɔmədeit] *v.* 适应

⑦ portion [pɔ:ʃən] *n.* 部分

⑧ exceed [ik'si:d] *v.* 超过

⑨ utter ['ʌtə] *v.* 发出

翌日，我们按照福尔摩斯事先的安排见了面，然后去查看了贝克大街二百二十一号乙的寓所，就是我们头一次见面时他提到的那一处。寓所有两间舒适的卧室，还有单独一间敞亮透气的客厅，客厅装饰得温馨明快，两扇大窗，令室内光线充足。寓所的条件各个方面都很合我们满意，租金由我们两个人分摊，非常合算。我们当场就把事情谈妥了，立刻租下了住房。我当晚就把自己的行李从旅馆搬了过来，翌日早上，福尔摩斯也跟着搬来了几只箱子和旅行包。紧接着的一两天里，我们忙着拆包裹，把东西摆放得妥妥帖帖的。一切安排妥当之后，我们慢慢地开始安顿下来了，熟悉了周围的新环境。

福尔摩斯确实不是个很难相处的人。他喜欢安静，生活挺有规律。他夜间极少十点钟之后上床睡觉，早上我还没起床，他总是用过了早餐出门了。他有时候一整天都待在化学试验室，或者在解剖室，偶尔也会散步到很远的地方，走到伦敦城的贫民区。当他工作热情高涨，干什么事情都有使不完的劲头。但时不时地也会出现相反的情况，一连几天，躺在客厅的沙发上，从早到晚不吭一声，一动不动。在这种时候，我注意到他眼里

such a dreamy, **vacant**① expression in his eyes, that I might have suspected him of being addicted to the use of some **narcotic**②, had not the **temperance**③ and cleanliness of his whole life forbidden such a notion.

As the weeks went by, my interest in him and my curiosity as to his aims in life, gradually deepened and increased. His very person and appearance were such as to strike the attention of the most casual observer. In height he was rather over six feet, and so excessively lean that he seemed to be considerably taller. His eyes were sharp and piercing, save during those intervals of **torpor**④ to which I have alluded; and his thin, hawk-like nose gave his whole expression an air of alertness and decision. His chin, too, had the **prominence**⑤ and squareness which mark the man of determination. His hands were invariably blotted with ink and stained with chemicals, yet he was possessed of extraordinary delicacy of touch, as I frequently had occasion to observe when I watched him manipulating his fragile philosophical instruments.

The reader may set me down as a hopeless busybody, when I confess how much this man stimulated my curiosity, and how often I endeavoured to break through the **reticence**⑥ which he showed on all that concerned himself. Before pronouncing judgment, however, be it remembered how objectless was my life, and how little there was to engage my attention. My health forbade me from venturing out unless the weather was exceptionally genial, and I had no friends who would call upon me and break the **monotony**⑦ of my daily existence. Under these circumstances, I eagerly **hailed**⑧ the little mystery which hung around my companion, and spent much of my time in endeavouring to unravel it.

He was not studying medicine. He had himself, in reply to a question, confirmed Stamford's opinion upon that point. Neither did he appear to have pursued any course of reading which might fit him for a degree in science or any other recognized **portal**⑨ which would give him an entrance into the learned world. Yet his **zeal**⑩ for certain studies was remarkable, and within eccentric limits his knowledge was so extraordinarily ample and minute that his observations have fairly **astounded**⑪ me. Surely no man would work so

① vacant ['veikənt] *a.* 茫然的；空白的
② narcotic [nɑ: 'kɔtik] *n.* 麻醉剂
③ temperance ['tempərəns] *n.* 节制
④ torpor ['tɔ:pə] *n.* 麻木
⑤ prominence ['prɔminəns] *n.* 突出
⑥ reticence ['retisəns] *n.* 沉默；谨严
⑦ monotony [mə'nɔtəni] *n.* 单调
⑧ hail [heil] *v.* 喝彩
⑨ portal [pɔ:təl] *n.* 大门
⑩ zeal [zi:l] *n.* 热情
⑪ astound [ə'staund] *v.* 使…震惊

流露出茫然若失的神情。若不是知道他平日生活严谨又爱干净，我真会怀疑他沾染上毒瘾。

几个礼拜后，我对他的兴趣与日俱增，对他人生目标的好奇心越来越强。他的身材相貌非同寻常，即使再不经意的旁观者都会予以关注。他身高六英尺多，但瘦骨嶙峋，似乎平添了身材的高度。目光犀利，但在我刚才所说那种慵懒期除外。细长的鹰钩鼻令他显得格外机敏果敢。下巴颏方正突出，说明他是个意志坚定的人。双手总是沾满了墨迹和化学药品，但手上动作显得异常灵巧，因为他在摆弄那些易碎的实验仪器时，我常常会注视着。

如果我承认，眼前这个人激起了我强烈的好奇心，而且常常想要冲破他把自己掩盖得严严实实的屏障，读者们兴许会把我看成是一个多管闲事的人。不过，在下此结论前，应该记住的是，我当时的生活多么漫无目标，吸引自己注意力的东西少之又少。由于身体不好，除非天气特别温暖宜人，否则我决不能贸然外出，而且也没有朋友上门来看我，每天的生活都过得单调沉闷。在这种状况下，我便迫不及待地想要探究我的同伴身上的种种小秘密，而且把大部分时间花费在揭秘上面。

他不是在研究医学。有一次在回答一个问题时，他亲口证实了斯坦福德的判断。看起来，他也不是在攻读什么课程，以便获得某个理学学位，或者赢得某种认可，跻身学界。但是，他对某些研究所表现出的热情令人觉得不可思议。他对某些生僻领域内的知识极为渊博精细，以致他的见解令我颇感惊讶。可以肯定地说，如果不是为了某一特定的目的，没人会如此孜孜不倦，掌握如此精确的知识。读书漫无目的人他们知识很难是非常精湛的。一般人不会费心劳神地专

hard or attain such precise information unless he had some definite end in view. Desultory readers are seldom remarkable for the exactness of their learning. No man burdens his mind with small matters unless he has some very good reason for doing so.

His ignorance was as remarkable as his knowledge. Of contemporary literature, philosophy and politics he appeared to know next to nothing. Upon my quoting Thomas Carlyle, he inquired in the naivest way who he might be and what he had done. My surprise reached a **climax**[①], however, when I found incidentally that he was ignorant of the Copernican Theory and of the composition of the Solar System. That any civilized human being in this nineteenth century should not be aware that the earth travelled round the sun appeared to be to me such an extraordinary fact that I could hardly realize it.

"You appear to be astonished," he said, smiling at my expression of surprise. "Now that I do know it I shall do my best to forget it."

"To forget it!"

"You see," he explained, "I consider that a man's brain originally is like a little empty attic, and you have to stock it with such furniture as you choose. A fool takes in all the **lumber**[②] of every sort that he comes across, so that the knowledge which might be useful to him gets crowded out, or at best is jumbled up with a lot of other things, so that he has a difficulty in laying his hands upon it. Now the skilful workman is very careful indeed as to what he takes into his brain-attic. He will have nothing but the tools which may help him in doing his work, but of these he has a large **assortment**[③], and all in the most perfect order. It is a mistake to think that that little room has **elastic**[④] walls and can **distend**[⑤] to any extent. Depend upon it there comes a time when for every addition of knowledge you forget something that you knew before. It is of the highest importance, therefore, not to have useless facts elbowing out the useful ones."

"But the Solar System!" I protested.

"What the deuce is it to me?" he interrupted impatiently; "you say that we go round the sun. If we went round the moon it would not make a pennyworth

注于琐碎的事情，除非有十分充足的理由这样做。

如同他的学识一样，他的无知也是显而易见的。关于当代文学、哲学和政治学，他几乎一无所知。当我引述托马斯·卡莱尔的文章时，他竟十分天真地问我卡莱尔是谁，做过些什么。然而，最让我感到惊讶的是，我无意中发现他对于哥白尼学说以及太阳系的构成，竟然也一无所知。十九世纪，一个有教养的人竟然不知道地球绕着太阳转。这在我看来实在是异乎寻常，简直不可理解。

① climax ['klaimæks] *n.* 高潮

"你似乎很惊讶啊，"他说，冲着我惊讶的表情露出了微笑，"即便我知道了，也会竭尽全力忘掉它的。"

"忘掉它！"

"你看吧，"他解释说，"我认为，人的大脑原本就像一间空的小阁楼，只能装入自己选中的家具。傻瓜才会不加选择，碰到什么都往里面放，以致那些对他有用的知识反而被挤得容不下了，或者最多也就是同其他东西挤成一团，结果使用起来很不方便。因此，一个熟练的技工在选择东西，放进小阁楼般的大脑时，会非常谨慎。除了对工作有用的东西外，什么都不会放进去。这些东西不但要样样俱全，而且须摆放得井井有条。如果你认为小阁楼的墙壁富有弹性，可以无止境地往外撑开的话，那就大错特错了。由此可知，迟早有一天，你的知识每增加一点，原有的知识就会忘掉一点。因此，最要紧的就是不能让那些无用的东西把有用的知识挤出去。"

② lumber [lʌmber] *n.* 杂物

③ assortment [ə'sɔ:tmənt] *n.* 混合物；分类

④ elastic [i'læstik] *a.* 有弹性的

⑤ distend [di'stend] *v.* 膨胀

"但那是太阳系啊！"我争辩说。

"这跟我又有什么关系呢？"他打断了我的话，显得不耐烦，"你说我们是围绕着太阳转的。但即便我们是绕着月亮转的，那也丝毫影响不到我和我的工作啊。"

of difference to me or to my work."

I was on the point of asking him what that work might be, but something in his manner showed me that the question would be an unwelcome one. I pondered over our short conversation, however, and endeavoured to draw my **deductions**[①] from it. He said that he would acquire no knowledge which did not bear upon his object. Therefore all the knowledge which he possessed was such as would be useful to him. I **enumerated**[②] in my own mind all the various points upon which he had shown me that he was exceptionally well-informed. I even took a pencil and jotted them down. I could not help smiling at the document when I had completed it. It ran in this way—

SHERLOCK HOLMES—his limits.

1. Knowledge of Literature.—Nil.
2. Knowledge of Philosophy.—Nil.
3. Knowledge of **Astronomy**[③].—Nil.
4. Knowledge of Politics.—Feeble.
5. Knowledge of **Botany**[④].—Variable. Well up in **belladonna**[⑤], opium, and poisons generally.Knows nothing of practical gardening.
6. Knowledge of Geology.—Practical, but limited. Tells at a glance different soils from each other. After walks has shown me **splashes**[⑥] upon his trousers, and told me by their colour and consistence in what part of London he had received them.
7. Knowledge of Chemistry.—Profound.
8. Knowledge of **Anatomy**[⑦].—Accurate, but unsystematic.
9. Knowledge of Sensational Literature.—**Immense**[⑧]. He appears to know every detail of every horror perpetrated in the century.
10. Plays the violin well.
11. Is an expert singlestick player, boxer, and swordsman.
12. Has a good practical knowledge of British law.

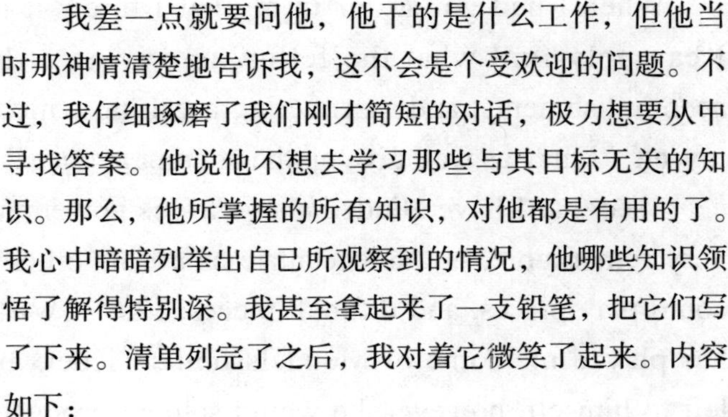

我差一点就要问他，他干的是什么工作，但他当时那神情清楚地告诉我，这不会是个受欢迎的问题。不过，我仔细琢磨了我们刚才简短的对话，极力想要从中寻找答案。他说他不想去学习那些与其目标无关的知识。那么，他所掌握的所有知识，对他都是有用的了。我心中暗暗列举出自己所观察到的情况，他哪些知识领悟了解得特别深。我甚至拿起来了一支铅笔，把它们写了下来。清单列完了之后，我对着它微笑了起来。内容如下：

夏洛克·福尔摩斯——其学识范围

一、文学知识——无。

二、哲学知识——无。

三、天文学知识——无。

四、政治学知识——粗浅。

五、植物学知识——因对象而异，在颠茄、鸦片方面知识丰富对毒药有一般了解，但在园艺方面一无所知。

六、地质学知识——掌握了实用性的知识，但很有限。一眼就能分辨不同土质。散步回来后，曾向我展示溅在他裤腿上的泥点，并根据泥点的颜色和黏稠度，告诉我是在伦敦的哪个区域溅上的。

七、化学知识——渊博。

八.解剖学知识——精准，但不成系统。

九、凶案文献知识——极丰富。他好像熟悉本世纪发生的每一桩恐怖案件的所有细节。

十、小提琴拉得很好。

十一、善于棍棒术，精于拳击和剑术。

十二、掌握了丰富的英国法律实用知识。

① deduction [di'dʌkʃən] *n.* 演绎，推论

② enumerate [i'nju:məreit] *v.* 例举

③ astronomy [ə'strɔnəmi] *n.* 天文学

④ botany ['bɔtəni] *n.* 植物学

⑤ belladonna [ˌbelə'dɔnə] *n.* 颠茄

⑥ splash [splæʃ] *n.* 污点

⑦ anatomy [ə'nætəmi] *n.* 解剖学

⑧ immense [i'mens] *a.* 丰富的

When I had got so far in my list I threw it into the fire in despair. "If I can only find what the fellow is driving at by **reconciling**[①] all these accomplishments, and discovering a calling which needs them all," I said to myself, "I may as well give up the attempt at once."

I see that I have alluded above to his powers upon the violin. These were very remarkable, but as eccentric as all his other accomplishments. That he could play pieces, and difficult pieces, I knew well, because at my request he has played me some of Mendelssohn's Lieder, and other favourites. When left to himself, however, he would seldom produce any music or attempt any recognized air. Leaning back in his arm-chair of an evening, he would close his eyes and **scrape**[②] carelessly at the fiddle which was thrown across his knee. Sometimes the chords were **sonorous**[③] and **melancholy**[④]. Occasionally they were fantastic and cheerful. Clearly they reflected the thoughts which possessed him, but whether the music aided those thoughts, or whether the playing was simply the result of a whim or fancy was more than I could determine. I might have rebelled against these **exasperating**[⑤] solos had it not been that he usually terminated them by playing in quick succession a whole series of my favourite airs as a slight compensation for the trial upon my patience.

During the first week or so we had no callers, and I had begun to think that my companion was as friendless a man as I was myself. Presently, however, I found that he had many acquaintances, and those in the most different classes of society. There was one little sallow rat-faced, dark-eyed fellow who was introduced to me as Mr. Lestrade, and who came three or four times in a single week. One morning a young girl called, fashionably dressed, and stayed for half an hour or more. The same afternoon brought a grey-headed, seedy visitor, looking like a Jew **pedlar**[⑥], who appeared to me to be much excited, and who was closely followed by a slip-shod elderly woman. On another occasion an old white-haired gentleman had an interview with my companion; and on another a railway porter in his

我把清单列到这儿后，接着便失望地把它扔到了火里。“如果我把这样一些特长糅合到一块儿，并且找到某种需要所有这些特长的行当，但结果却不能发现这家伙在干些什么，”我心里想着，“那还不如干脆打消这个念头呢。”

① reconcile ['rekənsail] *v.* 使…一致

上面我已经提到了他拉小提琴的能力，虽然可说是出类拔萃，但也像他的其他特长一样，有些怪异。我很清楚，他会拉很多曲目，而且是有难度的，因为他曾应我的请求，为我演奏一些门德尔松的《歌曲》，还有其他一些喜爱的曲目。然而，他自己一个人拉琴的时候，拉出的声音根本不成调，根本听不出他拉的是什么玩意儿。黄昏时刻，他会靠在椅背上，紧闭双眼，把小提琴放在腿上，手随意地拨弄琴弦。有时拨出的弦声高亢却又悲凉，有时怪异而又欢快。显然，琴音传递出他当时的心境，但是，究竟是琴声将他引入这样的心境呢，还是某种念头或情愫驱使他奏出这样的曲调呢？我无法做出判断。如果不是他往往会紧接着演奏好几首我喜欢的曲目，弥补一下对我耐性的折磨，我可能早就对他的独奏提出抗议了。

② scrape [skreip] *v.* 刮

③ sonorous ['sɔnərəs] *a.* 洪亮的

④ melancholy ['melənkəli] *a.* 忧郁的

⑤ exasperating [ig'zæspəreitiŋ] *a.* 使人恼怒的

开始的一两个星期时间里，我们没有任何朋友登门拜访。于是，我开始觉得，我的这位同伴和我自己一样，也没有一个朋友。不过，我很快就发现，他有许多熟人，那些人来自很不相同的社会阶层。其中有个身材矮小的人，脸色灰黄，面容不善，眼睛黑色，据介绍，他名叫莱斯特雷德，一个星期之内来过三四次。一天上午，有个打扮入时的姑娘上门了，待了半个多小时。同一天下午，来了个头发灰白、衣衫褴褛的客人，看上去像个犹太小商贩，在我面前显得很激动，身后还紧跟着一个邋遢肮脏的老妇人。另有一次，有位白发苍苍的老绅士同他进行了交谈。还有一次，来了个身穿棉绒制服的火车站搬运工。每当这些莫名

⑥ pedlar ['pedlə] *n.* 小贩

velveteen① uniform. When any of these **nondescript**② individuals put in an appearance, Sherlock Holmes used to beg for the use of the sitting-room, and I would retire to my bed-room. He always apologized to me for putting me to this inconvenience. "I have to use this room as a place of business," he said, "and these people are my clients." Again I had an opportunity of asking him a point blank question, and again my delicacy prevented me from forcing another man to **confide**③ in me. I imagined at the time that he had some strong reason for not alluding to it, but he soon dispelled the idea by coming round to the subject of his own accord.

It was upon the 4th of March, as I have good reason to remember, that I rose somewhat earlier than usual, and found that Sherlock Holmes had not yet finished his breakfast. The landlady had become so accustomed to my late habits that my place had not been laid nor my coffee prepared. With the unreasonable **petulance**④ of mankind I rang the bell and gave a curt intimation that I was ready. Then I picked up a magazine from the table and attempted to while away the time with it, while my companion munched silently at his toast. One of the articles had a pencil mark at the heading, and I naturally began to run my eye through it.

Its somewhat ambitious title was "The Book of Life," and it attempted to show how much an observant man might learn by an accurate and systematic examination of all that came in his way. It struck me as being a remarkable mixture of **shrewdness**⑤ and of **absurdity**⑥. The reasoning was close and intense, but the deductions appeared to me to be far-fetched and exaggerated. The writer claimed by a momentary expression, a twitch of a muscle or a glance of an eye, to fathom a man's inmost thoughts. Deceit, according to him, was an impossibility in the case of one trained to observation and analysis. His conclusions were as infallible as so many propositions of Euclid. So startling would his results appear to the uninitiated that until they learned the processes by which he had arrived at them they might well consider him as a **necromancer**⑦.

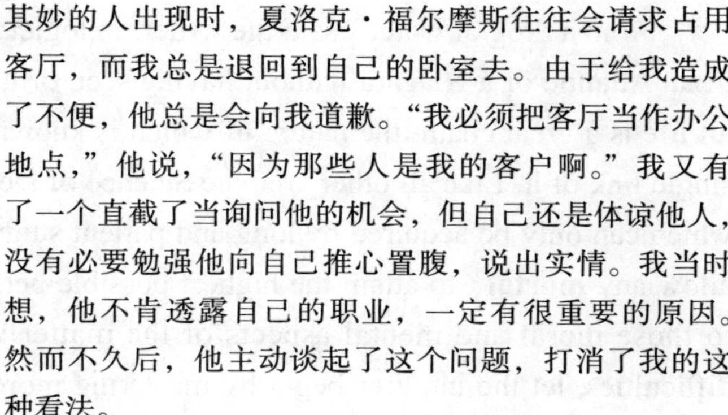

其妙的人出现时，夏洛克·福尔摩斯往往会请求占用客厅，而我总是退回到自己的卧室去。由于给我造成了不便，他总是会向我道歉。“我必须把客厅当作办公地点，”他说，“因为那些人是我的客户啊。”我又有了一个直截了当询问他的机会，但自己还是体谅他人，没有必要勉强他向自己推心置腹，说出实情。我当时想，他不肯透露自己的职业，一定有很重要的原因。然而不久后，他主动谈起了这个问题，打消了我的这种看法。

我清楚记得，那是在3月4日那天，我比平时起床早一点儿，结果发现，福尔摩斯还没有用完早餐。房东太太熟悉了我起床晚的习惯，所以，我的座位上没有摆好餐具，咖啡也没煮好。我莫名地生起气来了，按响了按铃，没好气地告诉房东太太，我要用早餐。然后，随手从桌上拿起一本杂志，打算用它来打发掉房东太太准备早餐的时间，而我的伙伴此时正在啃着面包，一声不吭。杂志上有篇文章，标题用铅笔标画了出来，我自然而然地就先看了这一篇。

文章的标题有点过于矫饰，叫做《生活指南》，文章企图说明，一个具有敏锐观察力的人通过对自己周围的所有事物进行精准和系统的观察，可以学到多少知识。我注意到，文章融精细缜密和荒诞不经于一体，可谓不同凡响。论证严丝合缝，但论断却显得过于牵强和夸大。作者声称，从一个人瞬间的表情、肌肉的颤抖或眼睛的眨动，都可洞悉他内心深处的想法。按照作者的说法，一个人如果受过观察和分析的训练的话，是不可能会受欺骗的。他所得出的结论就像欧几里德的定理一样，完全站得住脚。在一些外行看来，他的结论的确令人惊叹。如果没弄明白他推导出结论的步骤，他们真的会把他当作一个巫师。

① velveteen [ˌvelviˈtiːn] *n.* 棉绒衣服

② nondescript [ˈnɔndiˌskript] *a.* 难以归类的

③ confide [kənˈfaid] *v.* 吐露

④ petulance [ˈpetjuləns] *n.* 任性；坏脾气

⑤ shrewdness [ʃruːdnəs] *n.* 缜密

⑥ absurdity [əbˈsəːdəti] *n.* 荒诞

⑦ necromancer [ˈnekrəumænsə] *n.* 巫师

"From a drop of water," said the writer, "a logician could infer the possibility of an Atlantic or a Niagara without having seen or heard of one or the other. So all life is a great chain, the nature of which is known whenever we are shown a single link of it. Like all other arts, the Science of Deduction and Analysis is one which can only be acquired by long and patient study, nor is life long enough to allow any **mortal**① to attain the highest possible perfection in it. Before turning to those moral and mental aspects of the matter which present the greatest difficulties, let the inquirer begin by mastering more elementary problems. Let him, on meeting a fellow-mortal, learn at a glance to distinguish the history of the man, and the trade or profession to which he belongs. **Puerile**② as such an exercise may seem, it sharpens the faculties of observation, and teaches one where to look and what to look for. By a man's finger nails, by his coat-sleeve, by his boots by his trouser knees, by the **callosities**③ of his forefinger and thumb, by his expression, by his shirt cuffs—by each of these things a man's calling is plainly revealed. That all united should fail to enlighten the competent inquirer in any case is almost inconceivable."

"What **ineffable**④ **twaddle**⑤!" I cried, slapping the magazine down on the table, "I never read such rubbish in my life."

"What is it?" asked Sherlock Holmes.

"Why, this article," I said, pointing at it with my eggspoon as I sat down to my breakfast. "I see that you have read it since you have marked it. I don't deny that it is smartly written. It irritates me, though. It is evidently the theory of some arm-chair lounger who evolves all these neat little **paradoxes**⑥ in the seclusion of his own study. It is not practical. I should like to see him clapped down in a third-class carriage on the Underground, and asked to give the trades of all his fellow-travellers. I would lay a thousand to one against him."

"You would lose your money," Sherlock Holmes remarked calmly. "As for the article I wrote it myself."

"You!"

“从一滴水珠，”作者指出，“一个懂逻辑的人就能推测出他从未见过或听过的大西洋或尼亚加拉大瀑布的存在。所以，一个人所有的生活构成了巨大的链条，只要能够看见其中一环，整条链条的情况就完全可以推断出来。科学推理和分析正如其他技能一样，只有经过长期的耐心钻研才能够掌握。但人的生命是有限的，无论如何都难以把这种技能提高到登峰造极的地步。案件调查者应该把道德和心理等非常棘手的问题先搁置在一边，从最基本的问题入手。先学会一眼看出所遇到的人的经历和职业。虽然这种训练看起来好像很幼稚，但却能使一个人的观察力逐渐变得敏锐，教会我们应观察哪儿，观察些什么。一个人的指甲、衣袖、靴子和裤子膝盖处、大拇指和食指的茧子、表情、衬衣袖口等，任一细节都能明明白白地透露出他的职业信息。如果把这些细节联系起来，还不能让调查者开窍，那简直令人无法想象。”

“不知所云的废话！”我大声说，把杂志扔到桌上，“我有生以来都没有看过这样的垃圾文章。”

“什么文章？”福尔摩斯问。

“啊，这篇文章呢，”我说，一边坐下来用早餐，一边用蛋匙指了指那篇文章，“我想你看过了，因为你在上面做了记号。我不否认，这篇文章写得不错，不过，我看过后挺生气的。很显然，这是某个窝在扶手椅上的游手好闲之徒的理论，他待在自己的书房里凭空想象出了这样一些似是而非的东西，没有实际用途。我倒是想看到他被关在地铁的三等车厢里，请他说出所有同伴乘客的职业。我愿押一千跟他赌。”

“你会输钱的，”福尔摩斯说，态度很平静，“至于这篇文章，它是本人写的。”

“你！”

“对啊，我有两个方面的天赋，一是善于观察，二

① mortal ['mɔːtəl] *n.* 凡人

② puerile ['pjuːərail] *a.* 幼稚的

③ callosity [kæ'lɒsəti] *n.* 硬皮；茧子

④ ineffable [in'efəbl] *a.* 无法形容的

⑤ twaddle ['twɔdl] *n.* 废话

⑥ paradox ['pærədɔks] *n.* 悖论

"Yes, I have a turn both for observation and for deduction. The theories which I have expressed there, and which appear to you to be so chimerical, are really extremely practical—so practical that I depend upon them for my bread and cheese."

"And how?" I asked involuntarily.

"Well, I have a trade of my own. I suppose I am the only one in the world. I'm a consulting detective, if you can understand what that is. Here in London we have lots of government detectives and lots of private ones. When these fellows are at fault they come to me, and I manage to put them on the right scent. They lay all the evidence before me, and I am generally able, by the help of my knowledge of the history of crime, to set them straight. There is a strong family **resemblance**① about **misdeeds**②, and if you have all the details of a thousand at your finger ends, it is odd if you can't **unravel**③ the thousand and first. Lestrade is a well-known detective. He got himself into a fog recently over a forgery case, and that was what brought him here."

"And these other people?"

"They are mostly sent on by private inquiry agencies. They are all people who are in trouble about something and want a little enlightening. I listen to their story, they listen to my comments, and then I pocket my fee."

"But do you mean to say," I said, "that without leaving your room you can unravel some knot which other men can make nothing of, although they have seen every detail for themselves?"

"Quite so. I have a kind of **intuition**④ that way. Now and again a case turns up which is a little more complex. Then I have to bustle about and see things with my own eyes. You see I have a lot of special knowledge which I apply to the problem, and which **facilitates**⑤ matters wonderfully. Those rules of deduction laid down in that article which aroused your **scorn**⑥ are invaluable to me in practical work. Observation with me is second nature. You appeared to be surprised when I told you, on our first meeting, that you had come from Afghanistan."

是善于推理。我在文章中表达的观点，在你看来荒诞不经，但实际上极为实用——它们真的很实用，我可以据此谋生啊。”

“怎么谋生呢？”我不由自主地问了一句。

“嗯，我有自己的职业。我想，全世界这个职业仅有我一人。我是个‘咨询侦探’，不知你是否明白这是个怎样的行当。在伦敦，有许多官方侦探和私家侦探。案件一旦陷入困境，他们就会来找我。我设法为他们找出线索，指明侦破方向。他们把所有的证据都呈现给我看。一般情况下，凭借我对历史上各种刑事案件的了解，都能帮他们回到正确的思路上来。因为各种犯罪行为都有相似性，如果你对一千个案件的所有细节都了如指掌，却破不了第一千零一桩案件，那才真是怪事呢！莱斯特雷德是位著名侦探，最近为一桩伪造案件，弄得云里雾里，他就是为这事找我来了。”

“那另外那些人呢？”

“他们大多是由私家侦探机构派来的，都是碰到麻烦，需要我加以指点。我听他们叙述事情的原委，他们则听我陈述看法。就这样，钱就进我口袋了。”

“但是，你的意思是说，”我说，“别人即使亲眼目睹了一切，却也无从下手，而你足不出户，就能轻松解开谜团，对不对？”

“差不多是这么回事。我在这方面有一种直觉。时不时地，也会有一桩略微复杂的案件出现。那样的话，我不得不出去转一转，亲眼看一看情况。你知道的，我掌握了大量特殊知识，可以运用到破解案件上面去，而且效果极佳，令难题迎刃而解。虽然你对那篇文章里提出的推论法则嗤之以鼻，但在实际工作中，对我却具有非常宝贵的价值。我的观察力就是我的第二天性。记得我们初次见面时，我说，你来自阿富汗，你好像非常惊讶。”

① resemblance [ri'zembləns] *n.* 相似

② misdeed [ˌmis'diːd] *n.* 犯罪行为

③ unravel [ʌn'rævəl] *v.* 解开；解释，阐明

④ intuition [ˌintu'iʃən] *n.* 直觉

⑤ facilitate [fə'siliteit] *v.* 帮助；促进

⑥ scorn [skɔːn] *n.* 鄙视

"You were told, no doubt."

"Nothing of the sort. I *knew* you came from Afghanistan. From long habit the train of thoughts ran so swiftly through my mind that I arrived at the conclusion without being conscious of intermediate steps. There were such steps, however. The train of reasoning ran, 'Here is a gentleman of a medical type, but with the air of a military man. Clearly an army doctor, then. He has just come from the **tropics**①, for his face is dark, and that is not the natural tint of his skin, for his **wrists**② are fair. He has undergone hardship and sickness, as his haggard face says clearly. His left arm has been injured. He holds it in a **stiff**③ and unnatural manner. Where in the tropics could an English army doctor have seen much hardship and got his arm wounded? Clearly in Afghanistan.' The whole train of thought did not occupy a second. I then remarked that you came from Afghanistan, and you were astonished."

"It is simple enough as you explain it," I said, smiling. "You remind me of Edgar Allen Poe's Dupin. I had no idea that such individuals did exist outside of stories."

Sherlock Holmes rose and lit his pipe. "No doubt you think that you are complimenting me in comparing me to Dupin," he observed. "Now, in my opinion, Dupin was a very inferior fellow. That trick of his of breaking in on his friends' thoughts with an **apropos**④ remark after a quarter of an hour's silence is really very showy and superficial. He had some analytical genius, no doubt; but he was by no means such a phenomenon as Poe appeared to imagine."

"Have you read Gaboriau's works?" I asked. "Does Lecoq come up to your idea of a detective?"

Sherlock Holmes **sniffed**⑤ **sardonically**⑥. "Lecoq was a miserable bungler," he said, in an angry voice; "he had only one thing to recommend him, and that was his energy. That book made me positively ill. The question was how to identify an unknown prisoner. I could have done it in twenty-four hours. Lecoq took six months or so. It might be made a text-book for detectives to

“有人告诉你了，毫无疑问。”

“没有的事。我确实知道，你从阿富汗来。由于长期养成的习惯，一连串的思绪在我心中迅速掠过，速度快得来不及意识到中间的步骤，我就得出了结论。但是，中间的步骤还是存在的。我的推理过程是这样的：‘这位先生是个从事医务工作的人，但有着军人的气质。那么，很显然，是个军医。他刚从热带回来，因为脸色黝黑。但这并不是他原来的肤色，因为他手腕处露出的皮肤很白。他饱受过艰辛，罹患过疾病，因为他瘦削憔悴的脸上明明白白地显示着。他的左臂受过伤，动起来有些僵硬不自然。能让一个英国军医历经生死且手臂负伤的热带地方在哪里呢？显然是在阿富汗。’这一连串的思维过程还不到一秒钟，因此我说你是从阿富汗来的，你当时还感到很奇怪。”

① tropic ['trɔpik] *n.* 热带
② wrist [rist] *n.* 手腕
③ stiff [stif] *a.* 僵硬的

“听你一解释，这件事的确很简单，”我微笑着说，“你让我想起埃德加·爱伦·坡作品中的侦探杜宾来了。我真没想到现实生活中真会有这样的人。”

夏洛克·福尔摩斯站起身来，点燃他的烟斗。“毫无疑问，你认为，把我比作杜宾是对我的称赞，”他说，“啊，我倒是觉得，杜宾是个蹩脚的家伙。他惯用一种伎俩，那就是先沉默一刻钟，然后才突然道破他朋友的心事。这也太做作了，太没内涵了。不错，他有分析问题的天赋，但绝不是爱伦·坡想象中的那种奇才。”

④ apropos [ˌæprə'pəu] *a.* 恰当的

“你读过加博里约的作品吗？”我问，“勒考科那个人物在你心目中算得上是个侦探吗？”

夏洛克·福尔摩斯不屑地哼了一声。“勒考科是个可怜的笨蛋，”他说着，声音中透着愤怒，“他只有一件事还值得一提，那就是精力旺盛。那本书让我腻味透了。他在书中所遇到的难题只是如何找出隐藏的罪犯。我不用二十四小时就能办到。但勒考科却花费了六个多月时间。这都够做反面教材了，写给侦探看，教教他们

⑤ sniff [snif] *v.* 鄙视；嗤之以鼻
⑥ sardonically [sɑː'dɔnikli] *ad.* 嘲笑地

teach them what to avoid."

I felt rather **indignant**[1] at having two characters whom I had admired treated in this **cavalier**[2] style. I walked over to the window and stood looking out into the busy street. "This fellow may be very clever," I said to myself, "but he is certainly very **conceited**[3]."

"There are no crimes and no criminals in these days," he said, **querulously**[4]. "What is the use of having brains in our profession? I know well that I have it in me to make my name famous. No man lives or has ever lived who has brought the same amount of study and of natural talent to the detection of crime which I have done. And what is the result? There is no crime to detect, or, at most, some **bungling**[5] **villainy**[6] with a motive so transparent that even a Scotland Yard official can see through it."

I was still annoyed at his **bumptious**[7] style of conversation. I thought it best to change the topic.

"I wonder what that fellow is looking for?" I asked, pointing to a **stalwart**[8], plainlydressed individual who was walking slowly down the other side of the street, looking anxiously at the numbers. He had a large blue envelope in his hand, and was evidently the bearer of a message.

"You mean the retired sergeant of Marines," said Sherlock Holmes.

"**Brag**[9] and **bounce**[10]!" thought I to myself. "He knows that I cannot verify his guess."

The thought had hardly passed through my mind when the man whom we were watching caught sight of the number on our door, and ran rapidly across the roadway. We heard a loud knock, a deep voice below, and heavy steps ascending the stair.

"For Mr. Sherlock Holmes," he said, stepping into the room and handing my friend the letter.

Here was an opportunity of taking the conceit out of him. He little thought

如何避免犯同样的错误。”

他用这么傲慢的态度对待我所崇拜的两个小说人物，我感到愤愤不平。我走向窗户边，看着外面熙熙攘攘的街道。“这家伙可能聪明透顶，”我暗自思量着，“但他一定很傲慢。”

① indignant [in'dignənt] *a.* 愤怒的
② cavalier [ˌkævə'liə] *a.* 傲慢的
③ conceited [kən'siːtid] *a.* 自负的
④ querulously ['kweruləsli] *ad.* 抱怨地

“这些日子里，刑事案件和刑事罪犯都不见踪影了，”他抱怨着说，“干我们这行，有颗聪明的脑袋又有什么用呢？我很清楚，自己有头脑，足可以使自己闻名遐迩。古往今来，从来没有人像我一样把如此大量的研究和良好的天赋运用到侦破案件当中。但是，结果如何呢？没有有待去侦破的罪案，或者最多也就是些作案手法拙劣的案件，浅显易见的犯罪动机，就连伦敦警察厅的官方警探都能看透。”

⑤ bungling ['bʌŋgliŋ] *a.* 笨手笨脚地
⑥ villainy ['viləni] *n.* 罪行
⑦ bumptious ['bʌmpʃəs] *a.* 盲目自大的

我对他这种自以为是的态度还是感到不爽。我认为，还是换个话题的好。

“不知道那个人在寻找什么啊？”我问了一声，指着街对面一个身体健壮、衣着简朴的人，只见他一边慢慢地走着，一边焦急地看着一个个门牌号码，手里拿着个蓝色大信封，显然是个送信的。

⑧ stalwart ['stɔːlwət] *a.* 强壮的

“你是说那个退役了的海军陆战队中士吧？”夏洛克·福尔摩斯说。

“大言不惭啊！”我心里想着，“他知道我无法去验证他的猜测。”

⑨ brag [bræg] *v.* 自夸
⑩ bounce [bauns] *v.* 吹牛

我心里面刚刚冒出这样一个念头，只见我们一直看着的那个男人看见了我们的门牌号码，急忙跑过了街道。下面传来一阵响亮的敲门声，一个低沉的嗓音和上楼梯的沉重脚步声。

“给夏洛克·福尔摩斯先生的信，”他说着，走进了房间，把信交给了我的伙伴。

这可是杀杀他的傲气的好机会。他信口开河的时候，根本就想不到会这样。“我可不可以问一声，朋

of this when he made that random shot. "May I ask, my lad," I said, in the **blandest**① voice, "what your trade may be?"

"**Commissionaire**②, sir," he said, gruffly. "Uniform away for repairs."

"And you were?" I asked, with a slightly **malicious**③ glance at my companion.

"A sergeant, sir, Royal Marine Light Infantry, sir. No answer? Right, sir."

He clicked his heels together, raised his hand in a salute, and was gone.

① bland [blænd] *a.* 和蔼的

② commissionaire [kəˌmiʃə'nɛə] *n.* 听差

③ malicious [mə'liʃəs] *a.* 存心不良的

友，”我说，语气尽量平和，“您是干什么的？”

“送信跑腿的，先生，”他回答说，语气很生硬，“制服送去补了。”

“过去是干什么的呢？”我问，幸灾乐祸地瞥了一眼我的同伴。

“中士，先生，皇家海军陆战队轻步兵团的。先生，没有回信吗？好的，先生。”

他两腿一并，举手行了个礼，转身离开了。

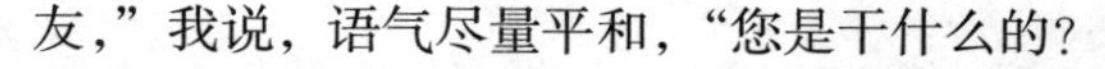

Chapter 3 The Lauriston Garden Mystery

I confess that I was considerably startled by this fresh proof of the practical nature of my companion's theories. My respect for his powers of analysis increased wondrously. There still remained some lurking suspicion in my mind, however, that the whole thing was a pre-arranged episode, intended to dazzle me, though what earthly object he could have in taking me in was past my comprehension. When I looked at him he had finished reading the note, and his eyes had assumed the vacant, **lack-lustre**① expression which showed mental abstraction.

"How in the world did you **deduce**② that?" I asked.

"Deduce what?" said he, **petulantly**③.

"Why, that he was a retired **sergeant**④ of Marines."

"I have no time for trifles," he answered, **brusquely**⑤; then with a smile, "Excuse my rudeness. You broke the thread of my thoughts; but perhaps it is as well. So you actually were not able to see that that man was a sergeant of Marines?"

"No, indeed."

"It was easier to know it than to explain why I knew it. If you were asked to prove that two and two made four, you might find some difficulty, and yet you are quite sure of the fact. Even across the street I could see a great blue **anchor**⑥ **tattooed**⑦ on the back of the fellow's hand. That **smacked**⑧ of the

第三章　劳里斯顿花园谜案

我承认，看到自己同伴的一套理论实用有效的新证据，我颇感惊讶。我对他分析问题能力的钦佩之情陡然增加。不过，心里面依旧潜藏着疑虑，认为整个事情都是事先安排好了的，旨在让我惊叹目眩。然而，他欺骗我是何目的，这我就无法理解了。我看他时，他刚看完了信，两眼茫然无神，暗淡无光，说明他心不在焉。

“这个你到底是如何推断出来啊？”我问了一声。

“推断出什么？”他说，态度粗鲁。

“啊，说他是退役的海军陆战队中士啊。”

“我没功夫纠缠细枝末节，”他回答说，语气生硬，但随即又露出了微笑，“请原谅我态度粗鲁，因为你打断了我的思路。不过，或许也没有什么关系。这么看来，你确实看不出，此人曾经是个海军陆战队中士啦？”

“对啊，确实看不出。”

“看出这一点倒是不难，但要解释我为何看得出来却挺难。如果有人要你证明二加二等于四，你可能会觉得有点困难，尽管你确认事实就是这样的。即便隔着一条街，我还是看清楚了那人手背上挺大一块蓝锚刺青，这是海洋上的标记啊。并且，他有军人的风度，两颊的

① lack-lustre [ˈlækˌlʌstə] *a.* 黯淡无光的

② deduce [diˈdjuːs] *v.* 推断

③ petulantly [ˈpetjuələntli] *ad.* 暴躁地

④ sergeant [ˈsɑːdʒənt] *n.* 中士

⑤ brusquely [ˈbruskli] *ad.* 生硬地

⑥ anchor [ˈæŋkə] *n.* 锚

⑦ tattoo [tæˈtuː] *n.* 刺青

⑧ smack of 带有…的迹象

sea. He had a military **carriage**[①], however, and regulation side **whiskers**[②]. There we have the marine. He was a man with some amount of self-importance and a certain air of command. You must have observed the way in which he held his head and swung his **cane**[③]. A steady, respectable, middle-aged man, too, on the face of him—all facts which led me to believe that he had been a sergeant."

"Wonderful!" I **ejaculated**[④].

"Commonplace," said Holmes, though I thought from his expression that he was pleased at my evident surprise and admiration. "I said just now that there were no criminals. It appears that I am wrong—look at this!" He threw me over the note which the commissionaire had brought.

"Why," I cried, as I cast my eye over it, "this is terrible!"

"It does seem to be a little out of the common," he remarked, calmly. "Would you mind reading it to me aloud?"

This is the letter which I read to him——

"MY DEAR MR. SHERLOCK HOLMES:

"There has been a bad business during the night at 3, Lauriston Gardens, off the Brixton Road. Our man **on the beat**[⑤] saw a light there about two in the morning, and as the house was an empty one, suspected that something was **amiss**[⑥]. He found the door open, and in the front room, which is bare of furniture, discovered the body of a gentleman, well dressed, and having cards in his pocket bearing the name of 'Enoch J. Drebber, Cleveland, Ohio, U.S.A.' There had been no robbery, nor is there any evidence as to how the man met his death. There are marks of blood in the room, but there is no wound upon his person. We are at a loss as to how he came into the empty house; indeed, the whole affair is a puzzler. If you can come round to the house any time before twelve, you will find me there. I have left everything ***in statu quo***[⑦] until I hear from you. If you are unable to come I shall give you fuller details, and would **esteem**[⑧] it a great kindness if you would favour me with your opinion.

"Yours faithfully,

"TOBIAS GREGSON."

① carriage ['kærɪdʒ] *n.* 举止，仪态

② whisker ['wiskə] *n.* 络腮胡子

③ cane [kein] *n.* 手杖

④ ejaculate [i'dʒækjə,leit] *v.* 突然说出

⑤ on the beat 在巡逻中

⑥ amiss [ə'mis] *a.* 出了差错的

⑦ in statu quo 维持现状

⑧ esteem [i'sti:m] *v.* 认为

胡须符合军队规定，这样我们就想到了海军陆战队了。此人有点自以为是，有种颐指气使的气势。你一定注意到了，他昂着头，挥舞着手杖的样子。从他的面容也可以看出，他是个沉稳持重、体面正派的中年人——所有这些事实帮助我得出结论，他曾经是个中士。"

"了不起啊！"我脱口说道。

"平凡小事而已，"福尔摩斯说，不过，从他脸部的表情，我觉得，自己显而易见的惊讶和钦佩之情令他很受用，"我刚才还说来着，说没有刑事罪犯，看起来我错了——看看这个！"他把刚才那个信差送过来的信扔给我看。

"啊，"我大声说，一边扫了一眼信，"这真可怕！"

"事情看上去超乎寻常啊，"他说着，语气平静，"请你大声念给我听好吗？"

下面就是我念给他听的信的内容：

尊敬的夏洛克·福尔摩斯先生：

昨天夜间，布里克斯顿大街的劳里斯顿花园三号发生一桩恶性案件。今天凌晨两点钟左右，我们巡逻的警察发现屋内有光亮，由于那所住宅平常空着没有人住，于是就怀疑发生了什么不测。他发现房门开着，前厅里没有家具，躺着一具男人的尸体，衣着讲究，衣袋中的名片上写着"伊诺克·J·德雷伯，美国俄亥俄州克利夫兰市"。现场无抢劫迹象，也无任何证据说明死者的死因。屋内有血迹，但尸体上并无伤痕。至于死者如何进入空屋，我们百思不得其解，深感此案诡秘怪异。请您十二点前亲临现场勘察，我将在场恭候。在您回复前，我会保护现场。若您不能亲临现场，我将向您提供更详尽的资料，如蒙指教，不胜感激。

您忠实的朋友

托比亚斯·格雷格森

"Gregson is the smartest of the **Scotland Yarders**[①]," my friend remarked; "he and Lestrade are the pick of a bad lot. They are both quick and energetic, but conventional—shockingly so. They have their knives into one another, too. They are as jealous as a pair of professional beauties. There will be some fun over this case if they are both put upon the scent."

I was amazed at the calm way in which he **rippled on**[②]. "Surely there is not a moment to be lost," I cried, "shall I go and order you a cab?"

"I'm not sure about whether I shall go. I am the most incurably lazy devil that ever stood in shoe leather—that is, when the fit is on me, for I can be **spry**[③] enough at times."

"Why, it is just such a chance as you have been longing for."

"My dear fellow, what does it matter to me. Supposing I unravel the whole matter, you may be sure that Gregson, Lestrade, and Co. will pocket all the credit. That comes of being an unofficial **personage**[④]."

"But he begs you to help him."

"Yes. He knows that I am his superior, and acknowledges it to me; but he would cut his tongue out before he would own it to any third person. However, we may as well go and have a look. I shall work it out **on my own hook**[⑤]. I may have a laugh at them if I have nothing else. Come on!"

He hustled on his overcoat, and bustled about in a way that showed that an energetic fit had **superseded**[⑥] the **apathetic**[⑦] one.

"Get your hat," he said.

"You wish me to come?"

"Yes, if you have nothing better to do." A minute later we were both in a hansom, driving furiously for the Brixton Road.

It was a foggy, cloudy morning, and a dun-coloured veil hung over the house-tops, looking like the reflection of the mud-coloured streets beneath. My companion was in the best of spirits, and **prattled**[⑧] away about Cremona **fiddles**[⑨], and the difference between a Stradivarius and an Amati. As for

① Scotland Yarder 伦敦警察厅的警察

② ripple on 传递，表现

③ spry [sprai] *a.* 活跃的

④ personage ['pə:sənidʒ] *n.* 名人

⑤ on one's own hook 独自

⑥ supersede [ˌsju:pə'si:d] *v.* 取代

⑦ apathetic [ˌæpə'θetik] *a.* 冷淡的

⑧ prattle ['prætl] *v.* 闲扯

⑨ fiddle ['fidl] *n.* 小提琴

“格雷格森是伦敦警察厅中最机敏睿智的人，”我朋友评价说，“他和莱斯特雷德是一群矮子中的高个儿。两个人都反应灵敏，精力充沛，但因循守旧——简直令人震惊。他们也会相互找茬儿，就像一对交际花，争风吃醋。如果他们两个一同来侦办这桩案件，那可就有点热闹了。”

福尔摩斯侃侃而谈，但态度平静，我感到很诧异。“毫无疑问，情况刻不容缓啊，”我大声说，“要我去帮你叫辆马车吗？”

“我是不是去，还不一定呢。我这个人慵懒倦怠，简直就不可救药了，不过，那也只是犯懒的时候才这样——也就是说，只是在懒劲上来了时才这样，平时还是挺有活力的。”

“怎么啦，这不正是你求之不得的良机吗？”

“亲爱的伙计啊，这关我什么事呢？即便我把整个案件给弄得水落石出，格雷格森和莱斯特雷德等人无疑都会把所有的功劳揽到自己头上的。这就是没有官方身份的下场啊。”

“但是，他恳请你帮助他啊。”

“没错，他知道我比他强，他在我面前也承认这一点，但是，他宁愿割下自己的舌头，也绝不愿让第三个人知道。得啦，我们还是去看看吧。我可以独自一人破案，即便什么都捞不到，也可以嘲笑他们一番，走吧！”

他急忙穿上外套，匆匆忙忙的，说明劲头上来了，不再慵懒倦怠了。

“你戴上帽子，”他说。

“想要我也去吗？”

“对啊，如果你没有别的事情可做的话。”片刻之后，我们坐上了马车，马车辘辘驶向布里克斯顿大街。

早晨雾气沉沉，乌云密布。所有的屋顶都笼罩上了一层暗褐色的雾纱，仿佛是土黄色街道的倒影。我同伴

myself, I was silent, for the dull weather and the melancholy business upon which we were engaged, depressed my spirits.

"You don't seem to give much thought to the matter in hand," I said at last, interrupting Holmes's musical **disquisition**[1].

"No data yet," he answered. "It is a capital mistake to theorize before you have all the evidence. It biases the judgment."

"You will have your data soon," I remarked, pointing with my finger; "this is the Brixton Road, and that is the house, if I am not very much mistaken."

"So it is. Stop, driver, stop!" We were still a hundred yards or so from it, but he insisted upon our **alighting**[2], and we finished our journey upon foot.

Number 3, Lauriston Gardens wore an **ill-omened**[3] and **minatory**[4] look. It was one of four which stood back some little way from the street, two being occupied and two empty. The latter looked out with three tiers of vacant melancholy windows, which were blank and dreary, save that here and there a "To Let" card had developed like a **cataract**[5] upon the bleared **panes**[6]. A small garden sprinkled over with a scattered eruption of sickly plants separated each of these houses from the street, and was **traversed**[7] by a narrow pathway, yellowish in colour, and consisting apparently of a mixture of clay and of gravel. The whole place was very sloppy from the rain which had fallen through the night. The garden was bounded by a three-foot brick wall with a fringe of wood rails upon the top, and against this wall was leaning a stalwart police **constable**[8], surrounded by a small knot of loafers, who craned their necks and strained their eyes in the vain hope of catching some glimpse of the proceedings within.

I had imagined that Sherlock Holmes would at once have hurried into the house and plunged into a study of the mystery. Nothing appeared to be further from his intention. With an air of **nonchalance**[9] which, under the circumstances, seemed to me to border upon **affectation**[10], he lounged up and

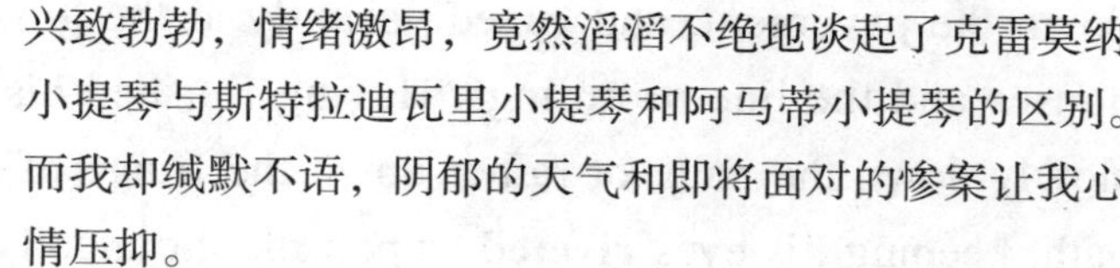

兴致勃勃，情绪激昂，竟然滔滔不绝地谈起了克雷莫纳小提琴与斯特拉迪瓦里小提琴和阿马蒂小提琴的区别。而我却缄默不语，阴郁的天气和即将面对的惨案让我心情压抑。

① disquisition [ˌdiskwi'ziʃən] *n.* 专题演讲

“你好像没怎么考虑眼前这桩案件啊，”我最后说，打断了福尔摩斯有关音乐的宏论。

“还没有掌握情况呢，”他回答说，“如果没有掌握所有证据就开始推理，那是大错特错的，会让我们的判断出现偏差。”

“你很快就会掌握情况的，”我说着，用手指指点着，“如果我没有弄错的话，这就是布里克斯顿大街，那就是出事的那幢房子。”

② alighting [ə'laitiŋ] *n.* 下车

“是这儿，停车，车夫，停车！”我们距离那幢房子还有一百码左右，他坚持我们就此下车。我们步行着走了过去。

③ ill-omened ['iləumənd] *a.* 不吉祥的

④ minatory ['minəˌtəri] *a.* 威胁性的

劳里斯顿花园三号笼罩着一种不祥的气氛，阴森可怕。距离街道有一段距离的地方，矗立着四幢住房，两幢住着人，另外两幢空着，三号楼就是其中一幢空的。空屋临街的一边有上下三排窗户，阴森凄凉。满是灰尘的玻璃上到处贴着“出租”的告示，就像是眼睛里长出的白内障。每幢房子前面都有一座小花园，把房子和街道隔开。花园里毫无规则地冒出了一些病恹恹的植物。花园里有条狭窄的小径穿过，呈淡黄色，显然是用粘土和砾石混合铺成的。昨晚下了一夜的雨，到处泥泞不堪。花园四周用三英尺高的砖墙围着，墙头上竖着木栅栏。倚墙站着一个身材高大魁梧的警察，旁边围着几个闲着没事看热闹的人，他们使劲伸长脖子拼命往里面张望，想看看里面的状况，但什么也看不到。

⑤ cataract ['kætəˌrækt] *n.* 白内障

⑥ pane [pein] *n.* 窗玻璃

⑦ traverse ['trævəs] *v.* 横穿

⑧ constable ['kənstəbəl] *n.* 警察

我本以为，夏洛克·福尔摩斯会立刻进入室内，一头扎入疑案分析工作中。但从他神态看，并不是这么回事。他一副漫不经心的样子，在那种情况下，我觉得，

⑨ nonchalance [nɔnʃələns] *n.* 漠不关心

⑩ affectation [ˌæfek'teiʃən] *n.* 装模作样，矫情

down the pavement, and gazed vacantly at the ground, the sky, the opposite houses and the line of railings. Having finished his **scrutiny**[①], he proceeded slowly down the path, or rather down the fringe of grass which **flanked**[②] the path, keeping his eyes **riveted**[③] upon the ground. Twice he stopped, and once I saw him smile, and heard him utter an **exclamation**[④] of satisfaction. There were many marks of footsteps upon the wet **clayey**[⑤] soil; but since the police had been coming and going over it, I was unable to see how my companion could hope to learn anything from it. Still I had had such extraordinary evidence of the quickness of his perceptive faculties, that I had no doubt that he could see a great deal which was hidden from me.

At the door of the house we were met by a tall, white-faced, **flaxen-haired**[⑥] man, with a notebook in his hand, who rushed forward and wrung my companion's hand with **effusion**[⑦]. "It is indeed kind of you to come," he said, "I have had everything left untouched."

"Except that!" my friend answered, pointing at the pathway. "If a herd of **buffaloes**[⑧] had passed along there could not be a greater mess. No doubt, however, you had drawn your own conclusions, Gregson, before you permitted this."

"I have had so much to do inside the house," the detective said **evasively**[⑨]. "My colleague, Mr. Lestrade, is here. I had relied upon him to look after this."

Holmes glanced at me and raised his eyebrows **sardonically**[⑩]. "With two such men as yourself and Lestrade upon the ground, there will not be much for a third party to find out," he said.

Gregson rubbed his hands in a self-satisfied way. "I think we have done all that can be done," he answered; "it's a queer case though, and I knew your taste for such things."

"You did not come here in a cab?" asked Sherlock Holmes.

"No, sir."

"Nor Lestrade?"

"No, sir."

他这是有点儿矫情，只见他在人行道上来回踱着步，表情茫然地俯视地面，仰望天空，平视正对面的住宅和那一排栅栏。仔细地察看完了一通之后，他接着便缓慢地沿着小径走，准确地说，应该是顺着小径边缘的草地走，眼睛一直盯着地面。他两次停下了脚步，有一次我看见他露出了微笑，听见他发出了满意的惊叹声。潮湿的泥地上有许多脚印。但是，因为警察已经在上面来回走过多次了，我真看不出福尔摩斯还能从中发现点什么。不过，我很清楚，他有敏锐的洞察力，因此坚信他一定能发现许多我所不能发现的东西。

到了房子的门口时，我们遇上了一位男士，身材高大，脸色白净，头发淡黄。他手里拿着一个记事本，急忙迎上前来热情地握住我同伴的手。“您能来真是太好了，”他说，“我已吩咐过，任何东西都不能动。”

“除了那儿！”我同伴回答说，指着那条小径，“即便是有一群野牛在上面踩过了，也不至于比那更加糟糕凌乱啊。不过，毫无疑问，您一定是有了结论了，格雷格森，否则您是不会允许他们这么干的。”

“室内有很多事情够我忙的，”警探说着，闪烁其词，“我同事莱斯特雷德先生在这儿，外面的事情我可指望着他负责的。”

福尔摩斯瞥了我一眼，讥讽地扬了扬眉头。“有了您和莱斯特雷德这样的能手坐镇现场，别人到场也不会有什么新发现啊，”他说。

格雷格森搓了搓双手，自鸣得意。“我认为，能够做的我们都做了，”他回答说，“不过，这是一桩诡异离奇的案件，我知道，这正对您的胃口呢。”

“您不是乘马车来的吧？”夏洛克·福尔摩斯问。

“不是，先生。”

“莱斯特雷德也不是吗？”

“不是，先生。”

① scrutiny ['skru:tini] *n.* 查看
② flank [flæŋk] *v.* 在…之侧
③ rivet ['rivit] *v.* 集中（目光）
④ exclamation [,ekskləˈmeiʃən] *n.* 惊叹
⑤ clayey ['kleii] *a.* 像黏土的
⑥ flaxen-haired ['flæksən hεəd] *a.* 淡黄色头发的
⑦ effusion [i'fju:ʒən] *n.* 感情迸发
⑧ buffalo ['bʌfələu] *n.* 野牛
⑨ evasively [i'veisivli] *ad.* 推脱地;含糊其辞地
⑩ sardonically [sɑ:'dɔnikəli] *ad.* 讽刺地

"Then let us go and look at the room." With which **inconsequent**[①] remark he strode on into the house, followed by Gregson, whose features expressed his astonishment.

A short passage, bare-planked and dusty, led to the kitchen and offices. Two doors opened out of it to the left and to the right. One of these had obviously been closed for many weeks. The other belonged to the dining-room, which was the apartment in which the mysterious affair had occurred. Holmes walked in, and I followed him with that subdued feeling at my heart which the presence of death inspires.

It was a large square room, looking all the larger from the absence of all furniture. A vulgar flaring paper **adorned**[②] the walls, but it was **blotched**[③] in places with **mildew**[④], and here and there great strips had become detached and hung down, exposing the yellow plaster beneath. Opposite the door was a showy fireplace, **surmounted**[⑤] by a mantelpiece of imitation white marble. On one corner of this was stuck the stump of a red wax candle. The solitary window was so dirty that the light was hazy and uncertain, giving a dull grey **tinge**[⑥] to everything, which was intensified by the thick layer of dust which coated the whole apartment.

All these details I observed afterwards. At present my attention was centred upon the single grim motionless figure which lay stretched upon the boards, with vacant sightless eyes staring up at the discoloured ceiling. It was that of a man about forty-three or forty-four years of age, middle-sized, broad shouldered, with crisp curling black hair, and a short **stubbly**[⑦] beard. He was dressed in a heavy broadcloth **frock**[⑧] coat and waistcoat, with light-coloured trousers, and **immaculate**[⑨] collar and cuffs. A top hat, well brushed and trim, was placed upon the floor beside him. His hands were clenched and his arms thrown abroad, while his lower **limbs**[⑩] were interlocked as though his death struggle had been a grievous one. On his rigid face there stood an expression of horror, and as it seemed to me, of hatred, such as I have never seen upon human features. This **malignant**[⑪] and terrible **contortion**[⑫], combined with the low forehead, **blunt**[⑬] nose, and **prognathous**[⑭] jaw gave the dead man a singularly **simious**[⑮] and

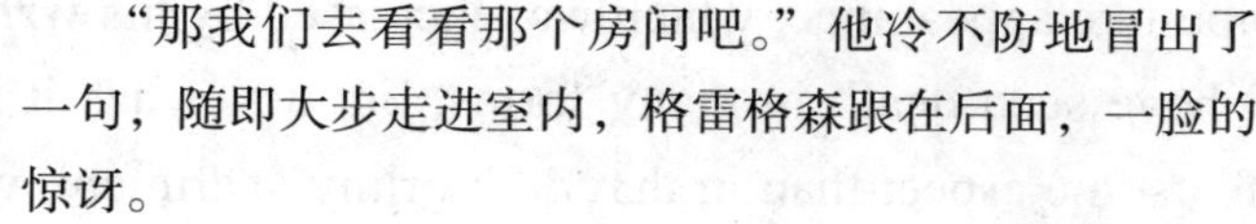

① inconsequent [in'kɔnsikwənt] *a.* 不连贯的，不切题的

“那我们去看看那个房间吧。”他冷不防地冒出了一句，随即大步走进室内，格雷格森跟在后面，一脸的惊讶。

一条很短的过道，没有铺上地毯，满是灰尘，直通厨房和杂物间。过道左右两侧各有一扇门。其中有一扇显然关闭了许多个星期。另一扇通向餐厅，扑朔迷离的案件就发生在那儿。福尔摩斯走了进去，我跟在他后面，心里充满了面对死亡现场所引起的压抑感。

② adorn [ə'dɔ:n] *v.* 装饰
③ blotch [blɔtʃ] *v.* 弄脏
④ mildew ['mil,dju:] *n.* 霉斑
⑤ surmount [sə'maunt] *v.* 覆盖在…之上
⑥ tinge [tindʒ] *n.* 细微的色彩

这是个正方形的大房间，里面没有任何家具，越发显得宽敞。墙壁上糊着花里胡哨的墙纸，俗不可耐，有些地方长出了大块霉斑。许多地方的墙纸已经大片剥落，露出了里面发黄的灰泥。正对着房门的是一个张扬醒目的壁炉，壁炉架是白色仿大理石做成的，炉台一端立着一截红蜡烛。仅有的一扇窗户肮脏不堪，室内光线昏暗，给里面的一切都抹上了一层晦暗阴郁的色彩，而室内厚厚的灰尘则更加重了这一色彩。

⑦ stubbly ['stʌbli] *a.* 又短又粗的
⑧ frock [frɔk] *n.* 长外衣
⑨ immaculate [i'mækjəlit] *a.* 整洁的
⑩ limb [lim] *n.* 肢
⑪ malignant [mə'lignənt] *a.* 恶毒的
⑫ contortion [kən'tɔ:ʃən] *n.* 扭曲
⑬ blunt [blʌnt] *a.* 不尖的
⑭ prognathous [prɔg'neiθəs] *a.* 下巴突出的
⑮ simious ['simiəs] *a.* 像猴子的

上述所有细节都是我后来才注意到的。我眼下的注意力全部集中在那具尸体上，孤零零的，满目狰狞，一动不动。尸体僵直地躺在地板上，一双空洞无神的眼睛凝视着褪色的天花板。死者四十三、四岁的样子，中等身材，肩膀很宽，一头黑色鬈发，留着胡茬。上身穿厚粗绒大衣，里面是件马甲，领子和袖口干干净净，下身穿着浅色的裤子。尸体旁的地板上有一顶整洁的礼帽。死者生前似乎有过一番痛苦的挣扎：他双手紧攥着，双臂向外伸展，双腿交织着，僵硬的脸上露出惊恐的神情。我想，这应该是一种愤恨的表情，活人的脸上不可能有如此表情。凶恶可怕的面容极度扭曲，加上低额，塌鼻和突下巴，使死者看起来非常像只猿猴。他那极不自然地痛苦扭曲的肢体，让他看起来更怪异可怕。我见过很多死人的样子，但却从没

ape-like appearance, which was increased by his **writhing**[①], unnatural posture. I have seen death in many forms, but never has it appeared to me in a more fearsome aspect than in that dark grimy apartment, which looked out upon one of the main arteries of suburban London.

Lestrade, lean and **ferret-like**[②] as ever, was standing by the doorway, and greeted my companion and myself.

"This case will make a stir, sir," he remarked. "It beats anything I have seen, and I am no chicken."

"There is no clue?" said Gregson.

"None at all," **chimed in**[③] Lestrade.

Sherlock Holmes approached the body, and, kneeling down, examined it **intently**[④]. "You are sure that there is no wound?" he asked, pointing to numerous **gouts**[⑤] and splashes of blood which lay all round.

"Positive!" cried both detectives.

"Then, of course, this blood belongs to a second individual—presumably the murderer, if murder has been committed. It reminds me of the circumstances **attendant**[⑥] on the death of Van Jansen, in Utrecht, in the year '34. Do you remember the case, Gregson?"

"No, sir."

"Read it up—you really should. There is nothing new under the sun. It has all been done before."

As he spoke, his **nimble**[⑦] fingers were flying here, there, and everywhere, feeling, pressing, unbuttoning, examining, while his eyes wore the same far-away expression which I have already remarked upon. So swiftly was the examination made, that one would hardly have guessed the minuteness with which it was conducted. Finally, he **sniffed**[⑧] the dead man's lips, and then glanced at the **soles**[⑨] of his patent leather boots.

"He has not been moved at all?" he asked.

"No more than was necessary for the purposes of our examination."

"You can take him to the **mortuary**[⑩] now," he said. "There is nothing more

见过像这幢面朝伦敦郊区主干道的阴暗肮脏的屋内这位死者这样狰狞恐怖的惨状。

莱斯特雷德一如既往，还是那么瘦削，一副侦探的派头。他站立在门口，向同伴和我打招呼。

“本案会引起轰动啊，先生，”他说，“我也不算是生手了，还真没有见过这样的案件呢。”

“毫无线索吗？”格雷格森问。

“一点儿也没有，”莱斯特雷德随口回答。

福尔摩斯走近尸体，跪下来专心致志地查看起来。“你们肯定，尸体上没有伤痕吗？”他问了一句，手指着四周斑斑点点的血迹。

“肯定！”两位侦探齐声回答说。

“那么，当然，这些血迹是另一个人留下的。如果这是一起凶杀案的话，那人有可能就是凶手。本案让我想起了1834年发生在乌得勒支市的一桩案件，范·杨森死亡的情形。您记得那桩案件吗，格雷格森？”

“不记得了，先生。”

“看看记载吧——您真的应该看看去。阳光底下没有什么新鲜玩意儿，都是先前出现过的。”

福尔摩斯说话的当儿，他那灵巧的手指四处移动着，这儿，那儿，到处摸一摸，按一按，解开死者衣扣，仔细观察。但如同我先前注意到的那样，他的目光依旧若即若离。检查工作进行得非常快，旁人几乎想象不到，他的检查其实非常精细。最后，他闻了闻死者的嘴唇，接着还瞥了一眼死者漆革靴子的底部。

“尸体一点儿都没有移动过吧？”他问。

“仅仅是做过必要的检查而已。”

“现在可以把尸体送去殡仪馆了，”他说，“没有什么可查的了。”

格雷格森已经安排好了一副担架和四个抬担架的人。在他召唤下，那些人进入到了房间，无名死者被抬了出

① writhing ['raiðiŋ] *a.* 扭曲的

② ferret-like ['feritlaik] *a.* 侦探派头的

③ chime in 紧跟着说

④ intently [in'tentli] *ad.* 专注地

⑤ gout [gaut] *n.* 一滴

⑥ attendant [ə'tendənt] *a.* 伴随的

⑦ nimble ['nimbl] *a.* 灵巧的

⑧ sniff [snif] *v.* 嗅

⑨ sole [səul] *n.* 鞋底

⑩ mortuary ['mɔ:tjuəri] *n.* 停尸间

to be learned."

Gregson had a **stretcher**[1] and four men at hand. At his call they entered the room, and the stranger was lifted and carried out. As they raised him, a ring **tinkled**[2] down and rolled across the floor. Lestrade grabbed it up and stared at it with **mystified**[3] eyes.

"There's been a woman here," he cried. "It's a woman's wedding-ring."

He held it out, as he spoke, upon the **palm**[4] of his hand. We all gathered round him and gazed at it. There could be no doubt that that circlet of plain gold had once adorned the finger of a bride.

"This complicates matters," said Gregson. "Heaven knows, they were complicated enough before."

"You're sure it doesn't simplify them?" observed Holmes. "There's nothing to be learned by staring at it. What did you find in his pockets?"

"We have it all here," said Gregson, pointing to a litter of objects upon one of the bottom steps of the stairs. "A gold watch, No. 97163, by Barraud, of London. Gold Albert chain, very heavy and solid. Gold ring, with **masonic**[5] **device**[6]. Gold pin—bull-dog's head, with **rubies**[7] as eyes. Russian leather card-case, with cards of Enoch J. Drebber of Cleveland, corresponding with the E. J. D. upon the linen. No purse, but loose money to the extent of seven pounds thirteen. Pocket edition of Boccaccio's '**Decameron**[8],' with name of Joseph Stangerson upon the **flyleaf**[9]. Two letters—one addressed to E. J. Drebber and one to Joseph Stangerson."

"At what address?"

"American Exchange, Strand—to be left till called for. They are both from the Guion Steamship Company, and refer to the sailing of their boats from Liverpool. It is clear that this unfortunate man was about to return to New York."

"Have you made any inquiries as to this man, Stangerson?"

"I did it at once, sir," said Gregson. "I have had advertisements sent to all the newspapers, and one of my men has gone to the American Exchange, but he has not returned yet."

① stretcher ['stretʃə] *n.* 担架

② tinkle ['tiŋkl] *v.* 发出叮当声

③ mystified ['mistə,faid] *a.* 困惑的

④ palm [pɑ:m] *n.* 手掌

⑤ masonic [mə'sɔnik] *a.* 共济会会员的

⑥ device [di'vais] *n.*（徽章）图案

⑦ ruby ['ru:bi] *n.* 红宝石

⑧ Decameron [di'kæmərən] *n.*《十日谈》

⑨ flyleaf ['flai,li:f] *n.* 扉页

去。他们抬起尸体时，一枚戒指叮当一声滚落在地板上。莱斯特雷德一把从地上抓起戒指，迷惑不解地盯着看。

"有个女人到过这儿，"他大声说，"这是一枚女式婚戒。"

说着，他把戒指放在手掌上递给在场的人看。我们都围上去看。毫无疑问，这枚足金戒指曾经套在一位新娘的手指上。

"案情更加复杂了，"格雷格森说，"天知道，案情先前就够复杂的。"

"您肯定这枚戒指没有使案情简单明了吗？"福尔摩斯说，"盯着看是得不出什么结论来的。你们在死者的衣服口袋里发现了些什么呢？"

"找到的东西全在这儿呢，"格雷格森说，指了指放在楼梯底层台阶上的一堆凌乱的东西，"一块由伦敦巴罗公司制造的金表，编号为97163。一条阿尔伯特金表链，粗重结实。一枚金戒指，上面刻有共济会标识。一枚金别针，呈斗牛狗头部形状，狗眼睛由两颗红宝石镶成。一个俄制名片夹，名片上印有克利夫兰的伊诺克·J·德雷伯字样，与死者衣袖上绣着的E.J.D三个缩写字母相吻合。没有钱包，只有些零钱，总共七英镑十三先令。一本薄伽丘的袖珍版小说《十日谈》，扉页上写有约瑟夫·斯坦格森的名字。还发现两封信，一封是写给德雷伯的，另一封是写给约瑟夫·斯坦格森的。"

"寄到什么地方的？"

"斯特兰德大街的美国交易所，信是留交收信人自取。两封信都是从盖恩轮船公司寄来的，信中提及他们的轮船已从利物浦起航。可见，这个不幸的人正要准备回纽约。"

"你们调查了斯坦格森这个人吗？"

"我当即就调查了，先生，"格雷格森说，"我已派人到各报社刊登寻人启事了，有个手下已经去美国交易所调查情况，现在还没回来呢。"

"Have you sent to Cleveland?"

"We telegraphed this morning."

"How did you word your inquiries?"

"We simply detailed the circumstances, and said that we should be glad of any information which could help us."

"You did not ask for particulars on any point which appeared to you to be **crucial**①?"

"I asked about Stangerson."

"Nothing else? Is there no circumstance on which this whole case appears to hinge? Will you not telegraph again?"

"I have said all I have to say," said Gregson, in an **offended**② voice.

Sherlock Holmes chuckled to himself, and appeared to be about to make some remark, when Lestrade, who had been in the front room while we were holding this conversation in the hall, reappeared upon the scene, rubbing his hands in a **pompous**③ and self-satisfied manner.

"Mr. Gregson," he said, "I have just made a discovery of the highest importance, and one which would have been overlooked had I not made a careful examination of the walls."

The little man's eyes sparkled as he spoke, and he was evidently in a state of suppressed **exultation**④ at having scored a point against his colleague.

"Come here," he said, bustling back into the room, the atmosphere of which felt clearer since the removal of its **ghastly**⑤ **inmate**⑥. "Now, stand there!"

He struck a match on his boot and held it up against the wall.

"Look at that!" he said, triumphantly.

I have remarked that the paper had fallen away in parts. In this particular corner of the room a large piece had peeled off, leaving a yellow square of **coarse**⑦ **plastering**⑧. Across this bare space there was **scrawled**⑨ in blood-red letters a single word—

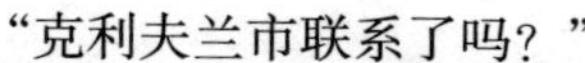

"克利夫兰市联系了吗？"

"我们今天早晨发了电报。"

"电报上是怎么说的？"

"只是详述了这里的状况，然后说希望他们能提供对我们有用的信息。"

"您难道没有具体问些您认为重要的情况吗？"

"我问了关于斯坦格森的情况。"

"没有别的了吗？整个案子就没个值得调查的关键点吗？您就只发了那一份电报吗？"

"我要说的在第一封电报上都说了，"格雷格森说，语气中窝着火。

夏洛克·福尔摩斯冲着自己咯咯地笑了起来，似乎正要说点什么，这时，莱斯特雷德又出现了。他搓着双手，一副洋洋自得的样子。刚才我们在厅堂里谈话时，他在前面的房间里。

"格雷格森先生，"他说，"我刚才有个重大的发现，如果我没有对墙壁进行仔细检查的话，说不定就忽略过去了。"

这个小个子说话时，眼睛里闪烁着光芒。很显然，由于胜过了自己的同事一筹，他心里洋溢着抑制不住的狂喜。

"请跟我来！"他说着，一边忙着走回前室。那具可怕的尸体被抬走了，屋里空气似乎清新了些，"好，就站在这儿！"

他拿根火柴在皮靴上划了一下，把火柴举着照亮墙壁。

"看看这个！"他说，态度很得意。

我先前已经提到过了，许多处墙纸都剥落了。就在室内这个特定的角落，在一大片墙纸脱落的地方露出了一方块粗糙泛黄的粉壁。空白的墙壁上潦潦草草写着几个血红色的字母，构成了一个单词——

① crucial ['kru:ʃəl] *a.* 关键性的

② offended [ə'fendid] *a.* 不高兴的

③ pompous ['pɔmpəs] *a.* 自负的

④ exultation [ˌegzʌl'teiʃən] *n.* 得意

⑤ ghastly ['ga:stli] *a.* 可怕的

⑥ inmate ['inmeit] *n.* 同室居住者，这里指尸体

⑦ coarse [kɔ:s] *a.* 粗糙的

⑧ plastering ['plɑ:stəriŋ] *n.* 灰泥面

⑨ scrawl [skrɔ:l] *v.* 潦草地写

RACHE

"What do you think of that?" cried the detective, with the air of a showman exhibiting his show. "This was overlooked because it was in the darkest corner of the room, and no one thought of looking there. The murderer has written it with his or her own blood. See this **smear**① where it has trickled down the wall! That **disposes**② of the idea of suicide anyhow. Why was that corner chosen to write it on? I will tell you. See that candle on the mantelpiece. It was lit at the time, and if it was lit this corner would be the brightest instead of the darkest portion of the wall."

"And what does it mean now that you have found it?" asked Gregson in a **depreciatory**③ voice.

"Mean? Why, it means that the writer was going to put the female name Rachel, but was disturbed before he or she had time to finish. You mark my words, when this case comes to be cleared up you will find that a woman named Rachel has something to do with it. It's all very well for you to laugh, Mr. Sherlock Holmes. You may be very smart and clever, but the old **hound**④ is the best, when all is said and done."

"I really beg your pardon!" said my companion, who had **ruffled**⑤ the little man's temper by bursting into an explosion of laughter. "You certainly have the credit of being the first of us to find this out, and, as you say, it bears every mark of having been written by the other participant in last night's mystery. I have not had time to examine this room yet, but with your permission I shall do so now."

As he spoke, he whipped a tape measure and a large round magnifying glass from his pocket. With these two **implements**⑥ he **trotted**⑦ noiselessly about the room, sometimes stopping, occasionally kneeling, and once lying flat upon his face. So **engrossed**⑧ was he with his occupation that he appeared to have forgotten our presence, for he **chattered**⑨ away to himself under his breath the whole time, keeping up a running fire of exclamations, groans, whistles, and little cries suggestive of encouragement and of hope.

RACHE

“这你们怎么看？”警探大声说，情形就像是演员在表演一样，“这一点之所以被大家忽略，是因为它出现在房间最昏暗的角落里，没人想到要查看这么个地方。这是凶手用自己的血写成的。看看这片血迹，顺着墙壁往下流呢！不管怎么说，自杀的看法是不成立的。凶手为何要选择这么样的一个角落写上字呢？我来告诉你们吧。看看壁炉架上的那支蜡烛，当时是亮着的。如果蜡烛是亮着的，那这个墙角就应该是房间里最亮而不是最暗的部分了。”

① smear [smiə] *n.* 污迹
② dispose [dis'pəuz] *v.* 去掉，排除

“你确实发现了这一点，但这是什么意思呢？”格雷格森说，态度不屑一顾。

③ depreciatory [di'priːʃiətəri] *a.* 蔑视的

“什么意思？啊，意思是，写字人正要把一个女人的名字‘蕾切尔’（Rachel）写上去，但他或者她还没有来得及写完，就被什么情况给打断了。你们记住我说过的话好啦，等到本案水落石出时，你们就会发现有个叫‘蕾切尔’的女人与本案有关。您尽可以嘲笑我，福尔摩斯先生。您可能非常聪明机敏，但说来说去，老猎犬还是最厉害的。”

④ hound [haund] *n.* 猎犬

⑤ ruffle ['rʌfl] *v.* 激怒

“我确实要恳请您谅解！”我同伴说，他忍不住放声大笑了起来，这下可把小个子警探给惹毛了，“您确实是我们中头一个发现这一点的，是您的功劳。正如您所说，所有迹象表明，这是昨晚谜案中的另一个在场的人留下的。但是，我还没来得及查看这间屋子呢。如果您允许的话，我现在就要查看了。”

他说话的当儿，从衣袋里掏出一把卷尺和一个大的圆形放大镜。他拿着这两样工具，悄无声息地四处走着，时而停下，时而跪下，甚至一度趴到了地上。他全神贯注地忙碌着，好像忘掉了我们的存在，不停地在喃喃自语，始终充满着火一样的热情。他时而惊叹，时而呻吟，时而打着响哨，时而低声叫喊，蕴含着鼓励与希

⑥ implement ['implimənt] *n.* 工具
⑦ trot [trɔt] *v.* 小跑
⑧ engross [in'grəus] *v.* 吸引；使全神贯注
⑨ chatter ['tʃætə] *v.* 喋喋不休

As I watched him I was irresistibly reminded of a pure-blooded well-trained foxhound as it dashes backwards and forwards through the **covert**①, **whining**② in its eagerness, until it comes across the lost scent. For twenty minutes or more he continued his researches, measuring with the most exact care the distance between marks which were entirely **invisible**③ to me, and occasionally applying his tape to the walls in an equally incomprehensible manner. In one place he gathered up very carefully a little pile of grey dust from the floor, and packed it away in an envelope. Finally, he examined with his glass the word upon the wall, going over every letter of it with the most minute exactness. This done, he appeared to be satisfied, for he replaced his tape and his glass in his pocket.

"They say that genius is an **infinite**④ **capacity**⑤ for taking pains," he remarked with a smile. "It's a very bad definition, but it does apply to detective work."

Gregson and Lestrade had watched the **manoeuvres**⑥ of their **amateur**⑦ companion with considerable curiosity and some **contempt**⑧. They evidently failed to appreciate the fact, which I had begun to realize, that Sherlock Holmes's smallest actions were all directed towards some definite and practical end.

"What do you think of it, sir?" they both asked.

"It would be robbing you of the credit of the case if I was to presume to help you," remarked my friend. "You are doing so well now that it would be a pity for anyone to interfere." There was a world of **sarcasm**⑨ in his voice as he spoke. "If you will let me know how your investigations go," he continued, "I shall be happy to give you any help I can. In the meantime I should like to speak to the constable who found the body. Can you give me his name and address?"

Lestrade glanced at his notebook. "John Rance," he said. "He is off duty now. You will find him at 46, Audley Court, Kennington Park Gate."

Holmes took a note of the address.

"Come along, Doctor," he said: "we shall go and look him up. I'll tell you

① covert ['kʌvət] *n.* 隐蔽处，这里指丛林
② whine [wain] *v.* 哀嚎
③ invisible [in'vizəbl] *a.* 看不见的
④ infinite ['infinit] *a.* 无限的
⑤ capacity [kə'pæsiti] *n.* 能力
⑥ manoeuvre [mə'nu:və] *n.* 动作
⑦ amateur ['æmətə] *a.* 业余的
⑧ contempt [kən'tempt] *n.* 轻蔑
⑨ sarcasm ['sɑ:kæzəm] *n.* 讽刺

望。我在看着他，心里不禁想到了一条训练有素的纯种猎狐犬，它正在猎物藏匿的丛林中来回奔跑着，急切地发出叫声，不找到猎物的气味绝不罢休。他查看了二十多分钟，仔仔细细地测量着一些印记间的距离，而这些印记我却压根儿什么也没看见。有时他还莫名其妙地拿卷尺在墙上来回比划着。他还非常小心翼翼地从地板的一处收集了一小撮灰色的粉末，装进一个信封。最后，他用放大镜仔细检查墙上的血字，小心翼翼地看着每一个字母。这一切完成之后，他似乎觉得足够了，便把卷尺和放大镜装入口袋里。

"人们都说，天才要吃得苦中苦，"他微笑着说，"这种说法很不准确，但是，用在侦探的工作上却很贴切。"

格雷格森和莱斯特雷德目睹着他们这位业余同行的种种招数，既显得很好奇，又有点不屑一顾。他们显然没有注意到这样的事实——而我都已经开始注意到了，夏洛克·福尔摩斯所有细微的举动都是有指向的，指向确切和实际的目标。

"这您怎么看呢，先生？"他们两位问。

"如果我贸然介入帮助你们，恐怕会抢了二位的功劳，"福尔摩斯说，"你们干得很出色，如果再有人插手的话，那会显得多此一举。"他说这些话时，语气中满含嘲讽。"如果你们愿意让我知道你们的调查进展情况的话，"他接着说，"我会乐于给你们提供力所能及的帮助。同时，我想要找那个发现尸体的警察谈谈，你们可以把他的姓名和住址告诉我吗？"

莱斯特雷德瞥了一眼自己的记事本。"约翰·兰斯，"他说，"现在下班了。您可以去肯宁顿公园大门的奥德利庭院四十六号找他。"

福尔摩斯拿笔记下了地址。

"走吧，医生，"他说。"我们去找他。我来告诉你

one thing which may help you in the case," he continued, turning to the two detectives. "There has been murder done, and the murderer was a man. He was more than six feet high, was in the **prime**① of life, had small feet for his height, wore coarse, square-toed boots and smoked a Trichinopoly cigar. He came here with his victim in a four-wheeled cab, which was drawn by a horse with three old shoes and one new one on his off **fore-leg**②. In all probability the murderer had a **florid**③ face, and the finger-nails of his right hand were remarkably long. These are only a few indications, but they may assist you."

Lestrade and Gregson glanced at each other with an **incredulous**④ smile.

"If this man was murdered, how was it done?" asked the former.

"Poison," said Sherlock Holmes **curtly**⑤, and strode off. "One other thing, Lestrade," he added, turning round at the door: "'Rache,' is the German for '**revenge**⑥;' so don't lose your time looking for Miss Rachel."

With which **Parthian shot**⑦ he walked away, leaving the two rivals open-mouthed behind him.

们一个对破案有帮助的情况，”他转身对着两位侦探继续说，“这儿发生了谋杀案，凶手是个男的，身高六英尺以上，年富力强，同其身高比较起来，脚显得小，穿着做工粗糙的方头皮靴，抽着特里其雪茄烟。他与被害人乘同一辆四轮马车来现场，拉车的马脚掌上有三块旧蹄铁，右前掌的蹄铁是新换的。凶手很有可能面色赤红，右手留有非常长的指甲。虽然这仅仅是些猜想，但也许对你们破案有用。”

莱斯特雷德和格雷格森交换了一下眼神，脸上露出疑惑的微笑。

“如果死者是被谋杀的，那他是如何遇害的呢？”莱斯特雷德问。

“毒死的，”夏洛克·福尔摩斯简略说了一声，然后大步离开了。“还有一个情况，莱斯特雷德，”他走到门口时又回头补充了一句，“‘Rache’是德语词，意为‘复仇’，您别浪费时间去找什么‘蕾切尔小姐’了。”

他说完这句尖刻的话之后便走开了，留下两个对手在他后面目瞪口呆。

① prime [praim] *n.* 年富力强的时期

② fore-leg ['fɔ:leg] *n.* 前肢

③ florid ['flɔrid] *a.* 红润的

④ incredulous [in'kredjuələs] *a.* 表示怀疑的

⑤ curtly [kə:tli] *ad.* 简短地

⑥ revenge [ri'vendʒ] *n.* 复仇

⑦ Parthian shot 临走时说的尖刻话

Chapter 4 What John Rance Had to Tell

It was one o'clock when we left No. 3, Lauriston Gardens. Sherlock Holmes led me to the nearest telegraph office, whence he **dispatched**① a long telegram. He then hailed a cab, and ordered the driver to take us to the address given us by Lestrade.

"There is nothing like first hand evidence," he remarked; "as a matter of fact, my mind is entirely made up upon the case, but still we may as well learn all that is to be learned."

"You amaze me, Holmes," said I. "Surely you are not as sure as you pretend to be of all those **particulars**② which you gave."

"There's no room for a mistake," he answered. "The very first thing which I observed on arriving there was that a cab had made two **ruts**③ with its wheels close to the **curb**④. Now, up to last night, we have had no rain for a week, so that those wheels which left such a deep impression must have been there during the night. There were the marks of the horse's **hoofs**⑤, too, the outline of one of which was far more clearly cut than that of the other three, showing that that was a new shoe. Since the cab was there after the rain began, and was not there at any time during the morning—I have Gregson's word for that—it follows that it must have been there during the night, and therefore, that it

第四章　约翰·兰斯的叙述

我们离开劳里斯顿花园三号时，已是下午一点钟了。夏洛克·福尔摩斯把我领到了最近的一家电报局，他在那儿发了一封很长的电报。随后，他雇了辆马车，让车夫按莱斯特雷德给的地址送我们过去。

“没有什么比第一手材料更加重要的了，”他说，“实际上，本案我心里已经完全有数了，但是，我们还是要把该了解的情况都了解一下。”

“你让我吃惊啊，福尔摩斯，”我说，“毫无疑问，你对自己说出的那些细节，并不像你装出来的那样有把握。”

“不可能出错的，”他回答说，“我一到那儿，注意到的第一件事情就是，紧挨着道路边上有两道车辙。对啦，直到昨天夜间，已经有一个星期没有下过雨了，所以昨夜一定有马车经过那里，才会留下那么深的车辙。另外，还有马蹄的印迹，其中一只蹄印比另外三只要清晰得多，说明这块蹄铁是新换的。下雨之后，那里才有马车经过，而整个早上那里都没有见到一辆马车——这一点是格雷格森告诉我的，可见，马车是晚上到那儿的，因此，就是这辆马车把那两个人送到

① dispatch [di'spætʃ] *v.* 发出

② particular [pə'tikjulə] *n.* 细节

③ rut [rʌt] *n.* 车辙

④ curb [kə:b] *n.*（马路）镶边

⑤ hoof [hu:f] *n.* 马蹄

brought those two individuals to the house."

"That seems simple enough," said I; "but how about the other man's height?"

"Why, the height of a man, in nine cases out of ten, can be told from the length of his **stride**[①]. It is a simple calculation enough, though there is no use my boring you with figures. I had this fellow's stride both on the clay outside and on the dust within. Then I had a way of checking my calculation. When a man writes on a wall, his instinct leads him to write about the level of his own eyes. Now that writing was just over six feet from the ground. It was child's play."

"And his age?" I asked.

"Well, if a man can stride four and a-half feet without the smallest effort, he can't be quite in the **sere**[②] and yellow. That was the breadth of a **puddle**[③] on the garden walk which he had evidently walked across. Patent-leather boots had gone round, and Square-toes had **hopped**[④] over. There is no mystery about it at all. I am simply applying to ordinary life a few of those precepts of observation and deduction which I advocated in that article. Is there anything else that puzzles you?"

"The finger nails and the Trichinopoly," I suggested.

"The writing on the wall was done with a man's forefinger dipped in blood. My glass allowed me to observe that the **plaster**[⑤] was slightly scratched in doing it, which would not have been the case if the man's nail had been trimmed. I gathered up some scattered ash from the floor. It was dark in colour and **flakey**[⑥]—such an ash as is only made by a Trichinopoly. I have made a special study of cigar ashes—in fact, I have written a **monograph**[⑦] upon the subject. I flatter myself that I can distinguish at a glance the ash of any known brand, either of cigar or of tobacco. It is just in such details that the skilled detective differs from the Gregson and Lestrade type."

"And the **florid**[⑧] face?" I asked.

"Ah, that was a more daring shot, though I have no doubt that I was right.

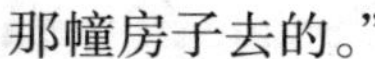

那幢房子去的。”

“这看起来够简单的，”我说，“但是，另外那个人的身高又是怎么回事呢？”

“啊，一个人的身高嘛，十之八九可以根据他的步长推算出来。这是道够简单的计算题，但我现在一步步教给你也无用。我从室外的泥土表面和室内的尘埃上获取了那个人的步长。我有一种检测计算的办法，一个人在墙上写字时，写字的高度会本能地与眼睛同高。他写的字距离地面六英尺多，连小孩子都猜得出来。”

“那他的年龄呢？”我问。

“是啊，如果一个人可以轻而易举地迈出四英尺半的步长，说明他不可能是个面色蜡黄的干瘦老头。花园小径上的一个水坑就有那么宽，而他显然是迈步跨过去的。穿漆皮靴的人是绕过去的，而穿方头靴的人却是跳过去的。这里面没有什么玄妙不解的东西，我只不过是把我那篇文章里提到的观察和推理，用于平常生活当中罢了。你还有什么别的东西迷惑不解的吗？”

“那手指甲和特里其雪茄烟呢？”我提议说。

“墙上的字是一个男人用食指蘸血写的。我用放大镜观察到，他写字时把一些墙灰刮了下来。如果此人修剪过指甲，那情况就不会是这样的。我还从地板上收集到一些散落的烟灰，颜色很深而且呈片状，只有特里其雪茄的烟灰才呈现那个样子。我专门研究过雪茄烟灰的特点——事实上，我还就这个问题写过一篇专门的论文呢。我不谦虚地说，不管是雪茄还是烟卷，只要瞥上一眼烟灰，任何知名品牌的烟我都可以识别出来。技艺高超的侦探之所以不同于格雷格森和莱斯特雷德之流，恰恰就是这些细节。”

“那红润的脸又是怎么回事呢？”我问。

“啊，那是个更大胆的推测了，不过我毫不怀疑，自己是正确的。眼下案件正在侦办中，这个问题你还是

① stride [straid] n.步长

② sere [siə] a. 干枯的

③ puddle ['pʌdl] n. 水坑

④ hop [hɔp] v. 跳

⑤ plaster ['plɑːstə] n. 墙灰

⑥ flakey [fleiki] a. 片状的

⑦ monograph ['mɔnəgrɑːf] n. 专论

⑧ florid ['flɔrid] a. 红红的

You must not ask me that at the present state of the affair."

I passed my hand over my brow. "My head is in a **whirl**①," I remarked; "the more one thinks of it the more mysterious it grows. How came these two men—if there were two men—into an empty house? What has become of the cabman who drove them? How could one man **compel**② another to take poison? Where did the blood come from? What was the object of the murderer, since robbery had no part in it? How came the woman's ring there? Above all, why should the second man write up the German word RACHE before **decamping**③? I confess that I cannot see any possible way of reconciling all these facts."

My companion smiled approvingly.

"You sum up the difficulties of the situation **succinctly**④ and well," he said. "There is much that is still obscure, though I have quite made up my mind on the main facts. As to poor Lestrade's discovery, it was simply a blind intended to put the police upon a wrong track, by suggesting Socialism and secret societies. It was not done by a German. The A, if you noticed, was printed somewhat after the German fashion. Now, a real German invariably prints in the Latin character, so that we may safely say that this was not written by one, but by a **clumsy**⑤ imitator who overdid his part. It was simply a ruse to divert inquiry into a wrong channel. I'm not going to tell you much more of the case, Doctor. You know a **conjurer**⑥ gets no credit when once he has explained his trick, and if I show you too much of my method of working, you will come to the conclusion that I am a very ordinary individual after all."

"I shall never do that," I answered; "you have brought detection as near an exact science as it ever will be brought in this world."

My companion flushed up with pleasure at my words, and the earnest way in which I uttered them. I had already observed that he was as sensitive to **flattery**⑦ on the score of his art as any girl could be of her beauty.

"I'll tell you one other thing," he said. "Patent leathers and Square-

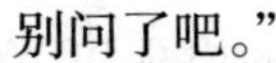

别问了吧。”

我一只手放在自己额头上。“我都晕头转向了，”我说，“越想越觉得案件扑朔迷离。那两个人怎么——如果真有两个人的话——会进入到那幢空房子里去呢？把他们送到那儿去的马车夫怎么样了呢？其中一个人如何能迫使另一个人服毒呢？血是哪来的？既然凶手不是图财害命，那他的杀人动机是什么？女式结婚戒指是哪儿来的？最重要的是，凶手逃离现场前为何要用德文写下‘复仇’呢？我承认，自己无法把这一切串联起来。”

我同伴会心地露出了微笑。

“你完整地总结了案件存在的难点，简明而又准确，”他说，“含糊不清的地方还有很多，不过我对主要的事实都已经了然于心了。至于可怜的莱斯特雷德的那个发现，那纯粹就是个障眼法，目的是为了转移警方的视线，暗示那是社会党或秘密团体所为。血字并不是德国人写的。如果你注意了一下的话，会发现A有点模仿德文体写上去的。但是真正的德国人总是会使用拉丁字体的，所以，我们可以很有把握地说，这不是德国人的手迹，而是个拙劣的模仿者所为，不过模仿得过了头了。这只不过是个诡异伎俩而已，目的是要把调查的方向引入歧途。关于案件，我不能对你说更多情况了。要知道，一位魔术师如果把自己的戏法说穿了，那就得不到人们的喝彩了。如果我把侦破方法全都讲给你听，你会得出结论，说我也只不过是个平凡之辈而已。”

“我才不会那么说呢，”我回答说，“你把侦破工作建立成了世界上一门精准的科学了。”

我同伴听到我这么一说，而且说得极为诚恳，高兴得涨红了脸了。我已经注意到了，他非常敏感，很爱听别人称赞他的侦破艺术，就像姑娘喜爱听人家赞扬其美貌一样。

“我告诉你另外一个情况，”他说，“穿漆革靴子的

① whirl [hwəːl] *n.* 旋转

② compel [kəm'pel] *v.* 强迫

③ decamp [di'kæmp] *v.* 逃走

④ succinctly [sək'siŋktli] *ad.* 简洁地

⑤ clumsy ['klʌmzi] *a.* 笨拙的

⑥ conjurer ['kʌndʒərə] *n.* 魔术师

⑦ flattery ['flætəri] *n.* 奉承话

toes came in the same cab, and they walked down the pathway together as friendly as possible—arm-in-arm, in all probability. When they got inside they walked up and down the room—or rather, Patent-leathers stood still while Square-toes walked up and down. I could read all that in the dust; and I could read that as he walked he grew more and more excited. That is shown by the increased length of his strides. He was talking all the while, and working himself up, no doubt, into a **fury**① . Then the tragedy occurred. I've told you all I know myself now, for the rest is mere **surmise**② and **conjecture**③ . We have a good working basis, however, on which to start. We must hurry up, for I want to go to Halle's concert to hear Norman Neruda this afternoon."

This conversation had occurred while our cab had been threading its way through a long succession of dingy streets and **dreary**④ byways. In the dingiest and dreariest of them our driver suddenly came to a stand. "That's Audley Court in there," he said, pointing to a narrow slit in the line of dead-coloured brick. "You'll find me here when you come back."

Audley Court was not an attractive locality. The narrow passage led us into a **quadrangle**⑤ paved with flags and lined by sordid dwellings. We picked our way among groups of dirty children, and through lines of discoloured linen, until we came to Number 46, the door of which was decorated with a small slip of brass on which the name Rance was engraved. On inquiry we found that the constable was in bed, and we were shown into a little front parlour to await his coming.

He appeared presently, looking a little **irritable**⑥ at being disturbed in his **slumbers**⑦ . "I made my report at the office," he said.

Holmes took a half-sovereign from his pocket and played with it pensively. "We thought that we should like to hear it all from your own lips," he said.

"I shall be most happy to tell you anything I can," the constable answered with his eyes upon the little golden disc.

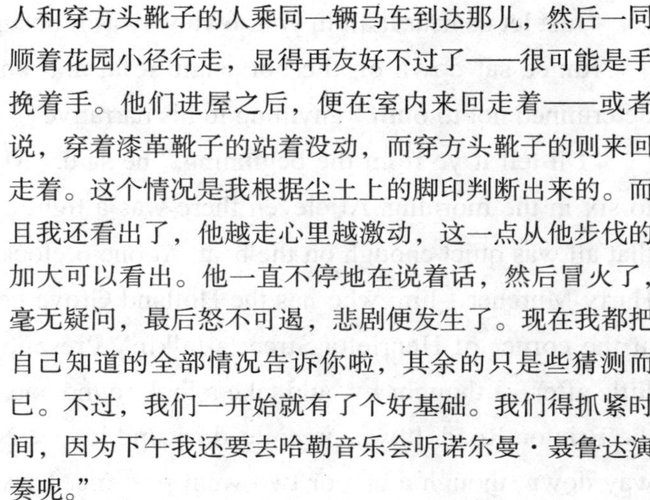

人和穿方头靴子的人乘同一辆马车到达那儿，然后一同顺着花园小径行走，显得再友好不过了——很可能是手挽着手。他们进屋之后，便在室内来回走着——或者说，穿着漆革靴子的站着没动，而穿方头靴子的则来回走着。这个情况是我根据尘土上的脚印判断出来的。而且我还看出了，他越走心里越激动，这一点从他步伐的加大可以看出。他一直不停地在说着话，然后冒火了，毫无疑问，最后怒不可遏，悲剧便发生了。现在我都把自己知道的全部情况告诉你啦，其余的只是些猜测而已。不过，我们一开始就有了个好基础。我们得抓紧时间，因为下午我还要去哈勒音乐会听诺尔曼·聂鲁达演奏呢。”

① fury ['fjuəri] *n.* 狂怒

② surmise [sə'maiz] *n.* 猜测

③ conjecture [kən'dʒektʃə] *n.* 猜测

我们说着这些话时，马车一直在穿街走巷地行进着，穿过了一条条肮脏漫长、阴郁沉闷的街道。在一处最最肮脏阴沉的地方，车夫突然停住了马车。“那边就是奥德利庭院，”车夫说，一边指着一排深暗色的砖墙处一个狭窄的入口，“你们返回时，到这儿来找我。”

④ dreary ['driəri] *a.* 沉闷的

奥德利庭院是个毫不起眼的所在。我们穿过了狭窄的过道，来到了一座方形的院落，里面的地面是石板铺的，四周是些鄙陋的住房。我们从一群脏兮兮的孩子中间挤过，又钻过一排排晒的褪色的衣服，找到了四十六号，门上钉着一个小铜牌，上面刻着兰斯的名字。一打听，才知道警察还在床上睡觉呢。于是，我们被领进一间小接待室候着他。

⑤ quadrangle ['kwɔdræŋgl] *n.* 四方院子

他很快就出现了，由于打断了他的好梦，看上去有点不爽。“我已经向局里报告过了，”他说。

⑥ irritable ['iritəbl] *a.* 易怒的

⑦ slumber ['slʌmbə] *n.* 熟睡

福尔摩斯从衣服口袋里掏出一个半镑的金币，若有所思地把玩着。“我们很想听听您亲口给我们讲述事情的经过，”他说。

“我很乐意把自己知道的一切情况告诉您，”警察回答说，两眼紧紧盯住那枚小小的金币。

"Just let us hear it all in your own way as it occurred."

Rance sat down on the horsehair sofa, and knitted his brows as though determined not to **omit**① anything in his narrative.

"I'll tell it ye from the beginning," he said. "My time is from ten at night to six in the morning. At eleven there was a fight at the 'White Hart'; but bar that all was quiet enough on the beat. At one o'clock it began to rain, and I met Harry Murcher—him who has the Holland Grove beat—and we stood together at the corner of Henrietta Street a-talkin'. Presently—maybe about two or a little after—I thought I would take a look round and see that all was right down the Brixton Road. It was precious dirty and lonely. Not a soul did I meet all the way down, though a cab or two went past me. I was a strollin' down, thinkin' between ourselves how uncommon handy a four of gin hot would be, when suddenly the **glint**② of a light caught my eye in the window of that same house. Now, I knew that them two houses in Lauriston Gardens was empty on account of him that owns them who won't have the **drains**③ seen to, though the very last **tenant**④ what lived in one of them died o' **typhoid**⑤ fever. I was knocked all in a **heap**⑥ therefore, at seeing a light in the window, and I suspected as something was wrong. When I got to the door——"

"You stopped, and then walked back to the garden gate," my companion interrupted. "What did you do that for?"

Rance gave a violent jump, and stared at Sherlock Holmes with the utmost amazement upon his features.

"Why, that's true, sir," he said; "though how you come to know it, Heaven only knows. Ye see, when I got up to the door it was so still and so lonesome, that I thought I'd be none the worse for some one with me. I ain't afeared of anything on this side o' the grave; but I thought that maybe it was him that died o' the typhoid inspecting the drains what killed him. The thought gave me a kind o' turn, and I walked back to the gate to see if I could see Murcher's lantern, but there wasn't no sign of him nor of anyone else."

“那您就按照自己的方式把事情的经过讲给我们听吧。”

兰斯在马毛沙发上坐了下来，眉头紧锁，像是在下定决心，确保叙述中不遗漏掉任何情节。

① omit [əu'mit] *v.* 省略

“我从刚一开始时讲起，”他说，“我值班的时间是从夜间十点钟到早晨六点钟。夜间十一点钟时，‘白鹿酒馆’有人在斗殴。但除此之外，我的整个巡逻期间都很平静的。一点钟时，天开始下雨了。我遇到了哈里·默切尔——他在荷兰树林区一带巡逻——我们两个站在亨利埃塔街的拐角处聊天。紧接着可能是两点钟，或者两点钟过一点点——我觉得自己要转过头看一看，布里克斯顿大街是否一切正常。那条街特别肮脏，特别僻静。我一路上都没有遇见一个人，不过身边有一两辆马车经过。我一边溜达，一边寻思着，如果能来杯温热的杜松子酒该多爽啊。这时，我瞥见了那幢房子的窗户里透出灯光。啊，我知道，劳里斯顿花园的那两幢房子一直空着，因为房东一直没请人把下水道修好。即使其中一幢房子的上一任房客得伤寒病死了，他也不愿意修。所以，看到窗口里有灯光，我吓了一大跳，怀疑情况不对头。当我到达门口时——”

② glint [glint] *n.* 闪光

③ drain [drein] *n.* 下水道
④ tenant ['tenənt] *n.* 房客
⑤ typhoid ['taifɔid] *n.* 伤寒
⑥ heap [hi:p] *n.* 堆积

“您停住了脚步，然后转身走回到花园门口，”我同伴打断了他的话，“您为何要那样做呢？”

兰斯猛然跳了起来，目不转睛看着福尔摩斯，一脸的惊讶。

“啊，确实如此，先生，”他说，“但您是怎么知道的呢？只有上帝才知道啊！您看，当我到达门口边时，周围十分安静，十分凄凉，我觉得，最好还是找个人来陪着自己。在这个世界上，我没有什么可害怕的，但自己当时想到，说不定是那个死于伤寒病的房客回来检查那段害得他丢了性命的下水道吧。这个念头吓得我怔了一下，于是转身返回到花园门口边，看看是不是还可以看见默切尔的提

"There was no one in the street?"

"Not a livin' soul, sir, nor as much as a dog. Then I pulled myself together and went back and pushed the door open. All was quiet inside, so I went into the room where the light was a-burnin'. There was a candle flickerin' on the **mantelpiece**[①]—a red wax one—and by its light I saw——"

"Yes, I know all that you saw. You walked round the room several times, and you knelt down by the body, and then you walked through and tried the kitchen door, and then——"

John Rance sprang to his feet with a frightened face and suspicion in his eyes. "Where was you hid to see all that?" he cried. "It seems to me that you knows a deal more than you should."

Holmes laughed and threw his card across the table to the constable. "Don't get arresting me for the murder," he said. "I am one of the **hounds**[②] and not the wolf; Mr. Gregson or Mr. Lestrade will answer for that. Go on, though. What did you do next?"

Rance **resumed**[③] his seat, without, however, losing his mystified expression. "I went back to the gate and sounded my whistle. That brought Murcher and two more to the spot."

"Was the street empty then?"

"Well, it was, as far as anybody that could be of any good goes."

"What do you mean?"

The constable's features broadened into a **grin**[④]. "I've seen many a drunk **chap**[⑤] in my time," he said, "but never anyone so cryin' drunk as that cove. He was at the gate when I came out, a-leanin' up agin the railings, and a-singin' at the pitch o' his lungs about Columbine's New-fangled Banner, or some such stuff. He couldn't stand, far less help."

"What sort of a man was he?" asked Sherlock Holmes.

John Rance appeared to be somewhat irritated at this **digression**[⑥]. "He was

灯，但是，他不见了，也没有别的人影儿。”

“街上也没有一个人吗？”

“别说没有一个活人，先生，连一条狗都没有。然后，我壮着胆子，走了回去，推开了房门。里面一片静谧，我于是走进了有灯光的那个房间。壁炉架上有支蜡烛亮着——是支红蜡烛——凭借着烛光，我看见了——”

“是啊，我知道您看见什么了。您在房间里面转了几个圈，在尸体旁边跪下，然后穿过房间去推了推厨房的门，然后——”

约翰·兰斯一跃身子站了起来，满脸惊恐，目光中充满了疑虑。“这一切您都是躲在什么地方看到的？”他大声说，“我感觉，您不应该知道这么多情况啊。”

福尔摩斯哈哈笑了起来，把自己的名片扔给桌子对面的警察。“您可别把我当成杀人嫌疑犯给逮捕起来啊，”他说，“我是猎犬之一，而不是狼。格雷格森和莱斯特雷德先生都可以证明这一点。那么，请继续讲，您接着做了什么？”

兰斯回到了座位上，不过，依旧满腹狐疑。“我返回到花园门口，吹响了警哨。结果默切尔和另外两个警察赶到了现场。”

“街上当时空无一人吗？”

“是啊，空无一人，肯定没有什么正经人。”

“您这话是什么意思？”

警察的面部五官舒展了，呲牙咧嘴地笑了起来。“我值班时看见了许多醉汉，”他说，“但没有看见过像那个家伙一样大喊大叫的醉汉。我从室内出来时，他正好在花园门口，身子倚靠在栅栏上，扯着嗓子，声嘶力竭地唱着科伦巴茵演唱的新流行歌曲，或者诸如此类的东西。他都站立不住了，更别说给我帮什么忙啦。”

“那是个怎样的人呢？”夏洛克·福尔摩斯问。

① mantelpiece ['mæntl,pi:s] *n.* 壁炉台

② hound [haund] *n.* 猎犬

③ resume [ri'zju:m] *v.* 回到（之前的位置）

④ grin [grin] *n.* 咧嘴笑

⑤ chap [tʃæp] *n.* 家伙

⑥ digression [dai'greʃən] *n.* 岔开

an uncommon drunk sort o' man," he said. "He'd ha' found hisself in the station if we hadn't been so took up."

"His face—his dress—didn't you notice them?" Holmes broke in impatiently.

"I should think I did notice them, seeing that I had to prop him up—me and Murcher between us. He was a long chap, with a red face, the lower part **muffled**① round——"

"That will do," cried Holmes. "What became of him?"

"We'd enough to do without lookin' after him," the policeman said, in an aggrieved voice. "I'll **wager**② he found his way home all right."

"How was he dressed?"

"A brown overcoat."

"Had he a whip in his hand?"

"A whip—no."

"He must have left it behind," muttered my companion. "You didn't happen to see or hear a cab after that?"

"No."

"There's a half-**sovereign**③ for you," my companion said, standing up and taking his hat. "I am afraid, Rance, that you will never rise in the force. That head of yours should be for use as well as **ornament**④. You might have gained your sergeant's stripes last night. The man whom you held in your hands is the man who holds the clue of this mystery, and whom we are seeking. There is no use of arguing about it now; I tell you that it is so. Come along, Doctor."

We started off for the cab together, leaving our **informant**⑤ incredulous, but obviously uncomfortable.

"The blundering fool," Holmes said, bitterly, as we drove back to our lodgings. "Just to think of his having such an incomparable bit of good luck, and not taking advantage of it."

"I am rather in the dark still. It is true that the description of this man tallies

他这么一打岔，约翰·兰斯有点不高兴了。“他不是那种普通的醉汉，”他说，“如果我们当时不是手忙脚乱，肯定会把带回到警局的。”

“他的面容——穿着打扮——您就没有注意一下吗？”福尔摩斯不耐烦地打断了他的话。

“我觉得，自己还真是注意了，因为我必须得把他给搀扶起来，我和默切尔一边一个架着。那家伙是个高个子，通红的脸庞，脸的下半部捂在——”

① muffle ['mʌfl] *v.* 裹着

“够了，”福尔摩斯大声说，“他后来怎样了？”

“我们够忙的，没有功夫管他，”警察说，语气中透着委屈，“我敢打赌，他找得到回家的路。”

② wager ['weidʒə] *v.* 打赌

“他穿的什么衣服？”

“穿了件棕褐色的外套。”

“手上拿了马鞭没有？”

“马鞭——没有。”

“他一定是把它放在马车里了，”我同伴喃喃地说，“从那之后，您没有看见或者听见马车经过吧？”

“没有。”

“这半镑金币是您的了，”我同伴说着，站起身，拿起帽子，“我担心啊，兰斯，您在警界永无出头之日了。您的这个脑袋不光是做摆设的，还应该使用使用才是啊。您昨晚本来有可能升任个警长什么的，因为您双手搀扶的那个人掌握着这桩疑案的线索，我们正在寻找他呢。现在说这些已经没用了，我只是把这事告诉您而已。走吧，医生。”

③ sovereign ['sɔvərin] *n.* 沙弗林（英国旧时面值一英镑的金币）

④ ornament ['ɔ:nəmənt] *n.* 装饰

我们一同朝着马车停的地方走去，给我们提供信息的那个警察留在那儿，将信将疑，但很显然，他心里不是滋味儿。

⑤ informant [in'fɔ:mənt] *n.* 提供消息的人

“十足的傻瓜蛋！”我们乘马车回寓所的途中，福尔摩斯尖刻地说，“想想看吧，他算是遇上了千载难逢的好机会，竟然没有好好地利用。”

with your idea of the second party in this mystery. But why should he come back to the house after leaving it? That is not the way of criminals."

"The ring, man, the ring: that was what he came back for. If we have no other way of catching him, we can always bait our line with the ring. I shall have him, Doctor—I'll lay you two to one that I have him. I must thank you for it all. I might not have gone but for you, and so have missed the finest study I ever came across: a study in scarlet, eh? Why shouldn't we use a little art **jargon**[①]. There's the scarlet thread of murder running through the colourless **skein**[②] of life, and our duty is to unravel it, and isolate it, and expose every inch of it. And now for lunch, and then for Norman Neruda. Her attack and her bowing are splendid. What's that little thing of Chopin's she plays so magnificently: Tra-la-la-lira-lira-lay."

Leaning back in the cab, this amateur bloodhound **carolled**[③] away like a lark while I **meditated**[④] upon the many-sidedness of the human mind.

"我还是云里雾里，确实，他对那个人的描述和你推测中谜案中的另一方很相符。但他既然离开了住宅，为何又返回来呢？这可不是罪犯通常的做法啊。"

"那枚戒指啊，伙计，那枚戒指，他返回是去寻找戒指的。如果我们没有别的方法逮住他，我们就可拿戒指来做诱饵，放出长线。我一定会逮住他的，医生——一定会逮住他，我敢押一赔二同你赌一把。这事我还真得要感谢你，要不是你，我还真不会去呢，那样的话，就错过了绝佳研究良机：就叫血字的研究，怎么样？我们为何不使用一个具有一点艺术性的术语呢？谋杀像一条红线贯穿在毫无色彩的生活当中，我们的责任就是要抽丝剥茧，把它分离出来，一点一滴地加以展示。得啦，要用午餐啦，然后去听诺尔曼·聂鲁达的演奏。她的指法和弓法可谓绝妙。肖邦的小夜曲经她一演奏妙不可言：特啦——啦——啦——哩啦——哩啦——唻。"

这位业余侦探倚靠在马车座上，像只云雀似的一路哼唱着，而我却在暗自忖量着人类头脑真是无所不能。

① jargon ['dʒɑ:gən] n.术语

② skein [skein] n. 一团

③ carol['kærəl] v. 欢乐地唱

④ meditate ['mediteit] v. 深思

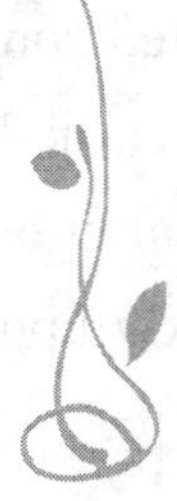

Chapter 5 Our Advertisement Brings a Visitor

Our morning's exertions had been too much for my weak health, and I was tired out in the afternoon. After Holmes's departure for the concert, I lay down upon the sofa and **endeavoured**[①] to get a couple of hours' sleep. It was a useless attempt. My mind had been too much excited by all that had occurred, and the strangest fancies and surmises crowded into it. Every time that I closed my eyes I saw before me the distorted **baboon-like**[②] **countenance**[③] of the murdered man. So **sinister**[④] was the impression which that face had produced upon me that I found it difficult to feel anything but gratitude for him who had removed its owner from the world. If ever human features **bespoke**[⑤] vice of the most malignant type, they were certainly those of Enoch J. Drebber, of Cleveland. Still I recognized that justice must be done, and that the **depravity**[⑥] of the victim was no **condonement**[⑦] in the eyes of the law.

The more I thought of it the more extraordinary did my companion's hypothesis, that the man had been poisoned, appear. I remembered how he had sniffed his lips, and had no doubt that he had detected something which had given rise to the idea. Then, again, if not poison, what had caused the man's death, since there was neither wound nor marks of **strangulation**[⑧]? But, on the other hand, whose blood was that which lay so thickly upon the floor? There

第五章　启事招来访客

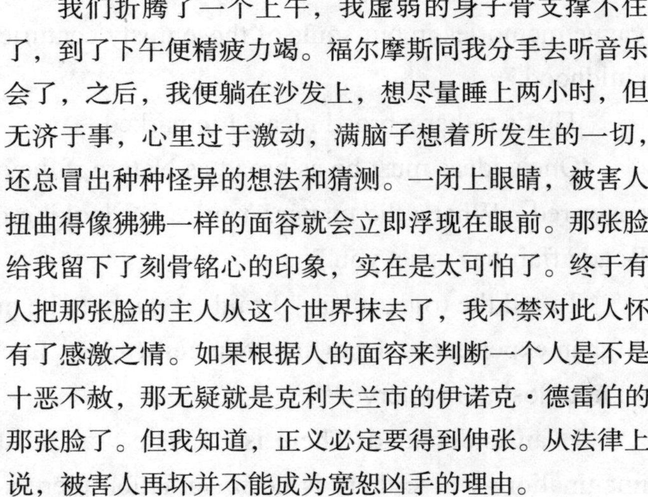

我们折腾了一个上午，我虚弱的身子骨支撑不住了，到了下午便精疲力竭。福尔摩斯同我分手去听音乐会了，之后，我便躺在沙发上，想尽量睡上两小时，但无济于事，心里过于激动，满脑子想着所发生的一切，还总冒出种种怪异的想法和猜测。一闭上眼睛，被害人扭曲得像狒狒一样的面容就会立即浮现在眼前。那张脸给我留下了刻骨铭心的印象，实在是太可怕了。终于有人把那张脸的主人从这个世界抹去了，我不禁对此人怀有了感激之情。如果根据人的面容来判断一个人是不是十恶不赦，那无疑就是克利夫兰市的伊诺克·德雷伯的那张脸了。但我知道，正义必定要得到伸张。从法律上说，被害人再坏并不能成为宽恕凶手的理由。

我同伴假设受害人是被毒死的，我越想越觉得这个假设不同寻常。我记得，他闻了闻死者的嘴唇，毫无疑问，他一定是发现了什么蛛丝马迹，才作如是推断的。还有就是，如果不是服了毒，那是什么原因致使那人死亡的呢？因为尸体上没有发现伤口，也没有勒痕。但是，从另一方面来说，地板上留下了那么多血迹，那会是谁的血呢？没有打斗过的迹象，受害人身边也没有

① endeavour [in'devə] *v.* 竭力

② baboon-like [bə'buːnˌlaik] *a.* 像狒狒的

③ countenance ['kauntinəns] *n.* 面容

④ sinister ['sinistə] *a.* 不祥的，不幸的

⑤ bespeak [bi'spiːk] *v.* 表明

⑥ depravity [di'præviti] *n.* 恶行

⑦ condonement [kən'dəunmənt] *n.* 宽恕

⑧ strangulation [stræŋgju'leiʃən] *n.* 勒死

were no signs of a struggle, nor had the victim any weapon with which he might have wounded an **antagonist**[①]. As long as all these questions were unsolved, I felt that sleep would be no easy matter, either for Holmes or myself. His quiet self-confident manner convinced me that he had already formed a theory which explained all the facts, though what it was I could not for an instant conjecture.

He was very late in returning—so late, that I knew that the concert could not have **detained**[②] him all the time. Dinner was on the table before he appeared.

"It was magnificent," he said, as he took his seat. "Do you remember what Darwin says about music? He claims that the power of producing and appreciating it existed among the human race long before the power of speech was arrived at. Perhaps that is why we are so subtly influenced by it. There are vague memories in our souls of those misty centuries when the world was in its childhood."

"That's rather a broad idea," I remarked.

"One's ideas must be as broad as Nature if they are to interpret Nature," he answered. "What's the matter? You're not looking quite yourself. This Brixton Road affair has upset you."

"To tell the truth, it has," I said. "I ought to be more case-hardened after my Afghan experiences. I saw my own **comrades**[③] **hacked**[④] to pieces at Maiwand without losing my nerve."

"I can understand. There is a mystery about this which **stimulates**[⑤] the imagination; where there is no imagination there is no horror. Have you seen the evening paper?"

"No."

"It gives a fairly good account of the affair. It does not mention the fact that when the man was raised up, a woman's wedding ring fell upon the floor. It is just as well it does not."

"Why?"

"Look at this advertisement," he answered. "I had one sent to every paper

足以使对手受到重创的器具。只要所有这些疑问得不到解答，我看，无论是福尔摩斯，还是我本人，都睡不安稳。福尔摩斯平静自信的态度令我坚信，他已经有了自己的看法，能够解释这一切事实，尽管那是什么样的一种看法，我还无法猜测。

福尔摩斯回来得很晚——从时间上来判断，我知道，他不可能一直在听音乐会。他回来时，晚饭早已经摆上餐桌了。

"音乐会妙不可言啊，"他说，一边坐了下来，"你还记得达尔文是怎样说音乐的吗？他认为，人类在使用语言之前，就拥有了创造和欣赏音乐的能力。或许这就是音乐能对我们产生微妙影响的原因。在我们灵魂的深处，对于原初世界的朦胧岁月，依然还有模糊的记忆。"

"这是一种不着边际的看法。"我说。

"如果人们想要理解大自然，那他们的思想就必须和大自然一样开阔，"他回答说，"怎么啦？你看起来不大对劲啊。布里克斯顿大街那桩案件弄得你心烦意乱了吧。"

"实话实说，还真是这么回事，"我说，"我有过在阿富汗的种种经历，本来应该是更加坚强才对。在迈万德战役中，我亲眼目睹自己的同伴们血肉横飞的场面，当时都没有胆怯。"

"我能够理解，本案存在一个谜团，令人浮想联翩。没有想象，就不会有恐惧。你看晚报了吗？"

"没有。"

"上面详细报道了本案，但报纸上没有提到尸体被抬起来时，一枚戒指掉到了地上。没有提到这个情节倒是更好。"

"为什么呢？"

"看看这则启事吧，"他回答说，"今天上午，离开

① antagonist [æn'tægənist] *n.* 对手

② detain [di'tein] *v.* 耽搁

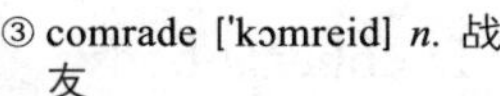

③ comrade ['kɔmreid] *n.* 战友

④ hack [hæk] *v.* 劈

⑤ stimulate ['stimjuleit] *v.* 激发

this morning immediately after the affair."

He threw the paper across to me and I glanced at the place indicated. It was the first announcement in the "Found" **column**[①]. "In Brixton Road, this morning," it ran, "a plain gold wedding ring, found in the roadway between the 'White Hart' Tavern and Holland Grove. Apply Dr. Watson, 221B, Baker Street, between eight and nine this evening."

"Excuse my using your name," he said. "If I used my own some of these **dunderheads**[②] would recognize it, and want to **meddle**[③] in the affair."

"That is all right," I answered. "But supposing anyone applies, I have no ring."

"Oh yes, you have," said he, handing me one. "This will do very well. It is almost a **facsimile**[④]."

"And who do you expect will answer this advertisement."

"Why, the man in the brown coat—our florid friend with the square toes. If he does not come himself he will send an **accomplice**[⑤]."

"Would he not consider it as too dangerous?"

"Not at all. If my view of the case is correct, and I have every reason to believe that it is, this man would rather risk anything than lose the ring. According to my notion he dropped it while **stooping**[⑥] over Drebber's body, and did not miss it at the time. After leaving the house he discovered his loss and hurried back, but found the police already in possession, owing to his own **folly**[⑦] in leaving the candle burning. He had to pretend to be drunk in order to **allay**[⑧] the suspicions which might have been aroused by his appearance at the gate. Now put yourself in that man's place. On thinking the matter over, it must have occurred to him that it was possible that he had lost the ring in the road after leaving the house. What would he do, then? He would eagerly look out for the evening papers in the hope of seeing it among the articles found. His eye, of course, would light upon this. He would be overjoyed. Why

现场后，我立刻让各家报纸登了一则启事。”

他把报纸从桌子对面递了过来，我看了一眼他所指的地方。是在“失物招领”栏里，第一则启事上写着：“今晨，在布里克斯顿大街，白鹿酒馆至荷兰树林间的路段上，拾到纯金婚戒一枚。失者请于今晚八时至九时到贝克大街二百二十一号乙华生先生处认领。”

“请原谅，用了你的名字登启事，”他说，“如果用我自己的名字，那些傻瓜蛋中有人可能会有所警觉，会来搅合此事的。”

“没有关系，”我回答说，“但是，如果有人前来认领，我可拿不出戒指啊。”

“噢，是的，你拿得出，”他说着，交给了我一枚，“这一枚足可以应付了，和原先那枚一模一样。”

“你觉得谁会来认领呢？”

“啊，那位穿棕褐色外套的男子，也就是我们那位红脸庞、穿方头靴子的朋友。他即便不亲自来，也会打发一个同伙来的。”

“他不会觉得这样做太冒险了吗？”

“绝对不会。如果我对本案的看法是正确的，而且我也有充分的理由相信是正确的，那人冒再大的风险，也会想要拿回那枚戒指的。根据我的判断，他是在弓着身子查看德雷伯的尸体时，把戒指掉在地上的，但当时他不知道。他离开了那幢住宅之后，发现戒指不见了，于是匆忙返回，但发现警察已经到达，一切都源于他的愚蠢之举，竟然让蜡烛亮着。他只得装作喝醉了酒，以免由于自己出现在门口引起警察怀疑。现在，你设身处地想一想，他把事情前前后后想过之后，一定会觉得，戒指可能是在离开住宅之后失落在路上了。他接着会怎么做呢？会急忙查看晚报，希望在‘失物招领栏’里找到它，看到这则广告后他一定会喜出望外的。他都会高兴得什么似的，怎么还会担心是个圈套呢？在他心目

① column ['kɔləm] *n.* 专栏

② dunderhead ['dʌndəhed] *n.* 傻瓜

③ meddle ['medl] *v.* 干涉

④ facsimile [fæk'simili] *n.* 复制品

⑤ accomplice [ə'kɔmplis] *n.* 同谋

⑥ stoop [stu:p] *v.* 弯腰，弓身

⑦ folly ['fɔli] *n.* 愚蠢的行为

⑧ allay [ə'lei] *v.* 减轻

should he fear a trap? There would be no reason in his eyes why the finding of the ring should be connected with the murder. He would come. He will come. You shall see him within an hour?"

"And then?" I asked.

"Oh, you can leave me to deal with him then. Have you any arms?"

"I have my old service **revolver**① and a few **cartridges**②."

"You had better clean it and load it. He will be a desperate man, and though I shall take him unawares, it is as well to be ready for anything."

I went to my bedroom and followed his advice. When I returned with the pistol the table had been cleared, and Holmes was engaged in his favourite occupation of scraping upon his violin.

"The plot thickens," he said, as I entered; "I have just had an answer to my American telegram. My view of the case is the correct one."

"And that is?" I asked eagerly.

"My fiddle would be the better for new strings," he remarked. "Put your **pistol**③ in your pocket. When the fellow comes speak to him in an ordinary way. Leave the rest to me. Don't frighten him by looking at him too hard."

"It is eight o'clock now," I said, glancing at my watch.

"Yes. He will probably be here in a few minutes. Open the door slightly. That will do. Now put the key on the inside. Thank you! This is a queer old book I picked up at a **stall**④ yesterday—*De Jure inter Gentes*—published in Latin at Liege in the Lowlands, in 1642. Charles' head was still firm on his shoulders when this little brown-backed volume was **struck off**⑤."

"Who is the printer?"

"Philippe de Croy, whoever he may have been. On the fly-leaf, in very faded ink, is written 'Ex libris Guliolmi Whyte.' I wonder who William Whyte was. Some **pragmatical**⑥ seventeenth century lawyer, I suppose. His writing has a legal twist about it. Here comes our man, I think."

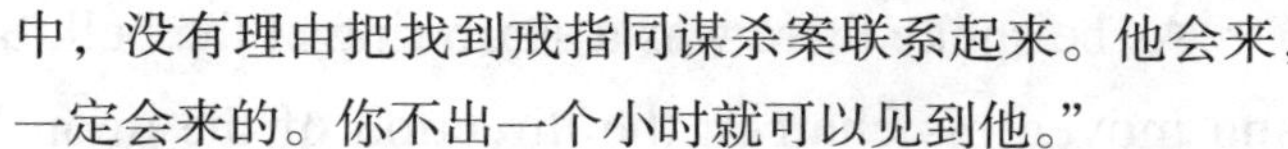

中，没有理由把找到戒指同谋杀案联系起来。他会来，一定会来的。你不出一个小时就可以见到他。”

“然后呢？”我问。

“噢，到时就让我来应付他吧，你有武器吗？”

“我有一支老式军用左轮手枪，还有几发子弹。”

① revolver [ri'vɔlvə] *n.* 左轮手枪

② cartridge ['kɑ:tridʒ] *n.* 子弹

“你最好把它擦一擦，装上子弹，他会狗急跳墙的。尽管我会在他还没有反应过来时制服他，但还是以防万一的好。”

我走进了卧室，照着他说的做了。拿着手枪返回到餐厅时，餐桌已经收拾干净了。福尔摩斯正撩拨着小提琴上的弦，这是他最喜欢的消遣方式。

“案情复杂起来了，”我进入房间时，他说，“我刚收到了美国的回电。我对本案的看法是正确的。”

“情况是——？”我迫不及待地问。

“我这把小提琴该换弦了，”他说，“你把手枪放到衣服口袋里。等到那家伙出现时，用平常的语气同他说话。其余的事情交由我来处理。不要死死地盯着他看，那样会惊动他的。”

③ pistol ['pistəl] *n.* 手枪

“现在是八点。”我瞥了一眼怀表说。

“不错，他可能过几分钟后就到了。房门虚掩着，这样就行。把钥匙插在内侧的锁孔上。谢谢！我昨天在书摊上买到了一本奇怪的旧书——《国际法》——是拉丁文的，1642年在低地国家的列日出版。这本棕褐色封面的小册子印刷出版时，查理一世的脑袋还安稳地长在脖子上呢。”

④ stall [stɔ:l] *n.* 小摊

⑤ strike off 印刷

“印刷商是谁？”

“菲利奇·德·克罗伊，谁知道他是个什么样的人啊。扉页上题签的字已经褪色了，内容是‘威廉·怀特藏书’。我不知道威廉·怀特是何许人。估计是十七世纪的某个实务的律师吧，因为他的字透着几分律师的气质。我想，我们的客人到了。”

⑥ pragmatical [præg'mætikəl] *a.* 实用主义的

As he spoke there was a sharp ring at the bell. Sherlock Holmes rose softly and moved his chair in the direction of the door. We heard the servant pass along the hall, and the sharp click of the **latch**① as she opened it.

"Does Dr. Watson live here?" asked a clear but rather harsh voice. We could not hear the servant's reply, but the door closed, and some one began to ascend the stairs. The footfall was an uncertain and **shuffling**② one. A look of surprise passed over the face of my companion as he listened to it. It came slowly along the passage, and there was a feeble tap at the door.

"Come in," I cried.

At my **summons**③, instead of the man of violence whom we expected, a very old and wrinkled woman hobbled into the apartment. She appeared to be dazzled by the sudden blaze of light, and after dropping a **curtsey**④, she stood blinking at us with her bleared eyes and **fumbling**⑤ in her pocket with nervous, shaky fingers. I glanced at my companion, and his face had assumed such a **disconsolate**⑥ expression that it was all I could do to keep my countenance.

The old **crone**⑦ drew out an evening paper, and pointed at our advertisement. "It's this as has brought me, good gentlemen," she said, dropping another curtsey; "a gold wedding ring in the Brixton Road. It belongs to my girl Sally, as was married only this time twelvemonth, which her husband is **steward**⑧ aboard a Union boat, and what he'd say if he come 'ome and found her without her ring is more than I can think, he being short enough at the best o' times, but more especially when he has the drink. If it please you, she went to the **circus**⑨ last night along with——"

"Is that her ring?" I asked.

"The Lord be thanked!" cried the old woman; "Sally will be a glad woman this night. That's the ring."

"And what may your address be?" I inquired, taking up a pencil.

"13, Duncan Street, Houndsditch. A weary way from here."

"The Brixton Road does not lie between any circus and Houndsditch," said

他说话的当儿，门铃刺耳地响了起来。福尔摩斯缓缓站起身，把自己的椅子朝着门口的方向移动了一下。我们听见仆人走过门厅的声音，门闩咔哒拔开了。

“华生医生是住这儿吗？”有个清晰但却刺耳的声音在问。我们没有听见女仆的回答，但听见门关上了，有人上楼梯了。脚步不均匀，而且显得很拖沓。我同伴听到脚步声时，脸上掠过惊讶的神情。脚步在过道上缓慢地前移，接着便听见微弱的敲门声。

“进来，”我大声说。

话音刚落，进入室内的不是我们想象中的那个凶恶男子，而是个步履蹒跚、满脸皱纹的老妇人。面对突如其来的强光，她似乎有点头晕目眩。行过屈膝礼后，她站立在那儿眨巴着昏花的眼睛看我们，神情紧张，抖动着的手指在衣服口袋里摸索着。我瞥了我同伴一眼，只见他表情很沮丧，我只好不动声色。

她拿出一张晚报，指着我们登载的启事。“我是看到了这个东西之后来的，好心的先生们，”她说，又屈身行了个礼，“在布里克斯顿大街遗失的金婚戒，那是我女儿萨莉的，她去年这个时候结的婚，丈夫是联合轮船公司的乘务员。如果他回家时发现她的戒指丢失了，我真不知道他会怎么说。他本来就脾气暴躁，喝了酒就会更加变本加厉。你们请听我说，她昨晚去看马戏时还——”

“是这枚戒指吗？”我问。

“谢天谢地！”老妇人大声说，“萨莉今晚可要开心死啦，是这枚。”

“您住在哪儿？”我询问了一句，拿起一支铅笔。

“霍恩兹蒂奇路邓肯街十三号，从这儿走过去可累人啦。”

“从霍恩兹蒂奇到马戏团不用经过布里克斯顿街啊。”夏洛克·福尔摩斯脱口而出。

① latch [lætʃ] *n.* 门闩

② shuffling [ˈʃʌfliŋ] *a.* 慢慢移动的

③ summon [ˈsʌmən] *n.* 召唤

④ curtsey [ˈkəːtsi] *n.*（女子的）屈膝礼

⑤ fumble [ˈfʌmbl] *v.* 笨拙地摸索

⑥ disconsolate [disˈkɔnsələt] *a.* 郁郁不乐的

⑦ crone [krəun] *n.* 干瘪的老太婆

⑧ steward [stjuəd] *n.* 乘务员

⑨ circus [ˈsəːkəs] *n.* 马戏场

Sherlock Holmes sharply.

The old woman faced round and looked keenly at him from her little red-rimmed eyes. "The gentleman asked me for my address," she said. "Sally lives in lodgings at 3, Mayfield Place, Peckham."

"And your name is——?"

"My name is Sawyer—her's is Dennis, which Tom Dennis married her—and a smart, clean **lad**①, too, as long as he's at sea, and no steward in the company more thought of; but when on shore, what with the women and what with **liquor**② shops——"

"Here is your ring, Mrs. Sawyer," I interrupted, in **obedience**③ to a sign from my companion; "it clearly belongs to your daughter, and I am glad to be able to **restore**④ it to the rightful owner."

With many **mumbled**⑤ blessings and **protestations**⑥ of gratitude the old crone packed it away in her pocket, and shuffled off down the stairs. Sherlock Holmes sprang to his feet the moment that she was gone and rushed into his room. He returned in a few seconds enveloped in an **ulster**⑦ and a **cravat**⑧. "I'll follow her," he said, hurriedly; "she must be an accomplice, and will lead me to him. Wait up for me." The hall door had hardly slammed behind our visitor before Holmes had descended the stair. Looking through the window I could see her walking feebly along the other side, while her **pursuer**⑨ **dogged**⑩ her some little distance behind. "Either his whole theory is incorrect," I thought to myself, "or else he will be led now to the heart of the mystery." There was no need for him to ask me to wait up for him, for I felt that sleep was impossible until I heard the result of his adventure.

It was close upon nine when he set out. I had no idea how long he might be, but I sat **stolidly**⑪ puffing at my pipe and skipping over the pages of Henri Murger's *Vie de Boheme.* Ten o'clock passed, and I heard the footsteps of the maid as they pattered off to bed. Eleven, and the more stately **tread**⑫ of the landlady passed my door, bound for the same destination. It was close upon twelve before I heard the sharp sound of his latch-key. The instant he entered

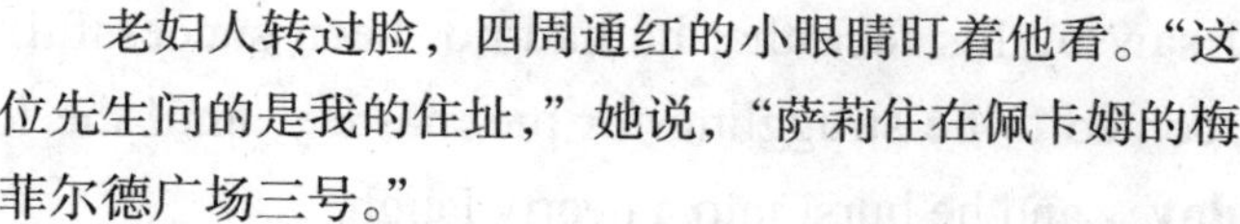

老妇人转过脸，四周通红的小眼睛盯着他看。“这位先生问的是我的住址，”她说，“萨莉住在佩卡姆的梅菲尔德广场三号。”

“您姓——？”

“我姓索耶，女儿姓丹尼斯，汤姆·丹尼斯娶了她——他只要待在海上，便是个机灵诚实的年轻人，全公司没有哪个船员比得上他。但是，一旦上了岸，有了女人和酒，那可就——”

“这是您的戒指，索耶太太，”我按照我同伴的示意打断了她的话，“很显然，这戒指是您女儿的。它能够物归原主，我很高兴。”

老妇人咕哝地说了一大堆祝福和感激的话后，把戒指装进了自己的衣服口袋，拖沓着脚步下楼了。老妇人刚一离开，夏洛克·福尔摩斯便立刻一跃而起，冲向他自己的卧室。过了几秒钟，他穿着乌尔斯特大衣，系着领巾，从房间里出来了。“我要去跟踪她，”他急匆匆地说，“她一定是个同谋，可以引导我找到凶手，你等着我。”来者离开时厅堂门刚刚关好，福尔摩斯便下楼了。透过窗子，我看见老妇人有气无力地在街道的另一边走着，而她的跟踪者则在她背后不远处尾随着。“要么他的整个看法都不对，”我心里想着，“要么，他现在正被人引导着走近谜案的真相。”他其实用不着吩咐我等着他，因为我觉得，没有得到他此番历险的结果，我是不可能睡着的。

他出发时已经快九点钟了。我不知道他要多久才能回来，只好百无聊赖地坐着，一边抽着烟斗，一边翻阅着亨利·米尔热的《放浪形骸》。十点过去了，我听到女仆啪嗒啪嗒回房睡觉的脚步声。十一点钟，房东太太更加沉稳的脚步从我的房门口经过，也要回房睡觉了。快到十二点了，我这才听见福尔摩斯用钥匙开门时发出的清脆的咔嗒声。他进入房间的瞬间，我便从他的脸色

① lad [læd] *n.* 小伙子

② liquor ['likə] *n.* 酒

③ obedience [ə'bi:diəns] *n.* 遵照

④ restore [ri'stɔ:] *v.* 交还

⑤ mumbled ['mʌmbld] *a.* 咕咕哝哝的

⑥ protestation [ˌprəutes'teiʃən] *n.* 声明

⑦ ulster ['ʌlstə] *n.* 乌尔斯特宽大衣

⑧ cravat [krə'væt] *n.* 领结

⑨ pursuer [pə'sju:ə] *n.* 追踪者

⑩ dog [dɔg] *v.* 跟随

⑪ stolidly [stɔlidli] *ad.* 不动感情地

⑫ tread [tred] *n.* 足音

I saw by his face that he had not been successful. Amusement and **chagrin**① seemed to be struggling for the mastery, until the former suddenly **carried the day**②, and he burst into a hearty laugh.

"I wouldn't have the Scotland Yarders know it for the world," he cried, dropping into his chair; "I have **chaffed**③ them so much that they would never have let me hear the end of it. I can afford to laugh, because I know that I will be even with them in the long run."

"What is it then?" I asked.

"Oh, I don't mind telling a story against myself. That creature had gone a little way when she began to **limp**④ and show every sign of being **footsore**⑤. Presently she came to a halt, and hailed a four-wheeler which was passing. I managed to be close to her so as to hear the address, but I need not have been so anxious, for she sang it out loud enough to be heard at the other side of the street, 'Drive to 13, Duncan Street, Houndsditch,' she cried. This begins to look genuine, I thought, and having seen her safely inside, I **perched**⑥ myself behind. That's an art which every detective should be an expert at. Well, away we rattled, and never drew rein until we reached the street in question. I hopped off before we came to the door, and strolled down the street in an easy, lounging way. I saw the cab pull up. The driver jumped down, and I saw him open the door and stand expectantly. Nothing came out though. When I reached him he was **groping**⑦ about **frantically**⑧ in the empty cab, and giving vent to the finest assorted collection of **oaths**⑨ that ever I listened to. There was no sign or trace of his passenger, and I fear it will be some time before he gets his fare. On inquiring at Number 13 we found that the house belonged to a respectable **paperhanger**⑩, named Keswick, and that no one of the name either of Sawyer or Dennis had ever been heard of there."

"You don't mean to say," I cried, in amazement, "that that **tottering**⑪, feeble old woman was able to get out of the cab while it was in motion, without either you or the driver seeing her?"

"Old woman be damned!" said Sherlock Holmes, sharply. "We were the old

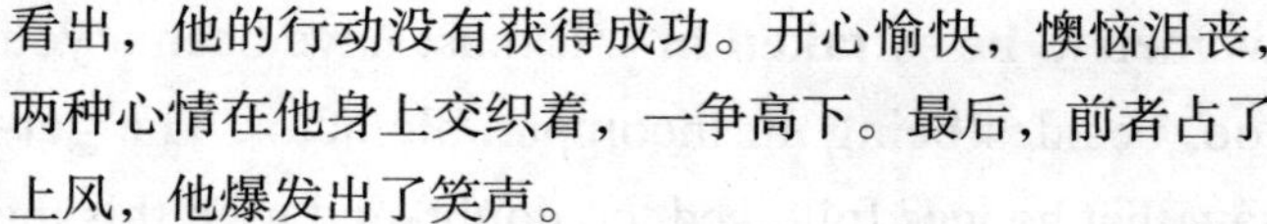

① chagrin [ʃæ'grin] *n.* 懊恼

② carry the day 获胜

③ chaff [tʃa:f] *v.* 嘲笑

④ limp [limp] *v.* 一拐一拐地走

⑤ footsore ['fut,sɔ:] *a.* 腿脚酸痛的

⑥ perch [pə:tʃ] *v.* 停留，这里指坐上马车

⑦ grope [grəup] *v.* 搜索

⑧ frantically ['fræntikəli] *ad.* 疯狂地

⑨ oath [əuθ] *n.* 咒骂

⑩ paperhanger ['peipə,hæŋə] *n.* 裱糊工

⑪ tottering ['tɔtəriŋ] *a.* 蹒跚的

看出，他的行动没有获得成功。开心愉快，懊恼沮丧，两种心情在他身上交织着，一争高下。最后，前者占了上风，他爆发出了笑声。

“我怎么也不能让伦敦警察厅知道这个情况，”福尔摩斯大声说着，重重地坐到自己的椅子上，“我常常嘲笑他们，如果他们知道了这件事情，他们决不会放过我的。我能够经受得起嘲笑，因为我知道，从长远来说，我总是能够摆平他们的。”

“那是怎么回事啊？”我问。

“噢，我也不在乎把自己窝囊的事情说出来。老妇人没走多远，就开始一瘸一拐的，看起来是走疼了脚。她很快就停了下来，叫了辆正从身边经过的四轮马车。于是，我尽量靠近她，想听听她说要去哪里。但是，我其实没有必要迫不及待，因为她说要去的地址时，高声大气，即便在街道对面都可以听清楚。‘到霍恩兹蒂奇的邓肯街十三号，’她大声说着。我当时以为这些都是真的。我看见她稳稳当当地坐进了马车里，我也悄悄坐在了后面。这是每个侦探必须精通的跟踪技巧。是啊，马车辚辚地驶出了，一路不停地奔向她说的那条街。快到门口时，我跳下马车，顺着街道悠哉游哉地往前走。我看见她的马车停了下来，车夫跳下车，打开车门等客人下车，然而，却没人下来。我走到跟前时，他显得很疯狂，徒劳地在空空如也的车厢里到处找，嘴里不停地骂着，那个骂人的话我可是从来都没有听过的。乘客没有了人影儿。他恐怕要想拿到乘车的钱，得等上一段时间才行啊。到十三号一打听才知道，那儿住着的是一位行为端正的糊裱工，名叫凯斯维克，根本就没有叫索耶或丹尼斯的人在那儿住过。”

“你不会是说，”我大声说，惊愕不已，“那个步履蹒跚，身体衰弱的老妇人能在马车行进过程中瞒过你和车夫的眼睛逃脱吧？”

women to **be** so **taken in**[①]. It must have been a young man, and an active one, too, besides being an incomparable actor. The **get-up**[②] was **inimitable**[③]. He saw that he was followed, no doubt, and used this means of giving me the **slip**[④]. It shows that the man we are after is not as lonely as I imagined he was, but has friends who are ready to risk something for him. Now, Doctor, you are looking **done-up**[⑤]. Take my advice and **turn in**[⑥]."

I was certainly feeling very weary, so I obeyed his **injunction**[⑦]. I left Holmes seated in front of the **smouldering**[⑧] fire, and long into the watches of the night I heard the low, melancholy wailings of his violin, and knew that he was still pondering over the strange problem which he had set himself to unravel.

① be taken in 上当受骗
② get-up ['getʌp] *n.* 乔装打扮
③ inimitable [i'nimitəbl] *a.* 无与伦比的
④ slip [slip] *n.* 逃脱
⑤ done-up ['dʌnʌp] *a.* 精疲力尽的
⑥ turn in 上床睡觉
⑦ injunction [in'dʒʌŋkʃən] *n.* 命令
⑧ smouldering [sməuldəriŋ] *a.* 微微燃烧着的

“见鬼的老妇人！”夏洛克·福尔摩斯说，语气尖刻，“我们才是老妇人呢，被人家这样骗了。一定是个年轻人，除了善于表演之外，还身手不凡。乔装改扮的本事也了不得。他发觉自己被跟踪了，毫无疑问，于是就用这样的伎俩把我给甩掉了。看起来，我们寻找的那个人并不像我们想象的那样孤身一人，而是有很多朋友，为了他可以铤而走险。对啊，医生，你看起来很累了。听我的，休息去吧。”

我确实感觉很疲倦了，所以就听从他的劝告，回卧室睡觉去了。留下福尔摩斯独自一人坐在微微燃烧着的壁炉前面。夜深人静了，我还能听见他拉出的低沉哀婉的小提琴声。我知道，他还在思索着手边这桩要破解的离奇案件。

Chapter 6 Tobias Gregson Shows What He Can Do

The papers next day were full of the "Brixton Mystery," as they termed it. Each had a long account of the affair, and some had leaders upon it in addition. There was some information in them which was new to me. I still retain in my **scrapbook**① numerous clippings and extracts bearing upon the case. Here is a **condensation**② of a few of them:—

The *Daily Telegraph* remarked that in the history of crime there had seldom been a tragedy which presented stranger features. The German name of the victim, the absence of all other motive, and the sinister inscription on the wall, all pointed to its **perpetration**③ by political **refugees**④ and revolutionists. The Socialists had many branches in America, and the **deceased**⑤ had, no doubt, **infringed**⑥ their unwritten laws, and been tracked down by them. After **alluding**⑦ airily to the Vehmgericht, aqua tofana, Carbonari, the Marchioness de Brinvilliers, the Darwinian theory, the principles of Malthus, and the Ratcliff Highway murders, the article concluded by **admonishing**⑧ the government and advocating a closer watch over foreigners in England.

The Standard commented upon the fact that lawless **outrages**⑨ of the sort usually occurred under a Liberal atdministration. They arose from the unsettling of the minds of the masses, and the consequent weakening of all authority. The

第六章　托比亚斯·格雷格森显示其能耐

翌日，各家报纸充斥着关于所谓的“布里克斯顿谜案”的新闻。每一家报纸都对事件给予了长篇报道，有些还加发了社论。有些情况我先前都不知道。直到现在，我的剪贴本里还保留着许多与本案有关的剪报和摘录。以下是其中一些的概要：

《每日电讯报》指出：纵观人类犯罪史，很少有惨案像本案一样，怪异离奇，独具特点。遇害人的德国名字，以及墙上写着的不祥的文字，所有这一切都指向一点，即罪行乃政治难民和革命分子所为，除此以外找不到其他任何犯罪动机。社会党在美国有很多分支，毫无疑问，死者一定是触犯了他们的不成文法，因此被人盯上了。文章还信马由缰地提到了秘密刑事法庭制度案，托法娜仙液案，意大利烧炭党人案，布兰维利耶侯爵夫人案，达尔文的进化论学说案，马尔萨斯的人口论原则案，还有拉特克利夫大道多人遇害案，最后，劝诫政府当局，严密关注侨居在英国的外国人的动向。

《旗帜报》对案件的评论是：这类无法无天的残暴行径通常发生在自由党执政期间。其原由是民心不稳，当局软弱无能。死者是位美国绅士，旅居伦敦已经几个

① scrapbook ['skræpˌbuk] *n.* 剪贴簿
② condensation [ˌkɔnden'seiʃən] *n.* 概要
③ perpetration [ˌpəːpi'treiʃən] *n.* 罪行
④ refugee [ˌrefju'dʒiː] *n.* 难民
⑤ deceased [di'siːst] *a.* 已经死亡的
⑥ infringe [in'frindʒ] *v.* 违反
⑦ allude [ə'luːd] *v.* 提及
⑧ admonish [æd'mɔniʃ] *v.* 劝告
⑨ outrage ['autreidʒ] *n.* 暴行

deceased was an American gentleman who had been residing for some weeks in the metropolis. He had stayed at the boarding-house of Madame Charpentier, in Torquay Terrace, Camberwell. He was accompanied in his travels by his private secretary, Mr. Joseph Stangerson. The two **bade adieu to**① their landlady upon Tuesday, the 4th inst., and departed to Euston Station with the **avowed**② intention of catching the Liverpool express. They were afterwards seen together upon the platform. Nothing more is known of them until Mr. Drebber's body was, as recorded, discovered in an empty house in the Brixton Road, many miles from Euston. How he came there, or how he met his fate, are questions which are still involved in mystery. Nothing is known of the whereabouts of Stangerson. We are glad to learn that Mr. Lestrade and Mr. Gregson, of Scotland Yard, are both engaged upon the case, and it is confidently **anticipated**③ that these well-known officers will speedily throw light upon the matter.

The *Daily News* observed that there was no doubt as to the crime being a political one. The **despotism**④ and hatred of Liberalism which **animated**⑤ the Continental governments had had the effect of driving to our shores a number of men who might have made excellent citizens were they not **soured**⑥ by the **recollection**⑦ of all that they had undergone. Among these men there was a **stringent**⑧ code of honour, any infringement of which was punished by death. Every effort should be made to find the secretary, Stangerson, and to ascertain some particulars of the habits of the deceased. A great step had been gained by the discovery of the address of the house at which he had boarded—a result which was entirely due to the **acuteness**⑨ and energy of Mr. Gregson of Scotland Yard.

Sherlock Holmes and I read these notices over together at breakfast, and they appeared to afford him considerable amusement.

"I told you that, whatever happened, Lestrade and Gregson would be sure to score."

"That depends on how it turns out."

"Oh, bless you, it doesn't matter in the least. If the man is caught, it will

星期了。他是在私人秘书约瑟夫·斯坦格森先生的陪同下来伦敦的，下榻在坎伯韦尔区托凯巷夏庞蒂埃太太的公寓里。两人于本月四日星期二告别房东太太，前往尤斯顿火车站，说是去赶乘开往利物浦的直达快车。有人后来在站台上看到过他们，但随后便不见了踪影。直到有新闻报道说，德雷伯先生的尸体被人发现在距离尤斯顿车站数英里远的布里克斯顿大街的一幢空住宅里。他是怎么到那儿的，又是怎样在那儿惨遭杀害的，至今仍是个谜。斯坦格森杳无音信。我们非常欣喜地获悉，伦敦警察厅的莱斯特雷德先生和格雷格森先生将一同负责办理此案，相信这两位声名赫赫的督察定能很快使案情真相大白。

《每日新闻》认为：毫无疑问，本案是桩政治案件。欧洲大陆的各国政府专横跋扈，仇视自由主义，结果把许多人士逼到了我国。那些人如果不是心中满怀着对自己境遇的痛苦记忆，悲观失望，本来可以成为优秀的公民。那些人当中有一套严苛的行为准则，一旦有人违犯，必被处死。我们必须不余遗力地寻找到死者的秘书斯坦格森，确认死者的一些生活习性。案件目前已取得重大进展，因为已经查明死者生前下榻的寓所了——这一结果完全归功于伦敦警察厅机敏睿智而又精力充沛的格雷格森先生。

我和福尔摩斯在早餐时看了这些报道。他觉得，这些报道很逗人。

“我对你说过了，不管情况如何，莱斯特雷德和格雷格森一定可以邀功。”

“这还要取决于最后的结果如何。”

“噢，天哪！这一点关系都没有。如果凶手被抓住了，那是他们尽心尽力的结果。如果凶手逃跑了，那他们也是尽了力的。如同猜钱币，无论正反面，他们都是赢家。不管他们做了什么，总是会有捧场的人。‘再愚

① bid adieu to 向…告别

② avowed [ə'vaud] *a.* 公开宣称的

③ anticipate [æn'tisipeit] *v.* 期望

④ despotism ['despə,tizəm] *n.* 专制统治

⑤ animate ['æni,meit] *v.* 驱动；激励

⑥ sour ['sauə] *v.* 使…变得阴郁

⑦ recollection [,rekə'lekʃən] *n.* 回忆

⑧ stringent ['strindʒənt] *a.* 严格的

⑨ acuteness [ə'kju:tnis] *n.* 敏锐

be *on account* of their **exertions**[①]; if he escapes, it will be *in spite* of their exertions. It's heads I win and tails you lose. Whatever they do, they will have followers. '*Un sot trouve toujours un plus sot qui l'admire.*'"

"What on earth is this?" I cried, for at this moment there came the pattering of many steps in the hall and on the stairs, accompanied by **audible**[②] expressions of disgust upon the part of our landlady.

"It's the Baker Street division of the detective police force," said my companion, gravely; and as he spoke there rushed into the room half a dozen of the dirtiest and most ragged street Arabs that ever I clapped eyes on.

"'Tention!" cried Holmes, in a sharp tone, and the six dirty little **scoundrels**[③] stood in a line like so many disreputable statuettes."In future you shall send up Wiggins alone to report, and the rest of you must wait in the street. Have you found it, Wiggins?"

"No, sir, we hain't," said one of the youths.

"I hardly expected you would. You must keep on until you do. Here are your wages." He handed each of them a shilling.

"Now, off you go, and come back with a better report next time."

He waved his hand, and they **scampered**[④] away downstairs like so many rats, and we heard their shrill voices next moment in the street.

"There's more work to be got out of one of those little beggars than out of a dozen of the force," Holmes remarked. "The mere sight of an official-looking person seals men's lips. These youngsters, however, go everywhere and hear everything. They are as sharp as needles, too; all they want is organisation."

"Is it on this Brixton case that you are employing them?" I asked.

"Yes; there is a point which I wish to ascertain. It is merely a matter of time. Hullo! we are going to hear some news now **with a vengeance**[⑤]! Here is Gregson coming down the road with **beatitude**[⑥] written upon every feature of his face. Bound for us, I know. Yes, he is stopping. There he is!"

There was a violent **peal**[⑦] at the bell, and in a few seconds the fair-

① exertion [ig'zəːʃən] *n.* 努力

② audible ['ɔːdibl] *a.* 听得见的

③ scoundrel ['skaundrəl] *n.* 无赖，这里指混混

④ scamper ['skæmpə] *v.* 蹦蹦跳跳地跑

⑤ with a vengeance 极度

⑥ beatitude [bi'æti,tuːd] *n.* 至福

⑦ peal [piːl] *n.* 洪亮的响声

蠢的人都会有更加愚蠢的崇拜者。'"

"到底怎么回事？"我大声说，因为就在这时，一阵杂乱的脚步声从厅堂和楼梯上传来，还掺杂着房东太太的埋怨声。

"是贝克大街刑警分队来了，"我同伴说，态度显得很严肃。他说话的当儿，六个街上的流浪儿冲了进来。他们蓬头垢面，衣衫褴褛，我还从来没有见过比他们更加邋遢的样子。

"立正！"福尔摩斯大声喊着，语气严厉，六个小邋遢鬼应声站成了一排，就像六尊破烂的雕像。"你们以后就让威金斯一个人来向我报告，其余的人在街上等着。威金斯，你们找到了吗？"

"没有，先生，还没有找到呢，"其中一个孩子说。

"我也没指望你们这么快就找到了，但你们必须一直找，直到找到为止。这是给你们的酬劳，"他说着发给了每人一个先令，"好啦，你们去吧！下次带好消息来。"

他挥了挥手，他们就像是一群耗子窜下楼去了。不一会儿，街上传来他们尖锐刺耳的叫声。

"这些个小乞丐，一个人的工作效力比十多个警察的都要高，"福尔摩斯说，"人们一旦看到有官方模样的人，就会三缄其口。而这些小家伙们哪儿都可以去，什么情况都听得到。他们还非常机灵，像枚针似的锐利。不足之处就是缺乏组织性。"

"你是雇佣他们来调查布里克斯顿案吗？"我问。

"对啊，因为我有个问题想要证实一下，只是个时间问题罢了。嘿！我们就要听到十足的好消息啦！格雷格森在街上走着呢，脸上洋溢着欢天喜地的表情。我知道，是找我们来了。他马上就要停下来了，他来了。"

门铃猛烈地响了起来，片刻之后，淡黄色头发的警

haired detective came up the stairs, three steps at a time, and burst into our sitting-room.

"My dear fellow," he cried, wringing Holmes's **unresponsive**[①] hand, "congratulate me! I have made the whole thing as clear as day."

A shade of anxiety seemed to me to cross my companion's expressive face.

"Do you mean that you are on the right track?" he asked.

"The right track! Why, sir, we have the man **under lock and key**[②]."

"And his name is?"

"Arthur Charpentier, **sub-lieutenant**[③] in Her Majesty's navy," cried Gregson, pompously, rubbing his fat hands and **inflating**[④] his chest.

Sherlock Holmes gave a sigh of relief, and relaxed into a smile.

"Take a seat, and try one of these cigars," he said. "We are anxious to know how you managed it. Will you have some whiskey and water?"

"I don't mind if I do," the detective answered. "The tremendous exertions which I have gone through during the last day or two have worn me out. Not so much bodily exertion, you understand, as the strain upon the mind. You will appreciate that, Mr. Sherlock Holmes, for we are both brain-workers."

"You do me too much honour," said Holmes, gravely. "Let us hear how you arrived at this most **gratifying**[⑤] result."

The detective seated himself in the armchair, and puffed **complacently**[⑥] at his cigar. Then suddenly he slapped his thigh in a **paroxysm**[⑦] of amusement.

"The fun of it is," he cried, "that that fool Lestrade, who thinks himself so smart, has gone off upon the wrong track altogether. He is after the secretary Stangerson, who had no more to do with the crime than the babe unborn. I have no doubt that he has caught him by this time."

The idea tickled Gregson so much that he laughed until he choked.

"And how did you get your clue?"

"Ah, I'll tell you all about it. Of course, Doctor Watson, this is strictly

探三步并作两步奔上了楼，紧接着冲进了我们的客厅。

“亲爱的朋友们啊，”他大声喊着，紧紧地握住福尔摩斯毫无反应的手，“祝贺我吧！我把整个案件查得像白昼一样明朗啦。”

我似乎看到了，福尔摩斯表情丰富的脸上掠过了一丝焦虑的阴影。

“您是说，您已经找到了正确的思路了吗？”他问。

“正确的思路！啊，先生，我们都已经把凶手关进牢房啦。”

“他叫什么？”

“阿瑟·夏庞蒂埃，皇家海军的中尉，”格雷格森大声说着，语气高调，不停地搓着满是肉的双手，昂首挺胸。

夏洛克·福尔摩斯松了口气，如释重负，继而轻松地微笑了。

“请坐，抽支雪茄吧，”他说，“我们很想知道您是怎么破的案，来点威士忌加水怎么样？”

“那就来点吧，”警探回答说，“我这一两天可是全力以赴啊，累得够呛了。您知道的，身体上的劳累倒是没有什么，主要是劳心啊。您会感同身受的，夏洛克·福尔摩斯先生，我们两个都是靠用脑来工作的人。”

“您这可是太过抬举我了，”福尔摩斯说，态度很严肃，“您取得了令人高兴的结果，说出来我们听听吧。”

警探坐在扶手椅上，洋洋得意地吸着烟。接着猛然拍了一下大腿，喜不自禁。

“很有意思的是，”他大声说，“莱斯特雷德那个傻瓜还自以为很聪明，这一次却完全把思路给搞错了。他一直在寻找那位秘书斯坦格森，但实际上，那人像个未出生的婴儿一样清白，与本案一丁点儿瓜葛都没有。我毫不怀疑，他此刻已经逮住人家了。”

格雷格森想到这事便乐不可支，笑得喘不过气来了。

“您是怎么找到线索的？”

① unresponsive [ˌʌnris'pɔnsiv] *a.* 毫无反应的

② under lock and key 把…囚禁

③ sub-lieutenant [ˌsʌblef'tenənt] *n.* 海军中尉

④ inflate [in'fleit] *v.* 膨胀，鼓起

⑤ gratifying ['grætifaiiŋ] *a.* 可喜的

⑥ complacently [kəm'pleisəntli] *ad.* 满足地

⑦ paroxysm ['pærəkˌsizəm] *n.* 突然发作

between ourselves. The first difficulty which we had to contend with was the finding of this American's **antecedents**[①]. Some people would have waited until their advertisements were answered, or until parties came forward and volunteered information. That is not Tobias Gregson's way of going to work. You remember the hat beside the dead man?"

"Yes," said Holmes; "by John Underwood and Sons, 129, Camberwell Road."

Gregson looked quite **crestfallen**[②].

"I had no idea that you noticed that," he said. "Have you been there?"

"No."

"Ha!" cried Gregson, in a relieved voice; "you should never **neglect**[③] a chance, however small it may seem."

"To a great mind, nothing is little," remarked Holmes, **sententiously**[④].

"Well, I went to Underwood, and asked him if he had sold a hat of that size and description. He looked over his books, and came on it at once. He had sent the hat to a Mr. Drebber, residing at Charpentier's Boarding Establishment, Torquay Terrace. Thus I got at his address."

"Smart—very smart!" murmured Sherlock Holmes.

"I next called upon Madame Charpentier," continued the detective. "I found her very pale and distressed. Her daughter was in the room, too—an uncommonly fine girl she is, too; she was looking red about the eyes and her lips **trembled**[⑤] as I spoke to her. That didn't escape my notice. I began to **smell a rat**[⑥]. You know the feeling, Mr. Sherlock Holmes, when you come upon the right scent—a kind of thrill in your nerves. 'Have you heard of the mysterious death of your late boarder Mr. Enoch J. Drebber, of Cleveland?' I asked.

"The mother nodded. She didn't seem able to get out a word. The daughter burst into tears. I felt more than ever that these people knew something of the matter.

"啊，我把这事的原委告诉你们吧。当然，华生医生，这事我们三个人知道就行了。我们首先要解决的难题，就是要查明那个美国人的来历。有些人会坐着等待，等着人家看了告示后来报告，或者等着各方人士前来主动提供信息。这可不是我托比亚斯·格雷格森的处事风格。你们还记得放在死者旁边的那顶帽子吗？"

① antecedent [ˌænti'siːdənt] *n.* 出身，来历

"记得，"福尔摩斯说，"是约翰·恩德伍德父子店的产品，店铺地址在坎伯韦尔大道一百二十九号。"

格雷格森看上去垂头丧气了。

② crestfallen ['krest,fɔːlən] *a.* 沮丧的

"没想到您也注意到了，"他说，"您去了那儿吗？"

"没有。"

"哈！"格雷格森大声说，松了一口气，"不能忽略任何机会啊，不管它看起来多么微不足道。"

③ neglect [ni'glekt] *v.* 忽略

"在智者的心目中，根本就不存在什么微不足道的事情，"福尔摩斯说道，摆出一副智者的神态。

④ sententiously [sen'tenʃəsli] *ad.* 简洁地

"是啊，我去找过恩德伍德，问他是否出售过那种型号和式样的帽子。他查了账目，立刻就查到了。那顶帽子是给德雷伯先生送去的，住在托凯巷的夏庞蒂埃公寓。就这样，我得到了他的住址。"

"聪明——非常聪明！"夏洛克·福尔摩斯喃喃地说。

"我接着去拜访了夏庞蒂埃太太，"警探接着说，"发现她脸色苍白，神情忧伤。她女儿也在家里——那姑娘长得非常漂亮。我对她说话时，她眼圈红了，嘴唇直哆嗦。这些都没有逃过我的眼神。我开始意识到事情不对劲，您知道那种感觉的，福尔摩斯先生，就是一旦发现了蛛丝马迹，神经就会高度兴奋起来。'你们听说了克利夫兰的伊诺克·德雷伯先生，也就是你们先前的房客，神秘死亡的消息了吗？'

⑤ tremble ['trembl] *v.* 颤抖

⑥ smell a rat 感到不妙

"做母亲的点了点头，看起来连话都说不出来了。她的女儿则哭了起来。我更加强烈地感觉到，这两个女人知道些情况。

"'At what o'clock did Mr. Drebber leave your house for the train?' I asked.

"'At eight o'clock,' she said, **gulping**① in her throat to keep down her **agitation**②. 'His secretary, Mr. Stangerson, said that there were two trains—one at 9:15 and one at 11. He was to catch the first.'

"'And was that the last which you saw of him?'

"A terrible change came over the woman's face as I asked the question. Her features turned perfectly **livid**③. It was some seconds before she could get out the single word 'Yes'—and when it did come it was in a **husky**④ unnatural tone.

"There was silence for a moment, and then the daughter spoke in a calm clear voice.

"'No good can ever come of falsehood, mother,' she said. 'Let us be frank with this gentleman. We *did* see Mr. Drebber again.'

"'God forgive you!' cried Madame Charpentier, throwing up her hands and sinking back in her chair. 'You have murdered your brother.'

"'Arthur would rather that we spoke the truth,' the girl answered firmly.

"'You had best tell me all about it now,' I said. 'Half-confidences are worse than none. Besides, you do not know how much we know of it.'

"'On your head be it, Alice!' cried her mother; and then, turning to me, 'I will tell you all, sir. Do not imagine that my agitation on behalf of my son arises from any fear **lest**⑤ he should have had a hand in this terrible affair. He is utterly innocent of it. My dread is, however, that in your eyes and in the eyes of others he may appear to be compromised. That however is surely impossible. His high character, his profession, his antecedents would all forbid it.'

"'Your best way is to **make a clean breast of**⑥ the facts,' I answered. 'Depend upon it, if your son is innocent he will be none the worse.'

"'Perhaps, Alice, you had better leave us together,' she said, and her daughter **withdrew**⑦. 'Now, sir,' she continued, 'I had no intention of telling you all this, but since my poor daughter has **disclosed**⑧ it I have no alternative. Having once decided to speak, I will tell you all without omitting any particular.'

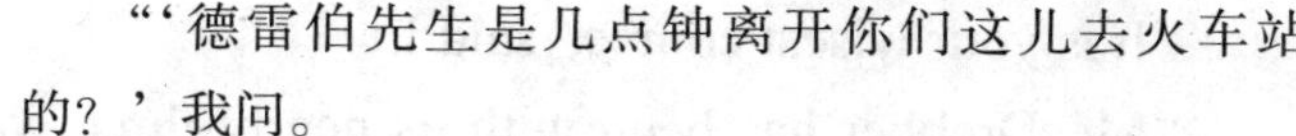

"'德雷伯先生是几点钟离开你们这儿去火车站的？'我问。

"'八点钟'她回答说，喉头哽咽，尽力压抑着内心的情绪波动，'他的秘书斯坦格森先生说有两趟火车，九点十五一趟，十一点一趟，他准备乘头一趟。'

"'那是你们最后见到他吗？'

"我这话刚出口，发现妇人脸色很难看，黯然失色，片刻之后，冒出了一个字'对'——嗓音干哑，语气很不自然。

"沉默了一会儿之后，女儿开口说话了，态度平静，声音清晰。

"'说谎不会有任何好处的，母亲，'姑娘说，'我们还是坦率地告诉这位先生吧，我们后来确实又见过德雷伯先生。'

"'愿上帝宽恕你吧！'夏庞蒂埃太太大声说，双手向上猛地一挥，瘫坐在椅子上，'你害死你哥哥了。'

"'阿瑟也肯定希望我们讲真话。'姑娘语气坚定地说。

"'你们现在最好把全部情况告诉我，'我说，'说半句留半句，还不如不说。再说，你们也不清楚我们到底掌握了多少情况。'

"'都是你惹的祸，艾丽斯！'她母亲大声说，然后转向我，'我会把全部情况告诉您的，先生。您可别以为，我为儿子的事情情绪激动，是因为担心他与这宗惨案有什么瓜葛，他绝对是清白无辜的。然而，我担心的是，在您或者别人看来，他好像脱不了干系。但这是不可能的。我儿子人品高尚，职业体面，从未有过不良记录。这些都能说明，他绝对与案件毫无关系。'

"'您最好还是把事情全部讲清楚，'我回应说，'请您相信，如果您儿子是无辜的，他自然就不会有事。'

"'艾丽斯，你还是让我们单独谈吧！'她说着，女儿离开了。'好啦，先生，'她继续说，'我本来不打算把一切告诉您的，但是，既然我可怜的女儿已经说出来

① gulp [gʌlp] *v.* 哽咽

② agitation [ˌædʒi'teiʃən] *n.* 焦虑

③ livid ['livid] *a.* 乌青色的；苍白的

④ husky ['hʌski] *a.* 嗓子干哑的

⑤ lest [lest] conj. 唯恐

⑥ make a clean breast of 彻底坦白

⑦ withdraw [wið'drɔː] *v.* 撤出；离开

⑧ disclose [dis'kləuz] *v.* 说出

"'It is your wisest course,' said I.

"'Mr. Drebber has been with us nearly three weeks. He and his secretary, Mr. Stangerson, had been travelling on the Continent. I noticed a "Copenhagen" label upon each of their trunks, showing that that had been their last stopping place. Stangerson was a quiet **reserved**① man, but his employer, I am sorry to say, was far otherwise. He was coarse in his habits and **brutish**② in his ways. The very night of his arrival he became very much the worse for drink, and, indeed, after twelve o'clock in the day he could hardly ever be said to be **sober**③. His manners towards the maid-servants were disgustingly free and familiar. Worst of all, he speedily assumed the same attitude towards my daughter, Alice, and spoke to her more than once in a way which, fortunately, she is too innocent to understand. On one occasion he actually seized her in his arms and embraced her—an outrage which caused his own secretary to **reproach**④ him for his unmanly conduct.'

"'But why did you stand all this,' I asked. 'I suppose that you can get rid of your boarders when you wish.'

"Mrs. Charpentier blushed at my **pertinent**⑤ question. 'Would to God that I had given him notice on the very day that he came,' she said. 'But it was a sore **temptation**⑥. They were paying a pound a day each—fourteen pounds a week, and this is the slack season. I am a widow, and my boy in the Navy has cost me much. I **grudged**⑦ to lose the money. I acted for the best. This last was too much, however, and I gave him notice to leave on account of it. That was the reason of his going.'

"'Well?'

"'My heart grew light when I saw him drive away. My son is on leave just now, but I did not tell him anything of all this, for his temper is violent, and he is passionately fond of his sister. When I closed the door behind them a load seemed to be lifted from my mind. Alas, in less than an hour there was a ring at the bell, and I learned that Mr. Drebber had returned. He was much excited, and evidently the worse for drink. He forced his way into the room, where I was sitting with my daughter, and made some **incoherent**⑧ remark about having

了，我也就别无选择了。我既然决定说，定会原原本本地告诉您，不会遗漏掉任何细节的。’

“‘您这样做是最明智的。’我说。

“‘德雷伯先生在我们这里住了将近三个星期。他和秘书斯坦格森先生一直在欧洲大陆旅行。我看见他们的行李箱上都贴了哥本哈根的标签，知道他们刚从那里来伦敦。斯坦格森话不多，很内敛。但他的雇主，不客气地说，与他差了去了。他举止粗鲁，行为蛮横。刚到的那天夜里，他就喝得酩酊大醉，到第二天中午十二点都还没完全清醒过来。对女仆举止轻浮，肆意妄为。最为恶劣的是，他很快对我女儿艾丽斯也是那副嘴脸。不止一次地对她说些不三不四的话，好在单纯的艾丽丝还听不懂。有一次，他居然把她搂进怀里，抱住她。他那样不知廉耻，连自己的秘书都义愤填膺地指责他。’

“‘那您为什么会容忍呢？’我问，‘我想，您随时都可以对自己的房客下逐客令。’

“我问到了关键点上，夏庞蒂埃太太不由得脸红了。‘如果他来的当晚就让他走人了就好啊，’她说，‘但是，挡不住的诱惑啊，他们住在这里每人每天付一英镑——一个星期就是十四英镑，况且现在又是租房的淡季。我是个寡妇，儿子在海军服兵役，花销很大。我不想失去这样一笔收入。我尽最大努力忍受着。然而，最后这次实在是太过分了，我这才责令他走人。他就是因为这个离开的。’

“‘嗯？’

“‘看到他乘马车离开了，我心里松了口气。我儿子正好在休假，但是，这事我对他没有吭一声，因为他火爆脾气，对妹妹疼爱有加。他们刚一离开，我就把门关上，心头的石头总算落了地。唉，不到一个小时之后，门铃就响了，没想到，德雷伯先生又回来了。他异常激动，一看就知道喝醉了。他闯进了房间，当时我和女

① reserved [ri'zə:vd] *a.* 沉默寡言的；矜持的

② brutish ['bru:tiʃ] *a.* 粗野的

③ sober ['səubə] *a.* 没喝醉的

④ reproach [ri'prəutʃ] *v.* 责备

⑤ pertinent ['pə:tinənt] *a.* 有关的

⑥ temptation [temp'teiʃən] *n.* 诱惑

⑦ grudge [grʌdʒ] *v.* 不情愿做

⑧ incoherent [,inkəu'hiərənt] *a.* 语无伦次的

missed his train. He then turned to Alice, and before my very face, **proposed**① to her that she should fly with him. "You are of age," he said, "and there is no law to stop you. I have money enough and to spare. Never mind the old girl here, but come along with me now straight away. You shall live like a princess." Poor Alice was so frightened that she shrunk away from him, but he caught her by the wrist and endeavoured to draw her towards the door. I screamed, and at that moment my son Arthur came into the room. What happened then I do not know. I heard oaths and the confused sounds of a **scuffle**②. I was too terrified to raise my head. When I did look up I saw Arthur standing in the doorway laughing, with a stick in his hand. "I don't think that fine fellow will trouble us again," he said. "I will just go after him and see what he does with himself." With those words he took his hat and started off down the street. The next morning we heard of Mr. Drebber's mysterious death.'

"This statement came from Mrs. Charpentier's lips with many **gasps**③ and pauses. At times she spoke so low that I could hardly catch the words. I made **shorthand**④ notes of all that she said, however, so that there should be no possibility of a mistake."

"It's quite exciting," said Sherlock Holmes, with a **yawn**⑤. "What happened next?"

"When Mrs. Charpentier paused," the detective continued, "I saw that the whole case hung upon one point. Fixing her with my eye in a way which I always found effective with women, I asked her at what hour her son returned.

"'I do not know,' she answered.

"'Not know?'

"'No; he has a latchkey, and he let himself in.'

"'After you went to bed?'

"'Yes.'

"'When did you go to bed?'

"'About eleven.'

"'So your son was gone at least two hours?'

"'Yes.'

"'Possibly four or five?'

① propose [prə'pəuz] *v.* 提议

② scuffle ['skʌfl] *n.* 扭打

③ gasp [gɑːsp] *n.* 喘气

④ shorthand ['ʃɔːthænd] *n.* 速记

⑤ yawn [jɔːn] *n.* 哈欠

儿在里面坐着。他前言不搭后语地说没有赶上火车。接着，他看着我女儿，当着我的面，让艾丽丝跟他私奔。“你已经长大了，”他说，“没有任何法律可以阻拦你跟我走。我有的是钱供你花，别管老妈子，现在就马上跟我走吧。你会过得像公主一样的。”可怜的艾丽丝被吓得战战兢兢，往后退缩，但他抓住了她的手腕，使劲把她往门口拽。我尖叫起来，就在那个当儿，我儿子阿瑟进来了。然后发生了什么，我就不清楚了，只听嘈杂声中夹杂着咒骂声和打斗声。我吓得没敢抬头看。后来我抬起头时，只见阿瑟拿着根棍子，站在门口大笑。“我想这小子再也不敢来找麻烦了，”他说，“我去跟着他，看看他还能怎样。”说完，他拿起帽子下楼出门了。第二天早上，我们听说德雷伯先生神秘遇害了。’

“这些都是夏庞蒂埃太太亲口断断续续告诉我的。她有时说话的声音很小，几乎听不清她在说什么。不过，她说的每句话，我都速记了下来，一字不差。”

“真是令人兴奋啊，”夏洛克·福尔摩斯说，打了个哈欠，“后来呢？”

“夏庞蒂埃太太说到这儿，”警探接着说，“我发现了整个案子的关键所在，眼睛盯着她看，用这种办法对付女人很奏效，问她儿子是什么时间回来的。

“‘我不知道，’她回答说。

“‘不知道？’

“‘对啊，他有钥匙，可以自己开门进来。’

“‘是在您去睡觉后才回来的吗？’

“‘是的。’

“‘您是几点钟去睡的？’

“‘十一点的样子。’

“‘这么说来，您儿子出去了至少有两个小时啦？’

“‘是啊。’

“‘还有可能四五个小时呢？’

"'Yes.'

"'What was he doing during that time?'

"'I do not know,' she answered, turning white to her very lips.

"Of course after that there was nothing more to be done. I found out where Lieutenant Charpentier was, took two officers with me, and arrested him. When I touched him on the shoulder and warned him to come quietly with us, he answered us **as bold as brass**①, 'I suppose you are arresting me for being concerned in the death of that scoundrel Drebber,' he said. We had said nothing to him about it, so that his alluding to it had a most suspicious aspect."

"Very," said Holmes.

"He still carried the heavy stick which the mother described him as having with him when he followed Drebber. It was a **stout**② **oak**③ **cudgel**④."

"What is your theory, then?"

"Well, my theory is that he followed Drebber as far as the Brixton Road. When there, a fresh **altercation**⑤ arose between them, in the course of which Drebber received a blow from the stick, in the pit of the stomach, perhaps, which killed him without leaving any mark. The night was so wet that no one was about, so Charpentier dragged the body of his victim into the empty house. As to the candle, and the blood, and the writing on the wall, and the ring, they may all be so many tricks to throw the police on to the wrong scent."

"Well done!" said Holmes in an encouraging voice. "Really, Gregson, you are getting along. We shall make something of you yet."

"I flatter myself that I have managed it rather neatly," the detective answered proudly. "The young man volunteered a statement, in which he said that after following Drebber some time, the latter **perceived**⑥ him, and took a cab in order to get away from him. On his way home he met an old shipmate, and took a long walk with him. On being asked where this old shipmate lived, he was unable to give any satisfactory reply. I think the whole case fits together uncommonly well. What amuses me is to think of Lestrade, who had started off

"'是啊。'

"'他那段时间里在干什么呢？'

"'我不知道，'她说，连嘴唇都变得煞白了。

"当然，至此，已经足够了。我打听到了夏庞蒂埃中尉的下落后，带了两个警探去逮捕他。当我触碰到他的肩膀，提醒他乖乖地跟我们走的时候，他却扯起来了大嗓门回应我。'我猜想，你们是因为德雷伯那个恶棍的死来抓我的吧？'他说。我们都根本没有提到这个事情，他倒是先提起来了，这够值得怀疑的。"

① as bold as brass 极为粗率无礼的

"很值得。"福尔摩斯说。

"正如他母亲说的，他跑去追德雷伯时带了根很粗的棍子，这时他仍然拿着那根棍子。是根很坚硬的橡木棍子。"

② stout [staut] *a.* 结实的
③ oak [əuk] *n.* 橡木
④ cudgel ['kʌdʒəl] *n.* 棍棒

"那您怎么看呢？"

"是啊，我的看法是，他一直追踪德雷伯先生到了布里克斯顿大街。两人在那里又吵起来了，德雷伯先生在争执中挨了一棍子，或许是打在腹部，所以要了他的命，但没有留下伤痕。夜间下雨了，周围没有什么人，因此，夏庞蒂埃把受害人的尸体拖进了那幢空住宅。至于蜡烛、血迹、墙上的血字，还有戒指，这些都是玩弄的伎俩，目的是要扰乱警方的视线。"

⑤ altercation [ˌɔːltə'keiʃən] *n.* 争吵

"分析得精妙！"福尔摩斯说，语气中充满了鼓励，"确实啊，格雷格森！您确实有长进了，我们真是看好您啊。"

"说句不谦虚的话，我自己也觉得这桩案件办得够利索的，"警探洋溢着自豪感说，"那个年轻人主动供认了。他说他跟踪了德雷伯一段时间之后，被发现了，后者坐上了一辆马车，以便把他给甩掉。他在回家途中遇上了自己昔日在船上的一位同事，于是与那个同事走了很远的路程。问他那位老同事住在什么地方，他却给不出令人满意的答案。我认为，整个案件已经严丝合缝地

⑥ perceive [pə'siːv] *v.* 觉察

upon the wrong scent. I am afraid he won't make much of Why, by Jove, here's the very man himself!"

It was indeed Lestrade, who had ascended the stairs while we were talking, and who now entered the room. The **assurance**① and **jauntiness**② which generally marked his **demeanour**③ and dress were, however, wanting. His face was disturbed and troubled, while his clothes were disarranged and untidy. He had evidently come with the intention of **consulting**④ with Sherlock Holmes, for on perceiving his colleague he appeared to be embarrassed and put out. He stood in the centre of the room, fumbling nervously with his hat and uncertain what to do."This is a most extraordinary case," he said at last—"a most incomprehensible affair."

"Ah, you find it so, Mr. Lestrade!" cried Gregson, triumphantly. "I thought you would come to that conclusion. Have you managed to find the secretary, Mr. Joseph Stangerson?"

"The secretary, Mr. Joseph Stangerson," said Lestrade gravely, "was murdered at Halliday's Private Hotel about six o'clock this morning."

串联起来了。莱斯特雷德从一开始就弄错了方向，一想起他，我就觉得好笑。恐怕他不会有什么结果。啊，天哪，说到他，他就到了！”

确实是莱斯特雷德到了。我们说话的当儿，他上了楼，此刻已进房间了。然而，他平常那种信心满满的态度和笔挺神气的装束不见了，一脸的困惑和焦虑，衣着凌乱邋遢。很显然，他是向福尔摩斯请教来了，但看到自己的同事也在，就尴尬得手足无措。他站在客厅中间，局促不安地捏着自己的帽子，不知怎样做才好。“这是一桩不可思议的案件啊，”他最后开口说——“一桩让人无法理解的案件。”

“啊，你也这样认为啊，莱斯特雷德先生！”格雷格森大声说，一副洋洋得意的样子，“我料到你会得出这样一个结论的。你找到了秘书约瑟夫·斯坦格森先生了吗？”

“秘书约瑟夫·斯坦格森先生，”莱斯特雷德，神情凝重，“今天早晨六点钟左右在哈利德私人旅馆被人杀害了。”

① assurance [ə'ʃuərəns] *n.* 把握，信心
② jauntiness ['dʒɔːntinis] *n.* 得意洋洋
③ demeanour [di'miːnə] *n.* 行为举止
④ consult [kən'sʌlt] *v.* 商量

Chapter 7 Light in the Darkness

The **intelligence**[①] with which Lestrade greeted us was so **momentous**[②] and so unexpected, that we were all three fairly **dumfoundered**[③]. Gregson sprang out of his chair and upset the remainder of his whiskey and water. I stared in silence at Sherlock Holmes, whose lips were **compressed**[④] and his brows drawn down over his eyes.

"Stangerson too!" he muttered. "The plot thickens."

"It was quite thick enough before," grumbled Lestrade, taking a chair. "I seem to have dropped into a sort of **council**[⑤] of war."

"Are you—are you sure of this piece of intelligence?" stammered Gregson.

"I have just come from his room," said Lestrade. "I was the first to discover what had occurred."

"We have been hearing Gregson's view of the matter," Holmes observed. "Would you mind letting us know what you have seen and done?"

"I have no **objection**[⑥]," Lestrade answered, seating himself. "I freely confess that I was of the opinion that Stangerson was concerned in the death of Drebber. This fresh development has shown me that I was completely mistaken. Full of the one idea, I set myself to find out what had become of the secretary. They had been seen together at Euston Station about half-past eight on the evening of the 3rd. At two in the morning Drebber had been found in the Brixton

第七章 黑暗中的光明

① intelligence [in'telidʒəns] *n.* 消息
② momentous [məu'mentəs] *a.* 重大的
③ dumfounder ['dʌm,faundə] *v.* =dumbfounder, 使惊讶
④ compresser [kəm'prest] *a.* 紧闭的
⑤ council ['kaunsəl] *n.* 会议
⑥ objection [əb'dʒekʃən] *n.* 反对

莱斯特雷德进门告诉我们的这个消息，非常重大，而且出人意料，我们三个人惊得目瞪口呆。格雷格森从坐着的椅子上一跃而起，把还没有喝完的威士忌加水都给打翻了。我一声没吭地盯着福尔摩斯看，只见他双唇紧闭，双眉紧锁。

"斯坦格森也遇害了，"他喃喃地说，"案情更复杂了。"

"先前就够复杂了，"莱斯特雷德抱怨着说，在椅子上坐了下来，"我好像参加了一个军事会议啊。"

"你这个——你这个消息可靠吗？"格雷格森结结巴巴地问。

"我刚从他的住处过来，"莱斯特雷德说，"我是第一个到现场的。"

"我们刚才在听格雷格森谈他对案件的看法呢，"福尔摩斯说，"能请您谈谈自己的看法和做法吗？"

"没有问题，"莱斯特雷德说，坐正了身子，"坦白地说，我先前以为，斯坦格森与德雷伯的死有关系，但出现这个新情况后，我明白，自己完全弄错了。我满脑子是这个想法，于是着手去寻找秘书的下落。3日晚上八点半钟左右，有人看见他们两个一同出现在尤斯顿火车站。凌晨两点，德雷伯的尸体在布里克斯顿大街被发

Road. The question which **confronted**[①] me was to find out how Stangerson had been employed between 8:30 and the time of the crime, and what had become of him afterwards. I telegraphed to Liverpool, giving a description of the man, and warning them to keep a watch upon the American boats. I then set to work calling upon all the hotels and lodging-houses in the **vicinity**[②] of Euston. You see, I argued that if Drebber and his companion had become separated, the natural course for the latter would be to put up somewhere in the vicinity for the night, and then to hang about the station again next morning."

"They would be likely to agree on some meeting-place beforehand," remarked Holmes.

"So it proved. I spent the whole of yesterday evening in making inquiries entirely without **avail**[③]. This morning I began very early, and at eight o'clock I reached Halliday's Private Hotel, in Little George Street. On my inquiry as to whether a Mr. Stangerson was living there, they at once answered me in the **affirmative**[④].

"'No doubt you are the gentleman whom he was expecting,' they said. 'He has been waiting for a gentleman for two days.'

"'Where is he now?' I asked.

"'He is upstairs in bed. He wished to be called at nine.'

"'I will go up and see him at once,' I said.

"It seemed to me that my sudden appearance might shake his nerves and lead him to say something unguarded. The **boots**[⑤] volunteered to show me the room: it was on the second floor, and there was a small corridor leading up to it. The boots pointed out the door to me, and was about to go downstairs again when I saw something that made me feel sickish, in spite of my twenty years' experience. From under the door there curled a little red **ribbon**[⑥] of blood, which had **meandered**[⑦] across the passage and formed a little pool along the skirting at the other side. I gave a cry, which brought the boots back. He nearly fainted when he saw it. The door was locked on the inside, but we put our shoulders to it, and knocked it in. The window of the room was open, and beside the window, all **huddled**[⑧] up, lay the body of a man in his nightdress.

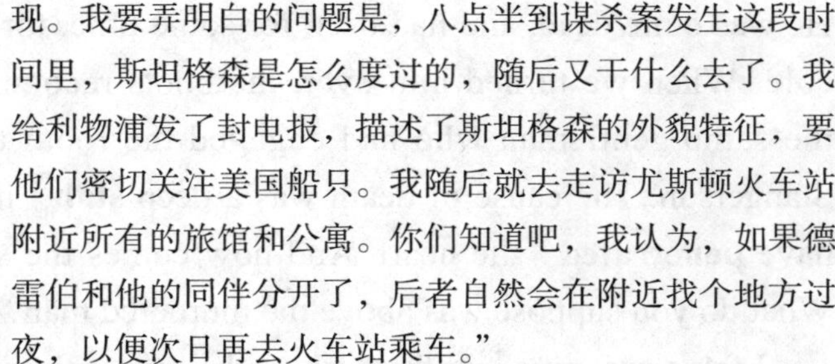

现。我要弄明白的问题是，八点半到谋杀案发生这段时间里，斯坦格森是怎么度过的，随后又干什么去了。我给利物浦发了封电报，描述了斯坦格森的外貌特征，要他们密切关注美国船只。我随后就去走访尤斯顿火车站附近所有的旅馆和公寓。你们知道吧，我认为，如果德雷伯和他的同伴分开了，后者自然会在附近找个地方过夜，以便次日再去火车站乘车。”

“他们可能事先约好了会面的地点呢。”福尔摩斯说。

“事实果然如此，我昨天整个傍晚都在寻访，但毫无结果。今天一大早，我就又开始了，八点钟时，寻访到小乔治街的哈利德私人旅馆，我问是否有一位叫斯坦格森的先生住在那儿时，他们立刻回答说有。”

“‘您肯定就是他一直在等的那位先生了吧！’他们说，‘他都等您两天了。’

“‘他在哪儿？’我问。

“‘在楼上，还没起床。他吩咐过，九点时叫醒他。’

“‘我这就上楼去找他，’我说。

“我当时想，自己突然出现，可能会令他措手不及，使他在猝不及防之下吐露出点实情来。旅馆里的擦鞋工主动领着我去那个房间，房间在三楼，一条狭窄的走廊直通到房门口。擦鞋工把房间的门指给了我之后，正要转身下楼，突然，我看到了让人非常恶心的景象，自己尽管有二十年的办案经历，但那景象还是让我感到恶心。一道由鲜血组成的细小的红线从门底下延伸出来，弯弯曲曲地流过过道，在对面的墙脚下形成了一个小小的血泊。我不禁大叫了一声，引得擦鞋工返回了。他看见血之后几乎要晕过去了。那房门反锁了，我们用肩撞开了门。房间的窗户敞开着，旁边躺着一具身穿睡衣的男尸，蜷缩成一团。他早就死了，因为四肢已经僵硬冰凉。我们给他翻了个身，

① confront [kən'frʌnt] *v.* 遭遇

② vicinity [vi'siniti] *n.* 附近

③ avail [ə'veil] *n.* 效益，收获

④ affirmative [ə'fə:mətiv] *a.* 肯定的

⑤ boots [bu:ts] *n.* 擦鞋人

⑥ ribbon ['ribən] *n.* 带子

⑦ meander [mi:'ændə] *v.* 蜿蜒而流

⑧ huddle ['hʌdl] *v.* 蜷缩

He was quite dead, and had been for some time, for his limbs were **rigid**[①] and cold. When we turned him over, the boots recognized him at once as being the same gentleman who had engaged the room under the name of Joseph Stangerson. The cause of death was a deep **stab**[②] in the left side, which must have **penetrated**[③] the heart. And now comes the strangest part of the affair. What do you suppose was above the murdered man?"

I felt a **creeping**[④] of the flesh, and a **presentiment**[⑤] of coming horror, even before Sherlock Holmes answered.

"The word RACHE, written in letters of blood," he said.

"That was it," said Lestrade, in an awe-struck voice; and we were all silent for a while.

There was something so **methodical**[⑥] and so incomprehensible about the deeds of this unknown **assassin**[⑦], that it imparted a fresh ghastliness to his crimes. My nerves, which were steady enough on the field of battle **tingled**[⑧] as I thought of it.

"The man was seen," continued Lestrade. "A milk boy, passing on his way to the dairy, happened to walk down the lane which leads from the **mews**[⑨] at the back of the hotel. He noticed that a ladder, which usually lay there, was raised against one of the windows of the second floor, which was wide open. After passing, he looked back and saw a man descend the ladder. He came down so quietly and openly that the boy imagined him to be some carpenter or **joiner**[⑩] at work in the hotel. He took no particular notice of him, beyond thinking in his own mind that it was early for him to be at work. He has an impression that the man was tall, had a reddish face, and was dressed in a long, brownish coat. He must have stayed in the room some little time after the murder, for we found blood-stained water in the basin, where he had washed his hands, and marks on the sheets where he had deliberately wiped his knife."

I glanced at Holmes on hearing the description of the murderer, which **tallied**[⑪] so exactly with his own. There was, however, no trace of exultation or satisfaction upon his face.

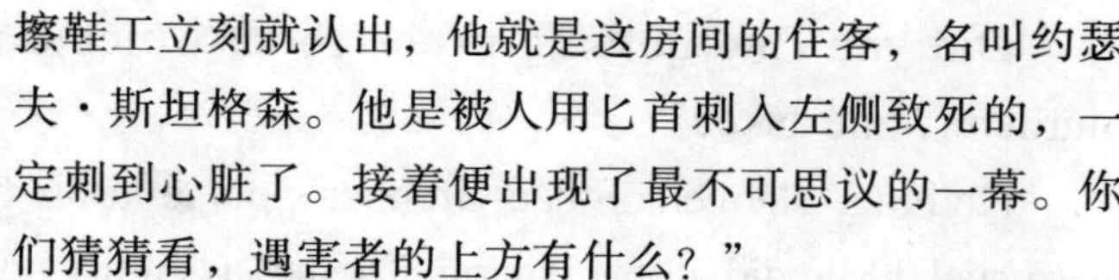

擦鞋工立刻就认出，他就是这房间的住客，名叫约瑟夫·斯坦格森。他是被人用匕首刺入左侧致死的，一定刺到心脏了。接着便出现了最不可思议的一幕。你们猜猜看，遇害者的上方有什么？”

福尔摩斯还没来得及回答，我就感觉全身肌肉发抖，预感到恐怖的情况要发生。

“‘RACHE’一词，是用血写的。”他说。

“就是这样。”莱斯特雷德说，语气中充满了恐惧。一时间，我们全都沉默不语。

那个不明身份的杀人凶手行动起来有条不紊，而且令人费解，这就使他犯下的罪行显得更加恐怖。我在战场上能够做到临危不惧，但一想到这一点，心里还是不禁发颤。

“有人见到过凶手，”莱斯特雷德接着说，“有个送牛奶的小伙子去牛奶店取奶，途中正好路过旅馆后面那条通往马厩的小巷。他注意到，有张梯子平常是倒着放在那儿的，这时却被支起来了，靠在三楼一个敞开着的窗户口。他走过之后，回头看了一眼，结果看到有个人从梯子上下来，从从容容，大大方方，小伙子认为他是在旅馆做事的木匠或者细木工什么的，所以便没有特别注意他，心里面只是嘀咕着，那人来干活儿也够早的。在他的印象中，那人个头挺高，红脸庞，穿了件很长的棕褐色外套。他杀了人之后一定还在房里逗留了一阵，因为我们发现脸盆里面有血水，他在盆里洗过手了。床单上有血迹，说明他从从容容地擦过刀。”

我听到对凶手相貌特征的描述与福尔摩斯所说的很相吻合之后，便瞥了他一眼。然而，他的脸上没有流露出半点兴奋或满意的神色。

“你们就没有在那房间里发现什么可以追寻凶手的线索吗？”他问。

① rigid ['ridʒid] *a.* 僵硬的

② stab [stæb] *v.* 刺入

③ penetrate ['penitreit] *v.* 穿透；刺入

④ creeping ['kri:piŋ] *n.* 蠕动，这里指麻木，战栗

⑤ presentiment [pri'zentimənt] *n.* 对不详事物的预感

⑥ methodical [mi'θɔdikəl] *a.* 有条不紊的

⑦ assassin [ə'sæsin] *n.* 行刺者，暗杀者

⑧ tingle ['tiŋgl] *v.* 有刺痛感；震颤

⑨ mews [mju:z] *n.* 马厩

⑩ joiner ['dʒɔinə] *n.* 细木工

⑪ tally ['tæli] *v.* 吻合

"Did you find nothing in the room which could furnish a clue to the murderer?" he asked.

"Nothing. Stangerson had Drebber's purse in his pocket, but it seems that this was usual, as he did all the paying. There was eighty **odd**① pounds in it, but nothing had been taken. Whatever the motives of these extraordinary crimes, robbery is certainly not one of them. There were no papers or **memoranda**② in the murdered man's pocket, except a single telegram, dated from Cleveland about a month ago, and containing the words, 'J. H. is in Europe.' There was no name **appended**③ to this message."

"And there was nothing else?" Holmes asked.

"Nothing of any importance. The man's novel, with which he had read himself to sleep was lying upon the bed, and his pipe was on a chair beside him. There was a glass of water on the table, and on the **window-sill**④ a small chip **ointment**⑤ box containing a couple of pills."

Sherlock Holmes sprang from his chair with an exclamation of delight.

"The last link," he cried, exultantly. "My case is complete."

The two detectives stared at him in amazement.

"I have now in my hands," my companion said, confidently, "all the threads which have formed such a tangle. There are, of course, details to be filled in, but I am as certain of all the main facts, from the time that Drebber parted from Stangerson at the station, up to the discovery of the body of the latter, as if I had seen them with my own eyes. I will give you a proof of my knowledge. Could you lay your hand upon those pills?"

"I have them," said Lestrade, producing a small white box; "I took them and the purse and the telegram, intending to have them put in a place of safety at the Police Station. It was the merest chance my taking these pills, for I am bound to say that I do not attach any importance to them."

"Give them here," said Holmes. "Now, Doctor," turning to me, "are those ordinary pills?"

They certainly were not. They were of a **pearly**⑥ grey colour, small,

“什么也没有发现。斯坦格森的衣服口袋里也放着德雷伯的钱包呢，这看起来很正常，因为付钱的事情都是他负责的。钱包里面有八十多英镑，分文不少。不管这两桩谋杀案的动机如何，但肯定不是为了谋财而害命的。被害人的衣服口袋里没有什么文件或日记本，只有一份电报，是一个月前从克利夫兰城发过来的，电文的内容是‘J.H.在欧洲’，没有落款。”

“就没有别的什么了吗？”福尔摩斯问。

“没什么重要东西了。死者有本小说放在床上，是他临睡前看的。其烟斗放在他旁边的一把椅子上。桌子上有一杯水。窗台上有个小药膏盒，里面装着两粒药丸。”

夏洛克·福尔摩斯从坐着的椅子一跃站起身，高兴得大喊了起来。

“这是最后的一个环节，”他大声说着，心情激动，“我对案情的分析完整了。”

两位警探眼睁睁地看着他，惊愕不已。

“缠绕在一起的线索，”我的同伴说，信心满满，“我现在全都掌握在手上了。当然，还需要补充一些细节，但是，我相信，主要的事实都已经全部弄清楚了，从德雷伯同斯坦格森在火车站分别，到发现后者的尸体，我就像是亲眼看见似的。我会把这些情况证明给你们看的。那两颗药丸您带来了吗？”

“带来了，”莱斯特雷德说着，随即拿出一个白色的小盒，“药丸、钱包和电报我都随身带着，准备放到警局去妥善保管。拿着药丸纯属巧合，因为说实在的，我并不觉得药丸有什么重要的。”

“请把药丸放在这儿吧，”福尔摩斯说。“对啦，医生，”他转身对着我说，“这两颗药丸是普通的那种吗？”

肯定不是普通药丸，就像是珍珠，呈灰白色，又小

① odd [ɔd] *a.* 零头的

② memorandum [ˌmemə'rændəm]（复数memoranda）*n.* 备忘录；便笺

③ append [ə'pend] *v.* 附加；签（名）

④ window-sill ['windəuˌsil] *n.* 窗台

⑤ ointment ['ɔintmənt] *n.* 软膏

⑥ pearly ['pə:li] *a.* 珍珠似的

round, and almost **transparent**① against the light. "From their lightness and transparency, I should imagine that they are **soluble**② in water," I remarked.

"Precisely so," answered Holmes. "Now would you mind going down and fetching that poor little devil of a **terrier**③ which has been bad so long, and which the landlady wanted you to put out of its pain yesterday."

I went downstairs and carried the dog upstair in my arms. It's laboured breathing and glazing eye showed that it was not far from its end. Indeed, its snow-white **muzzle**④ proclaimed that it had already exceeded the usual term of **canine**⑤ existence. I placed it upon a **cushion**⑥ on the rug.

"I will now cut one of these pills in two," said Holmes, and drawing his penknife he suited the action to the word. "One half we return into the box for future purposes. The other half I will place in this wine glass, in which is a teaspoonful of water. You perceive that our friend, the Doctor, is right, and that it readily **dissolves**⑦."

"This may be very interesting," said Lestrade, in the injured tone of one who suspects that he is being laughed at, "I cannot see, however, what it has to do with the death of Mr. Joseph Stangerson."

"Patience, my friend, patience! You will find in time that it has everything to do with it. I shall now add a little milk to make the mixture **palatable**⑧, and on presenting it to the dog we find that he laps it up readily enough."

As he spoke he turned the contents of the wine glass into a saucer and placed it in front of the terrier, who speedily licked it dry. Sherlock Holmes's earnest demeanour had so far convinced us that we all sat in silence, watching the animal intently, and expecting some startling effect. None such appeared, however. The dog continued to lie stretched upon the cushion, breathing in a laboured way, but apparently neither the better nor the worse for its **draught**⑨.

Holmes had taken out his watch, and as minute followed minute without result, an expression of the utmost **chagrin**⑩ and disappointment appeared

① transparent [træns'pεərənt] *a.* 透明的
② soluble ['sɔljubl] *a.* 可溶的
③ terrier ['teriə] *n.* 小猎犬
④ muzzle ['mʌzl] *n.* 鼻口部
⑤ canine ['keinain] *a.* 犬类的
⑥ cushion ['kuʃən] *n.* 垫子
⑦ dissolve [di'zɔlv] *v.* 溶解
⑧ palatable ['pælətəbl] *a.* 美味的
⑨ draught [drɑ:ft] *n.* 剂量
⑩ chagrin [ʃæ'grin] *n.* 懊恼

又圆，在光线下几乎是透明的。“分量轻，透明，根据这个情况，应该是可以溶于水的。”我说。

“一点没错，是这样的，”福尔摩斯回答说，“现在麻烦你下楼去把那只小猎狗抱上来好吗？可怜的小东西已经病了很久了，房东太太昨天还求你让它结束痛苦呢。”

我下楼把小狗抱上了楼。只见它呼吸困难，目光呆滞，离死不远了。确实，从它雪白的鼻翼就可以看出，其年龄已经超过了犬类通常的寿限。我把它放在地毯上的一个靠垫上。

“我现在把其中的一颗药丸切开，”福尔摩斯说着，用小刀把药丸切成两半，“半颗放回盒子，以备日后使用。另外半颗放进这个酒杯里，杯里有一茶匙水。你们看看，我的朋友华生医生说得没错，它在水里可以轻易溶解。”

“这可能很有趣，”莱斯特雷德说着，听他的语气，就好像是觉得有人在嘲笑他，自尊心倍受伤害一样，“然而，我看不出，这同约瑟夫·斯坦格森先生的死有什么关系。”

“耐心点，我的朋友啊，耐心点！您到时就会发现，关系可密切着呢。我这就往里面加点牛奶，味道就好了，端到这条狗面前，它马上就会舔个精光。”

说着，他就把酒杯里的液体倒进一个托盘，放在小猎狗的面前。小狗迅速就把盘子舔干了。福尔摩斯严肃的样子，早已使我们深信不疑。我们全都沉默不语地坐着，专注地盯着那条狗，看看会有什么惊人的事情发生。然而，什么事情也没有发生，小狗仍然趴在垫子上，呼吸急促。很显然，药丸既对它没有什么好处，也对它没有什么坏处。

福尔摩斯先前已经掏出了自己的怀表，看着时间一分一秒地过去，但毫无结果，他满脸懊恼沮丧，咬着嘴

upon his features. He **gnawed**[①] his lip, drummed his fingers upon the table, and showed every other **symptom**[②] of acute impatience. So great was his emotion, that I felt sincerely sorry for him, while the two detectives smiled **derisively**[③], by no means displeased at this check which he had met.

"It can't be a **coincidence**[④]," he cried, at last springing from his chair and pacing wildly up and down the room; "it is impossible that it should be a mere coincidence. The very pills which I suspected in the case of Drebber are actually found after the death of Stangerson. And yet they are **inert**[⑤]. What can it mean? Surely my whole chain of reasoning cannot have been false. It is impossible! And yet this wretched dog is none the worse. Ah, I have it! I have it!" With a perfect **shriek**[⑥] of delight he rushed to the box, cut the other pill in two, dissolved it, added milk, and presented it to the terrier. The unfortunate creature's tongue seemed hardly to have been **moistened**[⑦] in it before it gave a convulsive shiver in every limb, and lay as rigid and lifeless as if it had been struck by lightning.

Sherlock Holmes drew a long breath, and wiped the **perspiration**[⑧] from his forehead. "I should have more faith," he said; "I ought to know by this time that when a fact appears to be opposed to a long train of deductions, it invariably proves to be capable of bearing some other **interpretation**[⑨]. Of the two pills in that box one was of the most deadly poison, and the other was entirely harmless. I ought to have known that before ever I saw the box at all."

This last statement appeared to me to be so startling, that I could hardly believe that he was in his sober senses. There was the dead dog, however, to prove that his conjecture had been correct. It seemed to me that the mists in my own mind were gradually clearing away, and I began to have a dim, vague perception of the truth.

"All this seems strange to you," continued Holmes, "because you failed at the beginning of the inquiry to grasp the importance of the single real clue which was presented to you. I had the good fortune to seize upon that, and everything which has occurred since then has served to confirm my original **supposition**[⑩],

① gnaw [nɔ:] *v.* 咬

② symptom ['simptəm] *n.* 征兆

③ derisively [di'raisivli] *ad.* 嘲笑地

④ coincidence [kəu'insidəns] *n.* 巧合

⑤ inert [in'ə:t] *a.* 无效的

⑥ shriek [ʃri:k] *n.* 尖叫

⑦ moisten ['mɔisən] *v.* 使…变得潮湿

⑧ perspiration [ˌpə:spə'reiʃən] *n.* 汗

⑨ interpretation [ˌintə:pri'teiʃən] *n.* 解释

⑩ supposition [ˌsʌpə'ziʃən] *n.* 假设

唇，手指敲击着桌子，显得非常焦躁。看见他深情如此焦虑，我真的挺替他难受的。而两位警探的脸上却挂着嘲弄的笑容，见福尔摩斯受挫，他们一点儿都不难过。

"这不可能是巧合，"福尔摩斯大声说，最后从坐着的椅子上一跃站起身，在房间里来回踱着步，情绪狂躁，"这绝对不可能仅仅是巧合。看到德雷伯的尸体之后，我就怀疑是药丸毒死的，结果在斯坦格森死了之后发现了药丸。但竟然毫无作用，怎么回事呢？毫无疑问，我的整个推理过程不会有错的。绝对不可能！但可怜的小狗一点事都没有。啊，我明白啦！我明白啦！"他高兴地尖叫了一声，冲到药盒边，把另外一颗药丸切成两半，把其中半颗用水溶化，再加上牛奶，端到狗的跟前。不幸的小家伙刚把舌头沾湿，四肢便开始痉挛起来，然后就像被雷击了似的，直挺挺地死了。

福尔摩斯长长地舒了口气，擦了擦额头上的汗。"我本该信心更足些才对的，"他说，"到了这个时候，我应该知道了，如果某个事实同整个推理过程相悖，那这个事实就一定有其他解释。盒子里装的两颗药丸，一颗是剧毒的毒药，另外一颗则完全无毒。没见到这个盒子之前，我就该推断出来的。"

我觉得，他刚才这一席话真是令人惊愕，我几乎不相信他的神志是清醒的。然而，小狗死了，这证明了他的推测是正确的。我感觉到，自己满脑子的迷雾现在已经慢慢地开始消散了，对案件的真相开始有了隐隐约约的认识。

"你们觉得这一切很不可思议，"福尔摩斯接着说，"因为从调查之初开始，你们就没有认识到摆在面前的这条唯一真正的线索的重要性。我很幸运，抓住了这条线索。后来发生的一切情况都证实了我最初的假设，而且也确实是一个逻辑上的必然结果。因此，那些让你们

and, indeed, was the logical **sequence**[①] of it. Hence things which have **perplexed**[②] you and made the case more **obscure**[③], have served to enlighten me and to strengthen my conclusions. It is a mistake to confound strangeness with mystery. The most commonplace crime is often the most mysterious because it presents no new or special features from which deductions may be drawn. This murder would have been infinitely more difficult to unravel had the body of the victim been simply found lying in the roadway without any of those ***outré***[④] and sensational accompaniments which have **rendered**[⑤] it remarkable. These strange details, far from making the case more difficult, have really had the effect of making it less so."

Mr. Gregson, who had listened to this address with considerable impatience, could contain himself no longer. "Look here, Mr. Sherlock Holmes," he said, "we are all ready to acknowledge that you are a smart man, and that you have your own methods of working. We want something more than mere theory and **preaching**[⑥] now, though. It is a case of taking the man. I have made my case out, and it seems I was wrong. Young Charpentier could not have been engaged in this second affair. Lestrade went after his man, Stangerson, and it appears that he was wrong too. You have thrown out hints here, and hints there, and seem to know more than we do, but the time has come when we feel that we have a right to ask you straight how much you do know of the business. Can you name the man who did it?"

"I cannot help feeling that Gregson is right, sir," remarked Lestrade. "We have both tried, and we have both failed. You have remarked more than once since I have been in the room that you had all the evidence which you require. Surely you will not **withhold**[⑦] it any longer."

"Any delay in arresting the assassin," I observed, "might give him time to **perpetrate**[⑧] some fresh **atrocity**[⑨]."

Thus pressed by us all, Holmes showed signs of **irresolution**[⑩]. He continued to walk up and down the room with his head sunk on his chest and his brows drawn down, as was his habit when lost in thought.

① sequence ['si:kwəns] n. 结果
② perplex [pə'pleks] v. 使困惑
③ obscure [əb'skjuə] a. 模糊不清的
④ outré ['u:trei] a. 怪异的
⑤ render ['rendə] v. 致使
⑥ preach [pri:tʃ] v. 说教
⑦ withhold ['wið'həuld] v. 保留
⑧ perpetrate ['pə:pi,treit] v. 犯（罪）
⑨ atrocity [ə'trɔsiti] n. 暴行
⑩ irresolution [i,rezə'lju:ʃən] n. 犹豫

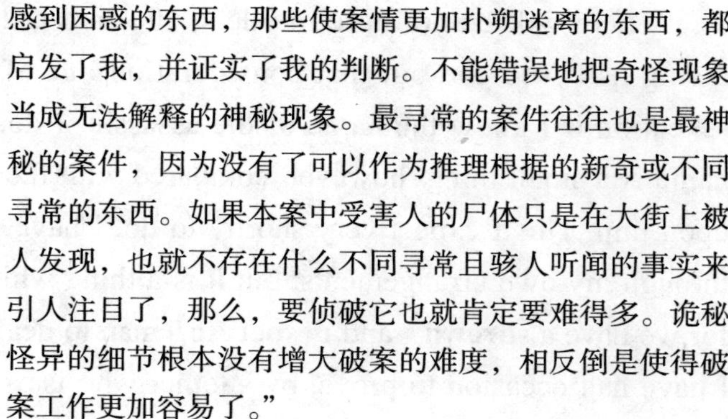

感到困惑的东西，那些使案情更加扑朔迷离的东西，都启发了我，并证实了我的判断。不能错误地把奇怪现象当成无法解释的神秘现象。最寻常的案件往往也是最神秘的案件，因为没有了可以作为推理根据的新奇或不同寻常的东西。如果本案中受害人的尸体只是在大街上被人发现，也就不存在什么不同寻常且骇人听闻的事实来引人注目了，那么，要侦破它也就肯定要难得多。诡秘怪异的细节根本没有增大破案的难度，相反倒是使得破案工作更加容易了。”

格雷格森本来就不耐烦地听着福尔摩斯的这一番话，现在更是无法忍受下去了。“您看吧，福尔摩斯先生，”他说，“我们打心眼里认可，您是个聪明睿智的人，有您自己的一套办案方法。不过，我们现在需要的不仅仅是理论和说教，而是要抓到凶手。我已经把自己侦破的经过说了一遍，看来是错了。小夏庞蒂埃是不可能同第二桩谋杀案有关系的。莱斯特雷德追查到了他的怀疑目标——斯坦格森。看起来，他也错了。您这儿露出一点口风，那儿又露出一点儿，好像知道的情况比我们要多。但是，是时候了，我们有权直截了当地问您，您对案情知道了多少。能够说出凶手的名字吗？”

“我不禁觉得，格雷格森说得很对，先生，”莱斯特雷德说，“我们两个都尝试过了，但都没有成功。从我进入到这个房间来之后，您不止一次说过，您已掌握了所有需要掌握的证据，您肯定不会再藏着掖着不说吧。”

“如果再拖延下去，不立刻逮捕凶手的话，”我说，“他可能还会继续作恶。”

我们大家这样催促，福尔摩斯反倒有些犹豫了。他仍然不停地在房间里来回踱着步，如同他平常陷入沉思时一样，头垂到了胸前，眉头紧锁。

"There will be no more murders," he said at last, stopping abruptly and facing us. "You can put that consideration **out of the question**[①]. You have asked me if I know the name of the assassin. I do. The mere knowing of his name is a small thing, however, compared with the power of laying our hands upon him. This I expect very shortly to do. I have good hopes of managing it through my own arrangements; but it is a thing which needs delicate handling, for we have a **shrewd**[②] and **desperate**[③] man to deal with, who is supported, as I have had occasion to prove, by another who is as clever as himself. As long as this man has no idea that anyone can have a clue there is some chance of securing him; but if he had the slightest suspicion, he would change his name, and **vanish**[④] in an instant among the four million inhabitants of this great city. Without meaning to hurt either of your feelings, I am bound to say that I consider these men to be more than a match for the official force, and that is why I have not asked your assistance. If I fail I shall, of course, **incur**[⑤] all the blame due to this omission; but that I am prepared for. At present I am ready to promise that the instant that I can communicate with you without **endangering**[⑥] my own combinations, I shall do so."

Gregson and Lestrade seemed to be far from satisfied by this assurance, or by the **depreciating**[⑦] **allusion**[⑧] to the detective police. The former had flushed up to the roots of his flaxen hair, while the other's beady eyes glistened with curiosity and **resentment**[⑨]. Neither of them had time to speak, however, before there was a tap at the door, and the spokesman of the street Arabs, young Wiggins, introduced his insignificant and **unsavoury**[⑩] person.

"Please, sir," he said, touching his **forelock**[⑪], "I have the cab downstairs."

"Good boy," said Holmes, **blandly**[⑫]. "Why don't you introduce this pattern at Scotland Yard?" he continued, taking a pair of steel **handcuffs**[⑬] from a drawer. "See how beautifully the **spring**[⑭] works. They fasten in an instant."

"The old pattern is good enough," remarked Lestrade, "if we can only find the man to put them on."

"不会再发生凶杀案了，"最后，他突然站住了，面对着我们说，"你们用不着担心。你们问我是否知道了凶手的名字，我知道了，不过，知道他的名字只不过是小事一桩。相比之下，我们能够把凶手抓住才是大事呢。我估计很快就可以实现了。我希望能由我来安排部署抓捕行动，这事需要周密的安排部署，因为我们面临的对手精明狡诈，不顾一切。而且我有理由证明，他还有一个同他一样精明的帮手。只要那个人还不知情，没有意识到有人找到了线索，那就有机会逮住他。但是，如果他有些许警觉，就会改名换姓，瞬间消失在这个有着四百万人口的大城市中。尽管我无意伤害你们二位的感情，但我还是要说，我认为官方警探真不是那些人的对手，这也就是我没有请求你们协助的原因。如果我失败了，当然难辞其咎，但即便如此，我还是初衷不改。现在，我可以保证，如果同你们的沟通不会影响我的全盘计划，我一定会及时把情况通报给你们。"

面对福尔摩斯的这种保证，或者说面对他对官方警探的简慢态度，格雷格森和莱斯特雷德似乎非常不满。前者的脸涨得通红，一直红到发根，而后者则眼睛睁得大大的，闪烁着惊奇而又愤恨的光芒。然而，他们两人都还没来得及开口，就听见有人敲门了，来者是毫不起眼而且不讨人喜欢的小威金斯，他是那帮街头流浪儿的代表。

"请吧，先生，"他说，触碰了一下自己的额发，"我叫了一辆马车在楼下呢。"

"好孩子，"福尔摩斯说，态度温和。"你们伦敦警察厅为何不用这种款式的呢？"他接着说，一面从一个抽屉里拿出一副钢手铐，"看看这个弹簧多管用啊，一下就铐上了。"

"老款式的也不错啊，"莱斯特雷德说，"只要我们能够找到罪犯铐上就成。"

① out of the question 不可能的
② shrewd [ʃru:d] *a.* 狡猾的
③ desperate ['despərit] *a.* 不顾一切的
④ vanish ['væniʃ] *v.* 消失
⑤ incur [in'kə:] *v.* 招致
⑥ endanger [in'deindʒə] *v.* 危及
⑦ depreciating [di'pri:ʃi:eitiŋ] *a.* 蔑视的
⑧ allusion [ə'lu:ʒən] *n.* 暗指，影射
⑨ resentment [ri'zentmənt] *n.* 愤恨
⑩ unsavoury [ʌn'seivəri] *a.* 讨厌的
⑪ forelock ['fɔ:lɔk] *n.* 额发
⑫ blandly [blændli] *ad.* 温和地
⑬ handcuffs ['hændkʌfs] *n.* 手铐
⑭ spring [spriŋ] *n.* 弹簧

"Very good, very good," said Holmes, smiling. "The cabman may as well help me with my boxes. Just ask him to step up, Wiggins."

I was surprised to find my companion speaking as though he were about to set out on a journey, since he had not said anything to me about it. There was a small portmanteau in the room, and this he pulled out and began to **strap**①. He was busily engaged at it when the cabman entered the room.

"Just give me a help with this **buckle**②, cabman," he said, kneeling over his task, and never turning his head.

The fellow came forward with a somewhat **sullen**③, **defiant**④ air, and put down his hands to assist. At that instant there was a sharp click, the **jangling**⑤ of metal, and Sherlock Holmes sprang to his feet again.

"Gentlemen," he cried, with flashing eyes, "let me introduce you to Mr. Jefferson Hope, the murderer of Enoch Drebber and of Joseph Stangerson."

The whole thing occurred in a moment—so quickly that I had no time to realize it. I have a vivid recollection of that instant, of Holmes's triumphant expression and the ring of his voice, of the cabman's **dazed**⑥, **savage**⑦ face, as he glared at the glittering handcuffs, which had appeared as if by magic upon his wrists. For a second or two we might have been a group of statues. Then, with an **inarticulate**⑧ roar of fury, the prisoner **wrenched**⑨ himself free from Holmes's grasp, and **hurled**⑩ himself through the window. Woodwork and glass gave way before him; but before he got quite through, Gregson, Lestrade, and Holmes sprang upon him like so many **staghounds**⑪. He was dragged back into the room, and then **commenced**⑫ a terrific conflict. So powerful and so fierce was he, that the four of us were shaken off again and again. He appeared to have the **convulsive**⑬ strength of a man in an **epileptic**⑭ fit. His face and hands were terribly mangled by his passage through the glass, but loss of blood had no effect in **diminishing**⑮ his resistance. It was not until Lestrade succeeded in getting his hand inside his neckcloth and half-strangling him that we made him realize that his struggles were of no avail; and even then we felt no security

“很好，很好，”福尔摩斯说着，露出了微笑，“最好让马车夫帮我搬箱子，请他上来吧，威金斯。”

听我同伴说话的语气，他好像是要外出旅行了，我感到很惊讶，因为他从来都没有向我提起过外出旅行的事。房间里面有一个小旅行箱，他把旅行箱拖了出来，开始捆绑。马车夫进入房间时，他还在忙碌着。

“请帮助我扣一下扣带，车夫，”他说着，跪着在忙碌，头都没有转过来。

车夫走上前，阴沉着脸，显得不情愿，但还是伸手帮起忙来了。就在这个瞬间，只听见一声金属发出的清脆的咔嚓声，福尔摩斯一跃身子站了起来。

“先生们，”他大声说，眼睛里闪烁着光芒，“我来向你们介绍一下，这是杰弗逊·霍普先生，就是杀害伊诺克·德雷伯先生和约瑟夫·斯坦格森先生的凶手。”

整个事情发生在一瞬间——迅速得我都没有反应过来。至今那一时刻还历历在目，我记得福尔摩斯脸上洋溢着的胜利的表情和他那洪亮的声音，记得闪亮的手铐像变魔术似地铐住马车夫时，他眼睁睁地看着，脸上露出的茫然而又凶狠的表情。有一两秒钟的时间，我们就像是一组雕像。紧接着，车夫发出了含混不清的怒吼，挣脱了福尔摩斯的控制，冲向窗外，窗框和玻璃都被他撞碎了。但是，没有等他窜出去，格雷格森，莱斯特雷德和福尔摩斯像三条猎犬似的猛扑了上去，把他给拽回来了，然后是一场激烈的搏斗。那家伙不但力气很大，而且非常凶狠，我们四个人一次次被他甩开。他就像癫狂病发作了，力量巨大。他在试图窜出窗户时，脸和手都被划破了，血流不止，但丝毫没有减弱抵抗。最后还是莱斯特雷德用手卡住了他的脖子，让他快透不过气来，他着才明白挣扎已毫无用处。然而，为了安全起见，我们还是把他的手和脚都捆了起来。一切完成之后，我们站起身，气喘吁吁。

① strap [stræp] *v.* 用皮带捆扎

② buckle ['bʌkl] *n.* 搭扣

③ sullen ['sʌlən] *a.* 阴郁的

④ defiant [di'faiənt] *a.* 公然违抗的

⑤ jangling ['dʒæŋgliŋ] *n.* 金属相碰发出的声音

⑥ dazed [deizd] *a.* 茫然的

⑦ savage ['sævidʒ] *a.* 凶恶的

⑧ inarticulate [ˌinɑː'tikjulət] *a.* 含混不清的

⑨ wrench [rentʃ] *v.* 拧，扳

⑩ hurl [həːl] *v.* 猛掷

⑪ staghound ['stægˌhaund] *n.* 狩鹿的猎犬

⑫ commence [kə'mens] *v.* 开始

⑬ convulsive [kən'vʌlsiv] *a.* 发疯似的

⑭ epileptic [ˌepi'leptik] *a.* 由癫痫引发的

⑮ diminish [di'miniʃ] *v.* 减少

PART 2
THE COUNTRY OF THE SAINTS

第二部
圣徒的区域

great flat plain-land, all dusted over with patches of alkali, and **intersected**[①] by clumps of the dwarfish **chaparral**[②] bushes. On the extreme verge of the horizon lie a long chain of mountain peaks, with their rugged summits **flecked**[③] with snow. In this great stretch of country there is no sign of life, nor of anything **appertaining**[④] to life. There is no bird in the steel-blue heaven, no movement upon the dull, grey earth—above all, there is absolute silence. Listen as one may, there is no shadow of a sound in all that mighty wilderness; nothing but silence—complete and heart-subduing silence.

It has been said there is nothing appertaining to life upon the broad plain. That is hardly true. Looking down from the Sierra Blanco, one sees a pathway traced out across the desert, which winds away and is lost in the extreme distance. It is **rutted**[⑤] with wheels and **trodden**[⑥] down by the feet of many adventurers. Here and there there are scattered white objects which glisten in the sun, and stand out against the dull deposit of alkali. Approach, and examine them! They are bones: some large and coarse, others smaller and more delicate. The former have belonged to oxen, and the latter to men. For fifteen hundred miles one may trace this ghastly **caravan**[⑦] route by these scattered remains of those who had fallen by the wayside.

Looking down on this very scene, there stood upon the fourth of May, eighteen hundred and forty-seven, a **solitary**[⑧] traveller. His appearance was such that he might have been the very genius or **demon**[⑨] of the region. An observer would have found it difficult to say whether he was nearer to forty or to sixty. His face was lean and **haggard**[⑩], and the brown **parchment-like**[⑪] skin was drawn tightly over the projecting bones; his long, brown hair and beard were all flecked and dashed with white; his eyes were sunken in his head, and burned with an unnatural **lustre**[⑫]; while the hand which grasped his rifle was hardly more fleshy than that of a **skeleton**.[⑬] As he stood, he leaned upon his weapon for support, and yet his tall figure and the massive framework of his bones suggested a wiry and vigorous **constitution**[⑭]. His **gaunt**[⑮] face, however, and his clothes, which

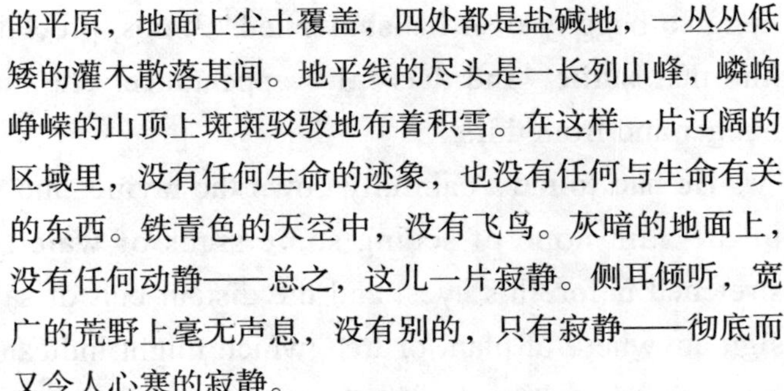

的平原，地面上尘土覆盖，四处都是盐碱地，一丛丛低矮的灌木散落其间。地平线的尽头是一长列山峰，嶙峋峥嵘的山顶上斑斑驳驳地布着积雪。在这样一片辽阔的区域里，没有任何生命的迹象，也没有任何与生命有关的东西。铁青色的天空中，没有飞鸟。灰暗的地面上，没有任何动静——总之，这儿一片寂静。侧耳倾听，宽广的荒野上毫无声息，没有别的，只有寂静——彻底而又令人心寒的寂静。

要说这片广阔无垠的荒原上没有一点和生命有关的东西，那倒并不完全属实。从布兰科山脉俯视，人们可以看到，沙漠中有条弯弯曲曲的小道，一直蜿蜒到了天尽头。小道上布满了车辙和许多探险者脚踏出的痕迹。那里处处散落着一些白色的物品，在太阳下闪闪发亮，在单调的盐碱地的衬托下，显得格外醒目。走向近处，仔细一看，原来全是骨头，有些大而粗糙，有些小而细腻。前者是牛骨，后者是人骨。恐怖的篷车小道绵延一千五百英里，人们根据散落在路边的遗骨沿途前行。

1847年5月4日，有位孤行者在高处俯视着眼前的一幕。他的音容相貌就像是这个地区的精灵或妖魔。外人很难判断，他是四十来岁，还是六十来岁。只见他面容憔悴消瘦，棕褐色的皮肤像羊皮纸似的，裹着嶙峋的骨架。长长的棕褐色头发和胡须已经花白了。两眼深陷，闪烁着异样的光芒。紧握着来复枪的手比骷髅骨也多不出半点肌肉。他用来复枪作支撑站立着，他那高大的身形和宽阔的骨架表明，他曾经有着强壮有力的体格。不过现在，他面容消瘦，衣衫松松垮垮地套在身上，一副衰老而枯朽的模样。此人濒临死亡——就要死于饥饿和干渴。

他在峡谷深处历经了千辛万苦，终于爬上了这处小的高地，指望着寻找到水源，但毫无结果。广袤

① intersect [ˌintə'sekt] *v.* 横穿
② chaparral [ˌtæpə'ræl] *n.* 灌木丛
③ fleck [flek] *v.* 使…有斑点
④ appertain [ˌæpə'tein] *v.* 有关联
⑤ rut [rʌt] *v.* 形成车辙
⑥ tread [tred] *v.* 踩出
⑦ caravan ['kærəvæn] *n.* 篷车
⑧ solitary ['sɔlitəri] *a.* 单独的
⑨ demon ['diːmən] *n.* 妖魔
⑩ haggard [hægəd] *a.* 面容憔悴的
⑪ parchment-like ['pɑːtʃməntlaik] *a.* 像羊皮纸的
⑫ lustre ['lʌstə] *n.* 光泽
⑬ skeleton ['skelitən] *n.* 骨架
⑭ constitution [ˌkɔnsti'tjuːʃən] *n.* 体格
⑮ gaunt [gɔːnt] *a.* 消瘦的

hung so baggily over his **shrivelled**[①] limbs, proclaimed what it was that gave him that **senile**[②] and **decrepit**[③] appearance. The man was dying—dying from hunger and from thirst.

He had **toiled**[④] painfully down the ravine, and on to this little **elevation**[⑤], in the vain hope of seeing some signs of water. Now the great salt plain stretched before his eyes, and the distant belt of savage mountains, without a sign anywhere of plant or tree, which might indicate the presence of moisture. In all that broad landscape there was no gleam of hope. North, and east, and west he looked with wild questioning eyes, and then he realized that his wanderings had come to an end, and that there, on that barren **crag**[⑥], he was about to die. "Why not here, as well as in a feather bed, twenty years hence," he muttered, as he seated himself in the shelter of a **boulder**[⑦].

Before sitting down, he had deposited upon the ground his useless rifle, and also a large **bundle**[⑧] tied up in a grey **shawl**[⑨], which he had carried **slung**[⑩] over his right shoulder. It appeared to be somewhat too heavy for his strength, for in lowering it, it came down on the ground with some little violence. Instantly there broke from the grey parcel a little moaning cry, and from it there **protruded**[⑪] a small, scared face, with very bright brown eyes, and two little speckled, dimpled fists.

"You've hurt me!" said a childish voice reproachfully.

"Have I though," the man answered **penitently**[⑫], "I didn't go for to do it." As he spoke he unwrapped the grey shawl and **extricated**[⑬] a pretty little girl of about five years of age, whose dainty shoes and smart pink **frock**[⑭] with its little linen apron, all bespoke a mother's care. The child was pale and **wan**[⑮], but her healthy arms and legs showed that she had suffered less than her companion.

"How is it now?" he answered anxiously, for she was still rubbing the **tousy**[⑯] golden curls which covered the back of her head.

"Kiss it and make it well," she said, with perfect gravity, showing the injured part up to him. "That's what mother used to do. Where's mother?"

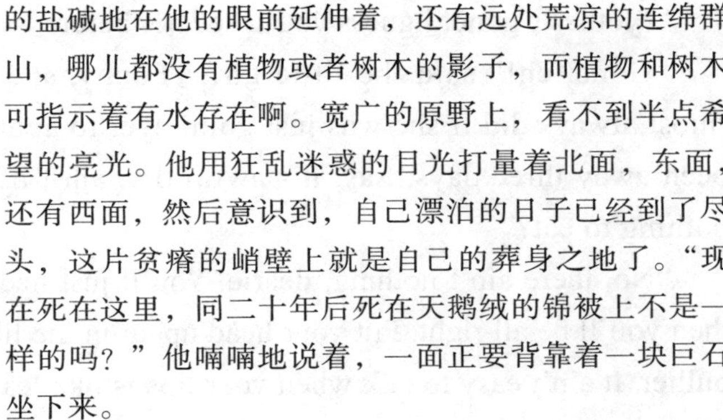

的盐碱地在他的眼前延伸着，还有远处荒凉的连绵群山，哪儿都没有植物或者树木的影子，而植物和树木可指示着有水存在啊。宽广的原野上，看不到半点希望的亮光。他用狂乱迷惑的目光打量着北面，东面，还有西面，然后意识到，自己漂泊的日子已经到了尽头，这片贫瘠的峭壁上就是自己的葬身之地了。“现在死在这里，同二十年后死在天鹅绒的锦被上不是一样的吗？”他喃喃地说着，一面正要背靠着一块巨石坐下来。

坐下之前，他把自己那支毫无用处的来复枪放在地上，同时把扛在自己右肩膀上的一个灰色大布包也放下来。看起来，布包太沉，他已经不堪重负了，因为放下时，布包在地上弄出了动静。紧接着，里面传出微弱的哭声，接着露出了一张受惊的，长着明亮褐色双眸的脸蛋，还伸出了两只长着雀斑的微凹的小拳头。

“您摔痛我啦！”一个稚嫩的声音说着，语气中透着埋怨。

“真的吗？”男人回答说，语气中带着歉疚，“我不是故意这样的。”他一边说话，一边解开布包，把里面一个年龄大概五岁左右的漂亮小姑娘抱出来。小姑娘脚穿着一双精致的鞋子，身穿着漂亮的粉红色连衣裙，外加一个亚麻布做的围兜。这一切体现了母亲的关爱。孩子显得面容苍白，神情倦怠，但四肢健康，说明她不像其同伴那样吃苦遭罪。

“现在感觉怎么样了？”他焦急地问了一声，因为看见她还在揉着脑后那团蓬乱的金色鬈发。

“您如果亲一亲，就会好的，”她说着，态度很认真，一边把受伤的地方亮给他看。“妈妈过去就是这样做的。妈妈哪儿去啦？”

“妈妈走了。我想你很快就可以见到她啦。”

① shrivelled ['ʃrivəld] *a.* 萎缩的
② senile ['si:ˌnail] *a.* 衰老的
③ decrepit [di'krepit] *a.* 老朽的
④ toil [tɔil] *v.* 跋涉
⑤ elevation [ˌelə'veiʃən] *n.* 高地
⑥ crag [kræg] *n.* 峭壁
⑦ boulder ['bəuldə] *n.* 巨石
⑧ bundle ['bʌndl] *n.* 包裹
⑨ shawl [ʃɔ:l] *n.* 大披肩
⑩ sling [sliŋ] *v.* 抛，掷
⑪ protrude [prəu'tru:d] *v.* 伸出
⑫ penitently ['penitəntli] *ad.* 悔过地
⑬ extricate ['ekstriˌkeit] *v.* 使脱身
⑭ frock [frɔk] *n.* 连衣裙
⑮ wan [wɔn] *a.* 苍白的
⑯ tousy ['tauzi] *a.* 蓬乱的

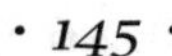

"Mother's gone. I guess you'll see her before long."

"Gone, eh!" said the little girl. "Funny, she didn't say good-bye; she 'most always did if she was just goin' over to auntie's for tea, and now she's been away three days. Say, it's awful dry, ain't it? Ain't there no water, nor nothing to eat?"

"No, there ain't nothing, dearie. You'll just need to be patient awhile, and then you'll be all right. Put your head up ag'in me like that, and then you'll feel bullier. It ain't easy to talk when your lips is like leather, but I guess I'd best let you know **how the cards lie**[①]. What's that you've got?"

"Pretty things! fine things!" cried the little girl enthusiastically, holding up two glittering fragments of **mica**[②]. "When we goes back to home I'll give them to brother Bob."

"You'll see prettier things than them soon," said the man confidently. "You just wait a bit. I was going to tell you though—you remember when we left the river?"

"Oh, yes."

"Well, we reckoned we'd strike another river soon, d'ye see. But there was somethin' wrong; **compasses**[③], or map, or somethin', and it didn't turn up. Water ran out. Just except a little drop for the likes of you and—and——"

"And you couldn't wash yourself," **interrupted**[④] his companion gravely, staring up at his grimy **visage**[⑤].

"No, nor drink. And Mr. Bender, he was the first to go, and then Indian Pete, and then Mrs. McGregor, and then Johnny Hones, and then, dearie, your mother."

"Then mother's a deader too," cried the little girl dropping her face in her **pinafore**[⑥] and sobbing bitterly.

"Yes, they all went except you and me. Then I thought there was some chance of water in this direction, so I **heaved**[⑦] you over my shoulder and we **tramped**[⑧] it together. It don't seem as though we've improved matters. There's

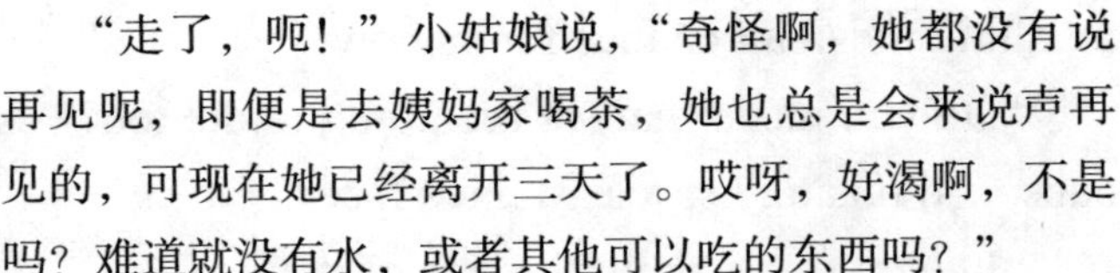

“走了，呃！”小姑娘说，“奇怪啊，她都没有说再见呢，即便是去姨妈家喝茶，她也总是会来说声再见的，可现在她已经离开三天了。哎呀，好渴啊，不是吗？难道就没有水，或者其他可以吃的东西吗？”

“没有，什么都没有，亲爱的。你所需要的就是忍耐一阵子，然后就一切都好了。你把头这样倚靠在我身上，这样会好受一点儿。嘴巴干透了，说话就费劲，但我觉得，最好还是把实际情况告诉你。你手里拿着什么东西？”

① how the cards lie 情况如何

② mica ['maikə] *n.* 云母

“漂亮的东西！精致的东西啊！”小姑娘热情洋溢地大声说着，一边举起两块亮晶晶的云母石，“等我们回家之后，我要把它们送给鲍勃弟弟。”

“你很快就可以看到更加漂亮的东西的，”男人信心百倍地说，“你只需要稍等片刻，我刚才正要告诉你的——你还记我们离开的那条河吗？”

“噢，记得。”

“对啊，我们本来指望着很快就可以到达另外一条河边，你知道的。但是，出差错了，可能是因为罗盘，或者地图，或者别的什么东西，那条河没有找到。水快要没有了，只剩下一点点，要留给你这样的小孩子喝。还有——还有——”

③ compass ['kʌmpəs] *n.* 指南针

④ interrupt [,intə'rʌpt] *v.* 打断

⑤ visage ['vizidʒ] *n.* 面容

“那您都洗刷不成了，”小姑娘打断了同伴的话，神情很严肃，抬起头看着他神情凝重的脸庞。

“对，喝的水都没有了。本德先生，他是第一个离开的，然后是印第安人皮特，然后是麦克格雷格太太，然后是约翰尼·霍尼斯，再后来，亲爱的，就是你妈妈。”

“这么说来，妈妈也死了，”小姑娘大声说着，把头垂在围兜上，伤心地抽泣起来了。

⑥ pinafore ['pinə,fɔ:] *n.* 围裙

“是啊，他们全都走了，就剩下我和你。后来，我以为往这个方向可以寻找到水源，于是，于是，我把你扛在肩膀上，一同艰难跋涉地到达了这儿。看起来，我们面前的形势并没有改善，现在我们希望渺茫啊！”

⑦ heave [hi:v] *v.* 举

⑧ tramp [træmp] *v.* 以沉重的步子走

an almighty small chance for us now!"

"Do you mean that we are going to die too?" asked the child, checking her sobs, and raising her tear-stained face.

"I guess that's about the size of it."

"Why didn't you say so before?" she said, laughing **gleefully**①. "You gave me such a fright. Why, of course, now as long as we die we'll be with mother again."

"Yes, you will, dearie."

"And you too. I'll tell her how awful good you've been. I'll bet she meets us at the door of heaven with a big **pitcher**② of water, and a lot of **buckwheat**③ cakes, hot, and toasted on both sides, like Bob and me was fond of. How long will it be first?"

"I don't know—not very long." The man's eyes were fixed upon the northern horizon. In the blue **vault**④ of the heaven there had appeared three little specks which increased in size every moment, so rapidly did they approach. They speedily resolved themselves into three large brown birds, which circled over the heads of the two wanderers, and then settled upon some rocks which overlooked them. They were buzzards, the **vultures**⑤ of the west, whose coming is the forerunner of death.

"Cocks and hens," cried the little girl gleefully, pointing at their ill-omened forms, and clapping her hands to make them rise. "Say, did God make this country?"

"In course He did," said her companion, rather startled by this unexpected question.

"He made the country down in Illinois, and He made the Missouri," the little girl continued. "I guess somebody else made the country in these parts. It's not nearly so well done. They forgot the water and the trees."

"What would ye think of offering up **prayer**⑥?" the man asked **diffidently**⑦.

"It ain't night yet," she answered.

"It don't matter. It ain't quite regular, but He won't mind that, you bet. You say over them ones that you used to say every night in the waggon when we

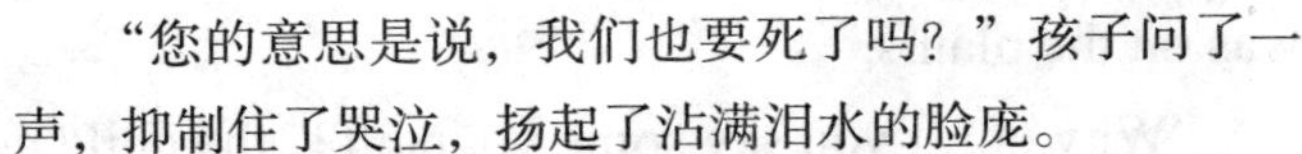

“您的意思是说，我们也要死了吗？”孩子问了一声，抑制住了哭泣，扬起了沾满泪水的脸庞。

“我看差不多了。”

“您先前为何不说啊？”小姑娘说，开心愉快地哈哈笑了起来，“您把我给吓了一大跳。啊，当然啦，只要我们死了，我们就又会同妈妈待在一块儿了。”

“对啊，你会的，宝贝儿。”

“您也会的。我会告诉妈妈，您有多么好。我敢打赌，妈妈会在天堂的大门口迎接我们的，提着一大壶水，还有很多荞麦饼，热乎乎的，两面烤得焦黄，那是我和鲍勃喜欢的。这还有多久啊？”

“我不知道——不会很久的。”男人的眼睛凝视着北方的地平线。天空中蓝色的苍穹下，出现了三个小黑点，形状不断增大，迅速在向他们靠近。三个黑点急速演变成了三只巨大的棕褐色飞鸟，盘旋在两个人的头顶，随即便落在了他们上方的岩石上。这是三只鹰，美国西部特有的那种秃鹰。它们的出现预示着死神即将降临。

“公鸡和母鸡，”小姑娘欣喜地大声喊着，一边指着三只不详的大鸟，一边拍着双手，想让它们受惊飞起来，“嘿，这个地方是上帝创造的吗？”

“当然是啦，”她的同伴说，听了这么一个突如其来的问题，显得很吃惊。

“上帝创造了伊里诺斯州，上帝也创造了密苏里州，”小姑娘接着说，“我猜，是别的什么人创造了这儿一片地方，造得不那么好，把水和树木都给忘掉了。”

“你觉得祈祷一下怎么样？”男人问了一声，显得底气不足。

“天还没有黑下来呢，”她回答说。

“没有关系啊，虽然现在做祈祷不太符合常规，但我敢肯定上帝是不会介意的。现在你就念那些我们在大平原上时你每天夜晚在大篷车上反复念的祈祷词。”

① gleefully ['gli:fuli] *ad.* 高兴地

② pitcher ['pitʃə] *n.* 大水罐

③ buckwheat ['bʌkwi:t] *n.* 荞麦

④ vault [vɔ:lt] *n.* 拱顶

⑤ vulture ['vʌltʃə] *n.* 秃鹫

⑥ prayer [prɛə] *n.* 祈祷词

⑦ diffidently ['difidəntli] *ad.* 缺乏底气地

was on the plains."

"Why don't you say some yourself?" the child asked, with wondering eyes.

"I disremember them," he answered. "I hain't said none since I was half the height o' that gun. I guess it's never too late. You say them out, and I'll stand by and come in on the **choruses**[1]."

"Then you'll need to kneel down, and me too," she said, laying the shawl out for that purpose. "You've got to put your hands up like this. It makes you feel kind o' good."

It was a strange sight had there been anything but the buzzards to see it. Side by side on the narrow shawl knelt the two wanderers, the little **prattling**[2] child and the reckless, hardened adventurer. Her **chubby**[3] face, and his haggard, angular visage were both turned up to the cloudless heaven in heartfelt **entreaty**[4] to that dread Being with whom they were face to face, while the two voices—the one thin and clear, the other deep and harsh—united in the entreaty for mercy and forgiveness. The prayer finished, they resumed their seat in the shadow of the boulder until the child fell asleep, **nestling**[5] upon the broad breast of her protector. He watched over her slumber for some time, but Nature proved to be too strong for him. For three days and three nights he had allowed himself neither rest nor **repose**[6]. Slowly the eyelids drooped over the tired eyes, and the head sunk lower and lower upon the breast, until the man's grizzled beard was mixed with the gold **tresses**[7] of his companion, and both slept the same deep and dreamless slumber.

Had the wanderer remained awake for another half hour a strange sight would have met his eyes. Far away on the extreme verge of the alkali plain there rose up a little spray of dust, very slight at first, and hardly to be distinguished from the mists of the distance, but gradually growing higher and broader until it formed a solid, well-defined cloud. This cloud continued to increase in size until it became evident that it could only be raised by a great **multitude**[8] of moving creatures. In more fertile spots the observer would have come to the conclusion

“您自己为什么不祈祷一下呢？”小姑娘问了一声，眼神中透着疑问。

“我忘了祈祷词了，”他回答说，“自从我长到像枪身一半高时，就没有再念过祈祷词了。我认为什么时候开始都不算晚。你把祈祷词说出来，我站在旁边听着，到了要一同说时我再说。”

“那么，您需要跪下来，我也要跪，”她说着，把披巾铺在地上，“像我这样，把手举起来。这样您会觉得心里更加舒服。”

只有那几只秃鹰目睹如此不可思议的一幕：狭窄的披肩布上，两个人并排跪着，一个是念念有词的小姑娘，一个是粗犷坚强的探险者。她那张圆乎乎的脸和他那张憔悴有棱角的脸一同仰望着没有云朵的天空，从内心深处向着威严的与他们同在的上帝发出恳求。两个人的声音——一个的稚嫩而清脆，另一个的低沉而沙哑——交织在了一起，祈求上帝的怜悯和宽恕。祈祷结束后，他们回到巨石阴处坐下，最后，小姑娘睡着了，依偎在其保护者宽阔的胸前。他看了一会儿她睡着的样子，但在大自然的力量面前，他还是显得无能为力。因为先前的三天三夜当中，他一直没有休息也没有合眼。慢慢地，他的眼睑耷拉下来了，脑袋越垂越下，都垂到了胸前了。最后，男人花白的胡须和他同伴金色的秀发混合在了一起，两人一同进入了深沉而又无梦的睡眠。

漫行者如果睁着眼睛再多支撑半个小时，就可以目睹奇异的景象。远方盐碱地平原的尽头，扬起了一抹小小的尘烟，刚一开始时很细微，很难同远处的雾霾区分。但是，慢慢地，它越升越高，越散越广，最后形成了一片严严实实、轮廓分明的云团。云团持续扩大，很显然，那只能是众多行进着的生灵扬起来的。如果是在肥沃的区域里，目击者会断定，向着他奔腾而来的，是

① chorus ['kɔːrəs] *n.* 齐声说

② prattling ['prætliŋ] *a.* 念念有词的

③ chubby ['tʃʌbi] *a.* 圆乎乎的

④ entreaty [en'triːti] *n.* 恳求

⑤ nestle ['nesl] *v.* 依偎

⑥ repose [ri'pəuz] *n.* 安眠

⑦ tress [tres] *n.* （女子的）长发

⑧ multitude ['mʌltitjuːd] *n.* 大量

that one of those great herds of **bisons**① which graze upon the prairie land was approaching him. This was obviously impossible in these arid wilds. As the whirl of dust drew nearer to the solitary **bluff**② upon which the two **castaways**③ were reposing, the **canvas-covered**④ tilts of waggons and the figures of armed horsemen began to show up through the haze, and the **apparition**⑤ revealed itself as being a great caravan upon its journey for the West. But what a caravan! When the head of it had reached the base of the mountains, the rear was not yet visible on the horizon. Right across the enormous plain stretched the straggling **array**⑥, waggons and **carts**⑦, men on horseback, and men on foot. Innumerable women who staggered along under burdens, and children who toddled beside the waggons or **peeped**⑧ out from under the white coverings. This was evidently no ordinary party of immigrants, but rather some **nomad**⑨ people who had been **compelled**⑩ from stress of circumstances to seek themselves a new country. There rose through the clear air a confused clattering and rumbling from this great mass of humanity, with the creaking of wheels and the neighing of horses. Loud as it was, it was not sufficient to rouse the two tired **wayfarers**⑪ above them.

At the head of the column there rode a score or more of grave ironfaced men, clad in **sombre**⑫ homespun **garments**⑬ and armed with rifles. On reaching the base of the bluff they halted, and held a short council among themselves.

"The wells are to the right, my brothers," said one, a hard-lipped, clean-shaven man with grizzly hair.

"To the right of the Sierra Blanco—so we shall reach the Rio Grande," said another.

"Fear not for water," cried a third. "He who could draw it from the rocks will not now abandon His own chosen people."

"Amen! Amen!" responded the whole party.

They were about to resume their journey when one of the youngest and keenest-eyed uttered an exclamation and pointed up at the rugged crag above them. From its summit there fluttered a little **wisp**⑭ of pink, showing up hard

① bison ['baisən] *n.* 野牛

② bluff [blʌf] *n.* 峭壁
③ castaway ['kɑ:stəwei] *n.* 流浪者
④ canvas-covered ['kænvəs,kʌvəd] *a.* 帆布覆盖的
⑤ apparition [,æpə'riʃən] *n.* 神奇现象

⑥ array [ə'rei] *n.* 队伍
⑦ cart [kɑ:t] *n.* 运货的马车

⑧ peep [pi:p] *v.* 偷看
⑨ nomad ['nəu,mæd] *n.* 游牧民
⑩ compel [kəm'pel] *v.* 迫使

⑪ wayfarer ['wei,fɛərə] *n.* 徒步旅行者

⑫ sombre ['sɔmbə] *a.* 暗淡的
⑬ garment ['gɑ:mənt] *n.* 衣服

⑭ wisp [wisp] *n.* 一缕

在草原上吃草的一大群野牛。但在这样一片贫瘠的荒凉之地显然不可能。飞旋着的尘烟离两个落魄者栖息的孤岩越来越近了，这时候，透过尘烟依稀可以看到一辆辆帆布顶棚的篷车和一个个武装骑手的身影。原来是一只浩浩荡荡的篷车队，正向着西部进发呢。但这是多么壮观的一支篷车队啊！队伍中领头的已经到达山麓了，后面的队伍还在一眼望不到头的远方。广袤的平原上，横贯着这样一支零零散散的队伍，有大小车辆，有马背上的男人，也有步行的男人。数不清的女人在重负之下步伐踉跄。孩子们或在篷车旁艰难前行，或坐在车里，在白色的篷布下面探出头向外张望。很显然，不是一支普通的迁徙队伍，而是一支受环境所迫不得不去寻找新家园的游牧民族。随着大队人马的到来，原本清新的空气中响起了咔嗒咔嗒、轰隆轰隆的声音，车辙辚辚，骏马萧萧，乱成一片。如此巨大的喧嚣声，都还不足以惊醒这两个疲惫不堪的漫行者。

队伍的前头是二十多个表情严肃、铁青着脸的骑手，他们身上穿着用色泽暗淡的手工布做成的衣服，带着来复枪。到达悬崖下面之后，便停下来，进行了简短的商议。

“泉水在右边啊，弟兄们，”有个人说话了，只见他头发灰白，嘴唇紧绷，胡子修得很干净。

“向着布兰科山脉的右侧——我们便可以到达格兰德河，”另一个人说。

“用不着替水的问题担心啊，”第三个人说，“能够从岩石缝里引出水来的上帝是不会抛弃他选定的臣民的。”

“阿门！阿门！”所有人都同声回应着。

他们正要继续前行，突然，有个年纪最轻、眼睛最敏锐的小伙子惊叫了起来，指着他们上方嶙峋的岩石。岩石的顶端飘动着小小的一缕粉红，在后面灰暗的岩石

and bright against the grey rocks behind. At the sight there was a general **reining**[①] up of horses and **unslinging**[②] of guns, while fresh horsemen came **galloping**[③] up to reinforce the **vanguard**[④]. The word `Redskins' was on every lip.

"There can't be any number of Injuns here," said the elderly man who appeared to be in command. "We have passed the Pawnees, and there are no other tribes until we cross the great mountains."

"Shall I go forward and see, Brother Stangerson," asked one of the band.

"And I," "And I," cried a dozen voices.

"Leave your horses below and we will **await**[⑤] you here," the Elder answered. In a moment the young fellows had **dismounted**[⑥], fastened their horses, and were ascending the precipitous slope which led up to the object which had excited their curiosity. They advanced rapidly and noiselessly, with the confidence and **dexterity**[⑦] of practised scouts. The watchers from the plain below could see them **flit**[⑧] from rock to rock until their figures stood out against the skyline. The young man who had first given the alarm was leading them. Suddenly his followers saw him throw up his hands, as though overcome with astonishment, and on joining him they were affected in the same way by the sight which met their eyes.

On the little **plateau**[⑨] which crowned the barren hill there stood a single giant boulder, and against this boulder there lay a tall man, long-bearded and hard-featured, but of an excessive thinness. His placid face and regular breathing showed that he was fast asleep. Beside him lay a little child, with her round white arms encircling his brown **sinewy**[⑩] neck, and her golden-haired head resting upon the breast of his velveteen **tunic**[⑪]. Her rosy lips were parted, showing the regular line of snow-white teeth within, and a playful smile played over her **infantile**[⑫] features. Her plump little white legs **terminating**[⑬] in white socks and neat shoes with shining buckles, offered a strange contrast to the long shrivelled members of her companion. On the ledge of rock above this strange couple there stood three solemn buzzards, who, at the sight of the new comers uttered **raucous**[⑭]

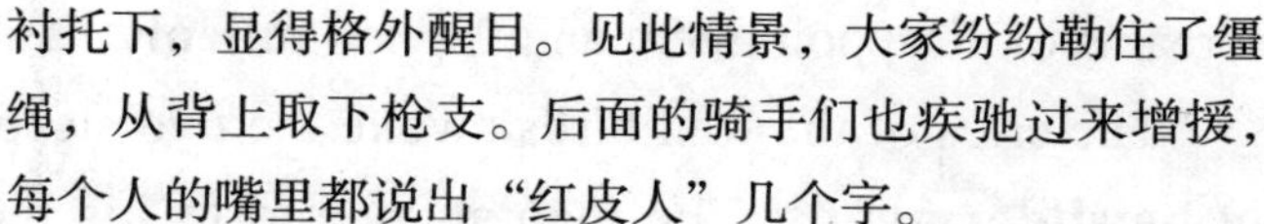

衬托下，显得格外醒目。见此情景，大家纷纷勒住了缰绳，从背上取下枪支。后面的骑手们也疾驰过来增援，每个人的嘴里都说出“红皮人”几个字。

“这儿不可能有印第安人啊，”有个上了年纪的人说，他看上去是领头的，“我们走过了有波尼人的地方了，要等到我们翻过了大山，才会有别的印第安人部落。”

“我过去看一看吧，斯坦格森兄弟，”人群中有个人说。

“还有我”，“还有我”十多个人大声说着。

“把你们的马留在下边，我们就在这儿等着你们，”年长者回答说。一时间，年轻人纷纷下了马，把马拴好后，开始攀登那道峻峭的山崖，向着那个引得他们好奇的目标进发。他们向前时行动敏捷，悄无声息，信心满满，身手敏捷，显出一副有经验的侦察人员的架势。在下面平地上观望的人们只见那些人的身影闪过一块又一块的岩石，直到登上岩石顶端。最先发现情况的那个年轻人领头，他的跟随者们突然看见他举起了双手，好像是受到了惊吓，等到他们走到他的跟前时，也同样被眼前的情形惊呆了。

荒凉的山顶部是一小块平地，上面孤零零地耸立着一块巨石。一个身材高大的男子斜靠在巨石上。男子胡须很长，五官粗犷，但瘦得出奇。他面容安详，呼吸匀称，说明他处在深深的睡眠中。身边躺着个小孩，她那又圆又白的手臂搂着大人露着条条青筋的脖子。孩子长着金发的脑袋依偎在他穿着棉绒服的胸口。红润的嘴唇张开着，露着整齐雪白的牙齿，满是稚气的小脸上挂着调皮的微笑。白白胖胖的小腿上穿着白色短袜，干净的鞋子上的搭扣闪闪发亮。这一切同她身边同伴瘦长的四肢形成了鲜明的对照，显得很怪异。两个怪人身后上方的岩石边上，落着三只神态庄严的秃鹰，它

① rein [rein] *v.* 勒缰绳使马停步
② unsling [ʌn'sliŋ] *v.* 取下
③ gallop ['gæləp] *v.* 奔驰
④ vanguard ['vængɑ:d] *n.* 先锋，这里指前面的骑手
⑤ await [ə'weit] *v.* 等待
⑥ dismount [dis'maunt] *v.* 下马
⑦ dexterity [dek'steriti] *n.* 敏捷
⑧ flit [flit] *v.* 轻快地掠过
⑨ plateau ['plætəu] *n.* 高原
⑩ sinewy ['sinju:i] *a.* 多肌腱的
⑪ tunic ['tju:nik] *n.* 束腰宽松外衣
⑫ infantile ['infən,tail] *a.* 稚气的
⑬ terminate ['tə:mineit] *v.* 终止，结束
⑭ raucous ['rɔ:kəs] *a.* 沙哑的

screams of disappointment and flapped **sullenly**[①] away.

The cries of the foul birds awoke the two sleepers who stared about them in **bewilderment**[②]. The man staggered to his feet and looked down upon the plain which had been so desolate when sleep had overtaken him, and which was now traversed by this enormous body of men and of beasts. His face assumed an expression of **incredulity**[③] as he gazed, and he passed his boney hand over his eyes. "This is what they call **delirium**[④], I guess," he muttered. The child stood beside him, holding on to the skirt of his coat, and said nothing but looked all round her with the wondering questioning gaze of childhood.

The rescuing party were speedily able to convince the two castaways that their appearance was no **delusion**[⑤]. One of them seized the little girl, and **hoisted**[⑥] her upon his shoulder, while two others supported her gaunt companion, and assisted him towards the waggons.

"My name is John Ferrier," the wanderer explained; "me and that little **un**[⑦] are all that's left o' twenty-one people. The rest is all dead o' thirst and hunger away down in the south."

"Is she your child?" asked someone.

"I guess she is now," the other cried, defiantly; "she's mine 'cause I saved her. No man will take her from me. She's Lucy Ferrier from this day on. Who are you, though?" he continued, glancing with curiosity at his stalwart, sunburned rescuers; "there seems to be a powerful lot of ye."

"**Nigh**[⑧] unto ten thousand," said one of the young men; "we are the **persecuted**[⑨] children of God—the chosen of the Angel Moroni."

"I never heard tell on him," said the wanderer. "He appears to have chosen a fair crowd of ye."

"Do not **jest**[⑩] at that which is sacred," said the other **sternly**[⑪]. "We are of those who believe in those sacred writings, drawn in Egyptian letters on plates of beaten gold, which were handed unto the holy Joseph Smith at Palmyra.

们一看到有新来者，便发出几声失望的哀鸣，气急败坏地飞走了。

① sullenly ['sʌlənli] *ad.* 不高兴地

不祥大鸟的尖叫声惊醒了两位沉睡者。他们迷惑不解地盯着四周看。男子挣扎着站了起来，看了看下面的平原。入睡前下面还是一片荒凉寂静，现在醒来却是人马聚集。他注视着，脸上露出了难以置信的表情，于是用一只瘦骨嶙峋的手捂住了眼睛。“我想这就是人们常说的神经错乱吧，”他喃喃地说。小姑娘站在边上，拽着他的衣角，她一声不吭，好奇地四下打量，目光中满是孩子特有的诧异。

② bewilderment [bi'wildəmənt] *n.* 困惑

③ incredulity [ˌinkri'djuːliti] *n.* 怀疑

④ delirium [di'liriəm] *n.* 神经错乱

前来救援的一群人很快就让两个落难者相信了，众人的出现不是什么幻觉。人群中有一位抱起了孩子，把她扛在肩上。另外两个人则搀扶着她孱弱无力的同伴，领着他走向大篷车队。

⑤ delusion [di'luːʒən] *n.* 幻觉

⑥ hoist [hɔist] *v.* 举起

⑦ un [ʌn] pron.（口语）人；东西

“我叫约翰·费里厄，”迷途者解释说，“我和这小孩是二十一人中的幸存者。其他人都渴死和饿死在南方了。”

“她是您孩子吗？”有人问。

“我想她现在是了，”对方大声说，语气很坚决。“我救了她的命，所以她就是我的孩子。没人可以把她从我身边抢走。从今天起，她就叫露茜·费里厄。但你们又是什么人啊？”他接着说，好奇地望着眼前这些身体壮实但晒得黝黑的救命恩人，“你们好像队伍很强大啊。”

“差不多有一万人，”年轻人中有一个说，“我们是受到迫害的上帝的孩子——天使梅洛纳的选民。”

⑧ nigh [nai] *ad.* 差不多

⑨ persecute ['pəːsikjuːt] *v.* 迫害

“我没有听说过这个天使的名字啊，”迷途者说，“他看起来选择了你们一大群人啊。”

“神圣的事情，可别拿来开玩笑，”另一个人说，态度很严肃，“我们信奉的神圣经文是用埃及文字书写成的，刻在黄金锻打的页片上。经文在帕尔迈拉传给了神圣的约瑟夫·史密斯。我们来自伊利诺斯州的瑙沃，因为我们先前在那儿有自己的神殿。我们到这儿寻求避难

⑩ jest [dʒest] *v.* 开玩笑

⑪ sternly ['stəːnli] *ad.* 严厉地

We have come from Nauvoo, in the state of Illinois, where we had founded our temple. We have come to seek a refuge from the violent man and from the godless, even though it be the heart of the desert."

The name of Nauvoo evidently recalled recollections to John Ferrier. "I see," he said, "you are the Mormons."

"We are the Mormons," answered his companions with one voice.

"And where are you going?"

"We do not know. The hand of God is leading us under the person of our **Prophet**①. You must come before him. He shall say what is to be done with you."

They had reached the base of the hill by this time, and were surrounded by crowds of the **pilgrims**②—pale-faced **meek-looking**③ women, strong laughing children, and anxious earnest-eyed men. Many were the cries of astonishment and of **commiseration**④ which arose from them when they perceived the youth of one of the strangers and the **destitution**⑤ of the other. Their **escort**⑥ did not halt, however, but pushed on, followed by a great crowd of Mormons, until they reached a waggon, which was **conspicuous**⑦ for its great size and for the **gaudiness**⑧ and smartness of its appearance. Six horses were **yoked**⑨ to it, whereas the others were furnished with two, or, at most, four apiece. Beside the driver there sat a man who could not have been more than thirty years of age, but whose massive head and resolute expression marked him as a leader. He was reading a brown-backed volume, but as the crowd approached he laid it aside, and listened attentively to an account of the episode. Then he turned to the two castaways.

"If we take you with us," he said, in solemn words, "it can only be as believers in our own **creed**⑩. We shall have no wolves in our fold. Better far that your bones should bleach in this wilderness than that you should prove to be that little speck of decay which in time **corrupts**⑪ the whole fruit. Will you come with us on these terms?"

"Guess I'll come with you on any terms," said Ferrier, with such

之所，远离那些充满暴力的人，不信神的人，即便这儿是沙漠深处也罢。”

很显然，瑙沃这个名字勾起来约翰·费里厄的种种回忆。“我明白了，”他说，“你们是摩门教徒。”

“我们是摩门教徒。”其同伴们回答说。

“那你们这是要去哪儿呢？”

“我们也不知道，上帝之手通过我们的先知引领着我们向前，您得到我们的先知跟前去，如何安置您，他会做出安排的。”

他们这时已经来到了山脚下，然后被人群团团围住——人群中有妇女，她们脸色苍白，神情温顺；有儿童，他们身体强壮，欢声笑语；有男人，他们焦虑不安，目光坦诚。他们看到两个陌生人中一个年幼，另一个身体虚弱，许多人大声叫了起来，充满着震惊和同情。然而，护送他们的行动没有停下，而是不断向前推动，后面跟随着大群摩门教徒，直到他们到达了一辆篷车边，篷车显得格外醒目，因为其结构庞大，外观鲜艳华丽。大篷车由六匹马拉着，而其他的都是由两匹马拉着的，或者最多也就是四匹马。车夫旁边坐着个年龄不超过三十岁的男子，但他头颅硕大，神态坚毅，显然是个领头的。他正在看一本棕色封面的书，但看到人群涌了过来，便把书籍放到了一旁，认真地倾听了事情的始末。然后把目光转向了两个落难者。

“如果我们要带着你们一起走，”他说着，言辞很庄严，“你们就只能信奉我们的教义。我们的羊圈里不允许有狼出现。即便让你们抛尸荒野，尸骨经风吹日晒变成白色，也比让你们成为水果上小小的烂斑最后导致整个果实腐烂要强得多。面对这样的条件，你们还愿意同我们一起走吗？”

“我觉得，面对任何条件，我都会跟随着你们，”费里厄说，说得郑重其事，连那些神情严肃的老者都忍不

① prophet ['prɔfit] *n.* 先知

② pilgrim ['pilgrim] *n.* 朝圣者

③ meek-looking ['mi:klukiŋ] *a.* 看起来温顺的

④ commiseration[kəˌmizə'reiʃən] *n.* 同情

⑤ destitution [ˌdesti'tju:ʃən] *n.* 穷困

⑥ escort ['eskɔ:t] *n.* 护送

⑦ conspicuous [kən'spikjuəs] *a.* 明显的

⑧ gaudiness ['gɔ:dinis] *n.* 华丽

⑨ yoke [jəuk] *v.* 给…上轭

⑩ creed [kri:d] *n.* 教条

⑪ corrupt [kə'rʌpt] *v.* 腐烂

⑫ emphasis ['emfəsis] *n.* 强调

emphasis[12] that the grave Elders could not **restrain**[1] a smile. The leader alone retained his stern, impressive expression.

"Take him, Brother Stangerson," he said, "give him food and drink, and the child likewise. Let it be your task also to teach him our holy creed. We have delayed long enough. Forward! On, on to Zion!"

"On, on to Zion!" cried the crowd of Mormons, and the words rippled down the long caravan, passing from mouth to mouth until they died away in a dull murmur in the far distance. With a cracking of whips and a creaking of wheels the great waggons got into motion, and soon the whole caravan was winding along once more. The Elder to whose care the two **waifs**[2] had been committed, led them to his waggon, where a meal was already awaiting them.

"You shall remain here," he said. "In a few days you will have recovered from your **fatigues**[3]. In the meantime, remember that now and for ever you are of our religion. Brigham Young has said it, and he has spoken with the voice of Joseph Smith, which is the voice of God."

① restrain [ris'trein] *v.* 抑制

② waif [weif] *n.* 流浪者

③ fatigue [fə'ti:g] *n.* 疲劳

住露出了微笑，但唯有那位领头的依旧表情严肃，不苟言笑。

“带上他吧，斯坦格森兄弟，”他说，“给他吃的和喝的，孩子也一样。你还要负责给他讲一讲我们神圣的教义。我们已经耽搁够长时间了，前进吧！继续前进，向着锡安进发！”

“继续前进，向着锡安进发！”摩门教众教徒大声说。领头人的号令在队伍中一路相传着，犹如翻滚的浪花，沿着大篷车队组成的长龙，一直传到很远很远，声音不断减弱，最后成了远方喃喃细语。马鞭啪啪，车轮辘辘，大篷车队动起来了，很快，整个队伍再次蜿蜒向前进。遵命照料两位落难者的长老把他们领到了他自己的马车上，那儿已经为他们准备好了饮食。

“你们就待在这儿吧，”他说，“过几天，你们身体就可以恢复过来。同时，要永远记住，你们已经皈依了我们的宗教。杨百翰已有了训诫，他是代表约瑟夫·史密斯说话的，也就是等于上帝的旨意。”

Chapter 2 The Flower of Utah

This is not the place to **commemorate**① the trials and **privations**② endured by the immigrant Mormons before they came to their final **haven**③. From the shores of the Mississippi to the western slopes of the Rocky Mountains they had struggled on with a constancy almost **unparalleled**④ in history. The savage man, and the savage beast, hunger, thirst, fatigue, and disease—every **impediment**⑤ which Nature could place in the way, had all been overcome with Anglo-Saxon **tenacity**⑥. Yet the long journey and the accumulated terrors had shaken the hearts of the stoutest among them. There was not one who did not sink upon his knees in heartfelt prayer when they saw the broad valley of Utah bathed in the sunlight beneath them, and learned from the lips of their leader that this was the promised land, and that these **virgin**⑦ acres were to be theirs for evermore.

Young speedily proved himself to be a skilful administrator as well as a resolute chief. Maps were drawn and charts prepared, in which the future city was sketched out. All around farms were **apportioned**⑧ and **allotted**⑨ in proportion to the standing of each individual. The tradesman was put to his trade and the **artisan**⑩ to his calling. In the town streets and squares sprang up, as if by magic. In the country there was draining and hedging, planting and clearing, until the next summer saw the whole country golden with the wheat crop. Everything **prospered**⑪ in the strange settlement. Above all, the great temple which they had **erected**⑫ in the

第二章　犹他之花

① commemorate [kə'memərеit] *v.* 纪念
② privation [prai'veiʃən] *n.* 艰难
③ haven ['heivən] *n.* 安全的地方
④ unparalleled[ʌn'pærə,leld] *a.* 空前的
⑤ impediment [im'pedimənt] *n.* 障碍
⑥ tenacity [tə'næsiti] *n.* 顽强
⑦ virgin ['və:dʒin] *a.* 处女的
⑧ apportion [ə'pɔ:ʃən] *v.* 分配
⑨ allot [ə'lɔt] *v.* 摊派
⑩ artisan ['ɑ:tizən] *n.* 工匠
⑪ prosper ['prɔspə] *v.* 兴旺
⑫ erect [i'rekt] *v.* 建立

迁徙的摩门教徒们历尽了磨难与艰辛，最后到达了他们的避难所。关于这一过程的情况，此处不予追忆。从密西西比河畔到落基山脉的西麓，他们凭着人类历史上几乎是无可比拟的坚定意志，一路奋力向前。凶悍的野蛮人，凶猛的野兽，饥饿干渴，劳累疾病——一路上，大自然能够设置的种种障碍，应有尽有——但全都被他们以盎格鲁-撒克逊人特有的顽强意志给征服了。然而，漫长的旅途，积累的恐惧，曾令他们中最坚忍不拔者都心有动摇，但是，他们看到了自己的下方辽阔的犹他峡谷沐浴在阳光下，听到他们的头领亲口说出，那就是上帝赐予的乐土，那片处女地永远属于他们的，这时候，所有人都双膝跪地，虔诚祈祷。

杨百翰很快就证明了自己既是个坚毅果敢的头领，也是个卓越的管理者。他绘制了一张张地图，制作了一张张图表，其中勾勒出了未来城市的蓝图。周围的耕地进行了分配，按照每个人的地位不同进行分发。商人开始经商了，工匠干起了自己的行当。城里的街道和广场像变魔术似的出现了。乡野里，人们有的挖水沟，有的扎篱笆，有的种庄稼，有的平土地，到了次年的夏天，整个乡野处处是金黄的麦浪。在这个陌生的居住地，一切都兴兴向荣起来了。最值得一提的

centre of the city grew ever taller and larger. From the first blush of dawn until the closing of the twilight, the clatter of the hammer and the rasp of the saw was never absent from the **monument**① which the immigrants erected to Him who had led them safe through many dangers.

The two castaways, John Ferrier and the little girl who had shared his fortunes and had been adopted as his daughter, accompanied the Mormons to the end of their great pilgrimage. Little Lucy Ferrier was borne along pleasantly enough in Elder Stangerson's waggon, a **retreat**② which she shared with the Mormon's three wives and with his son, a **headstrong**③ forward boy of twelve. Having rallied, with the **elasticity**④ of childhood, from the shock caused by her mother's death, she soon became a pet with the women, and **reconciled**⑤ herself to this new life in her moving canvas-covered home. In the meantime Ferrier having recovered from his privations, distinguished himself as a useful guide and an **indefatigable**⑥ hunter. So rapidly did he gain the esteem of his new companions, that when they reached the end of their wanderings, it was **unanimously**⑦ agreed that he should be provided with as large and as fertile a tract of land as any of the settlers, with the exception of Young himself, and of Stangerson, Kemball, Johnston, and Drebber, who were the four principal Elders.

On the farm thus acquired John Ferrier built himself a **substantial**⑧ log-house, which received so many additions in succeeding years that it grew into a roomy villa. He was a man of a practical turn of mind, keen in his dealings and skilful with his hands. His iron constitution enabled him to work morning and evening at improving and tilling his lands. Hence it came about that his farm and all that belonged to him prospered exceedingly. In three years he was better off than his neighbours, in six he was well-to-do, in nine he was rich, and in twelve there were not half a dozen men in the whole of Salt Lake City who could compare with him. From the great inland sea to the distant Wahsatch Mountains there was no name better known than that of John Ferrier.

是，人们在城市中心建设的那座大教堂，日益高大，日益雄伟。黎明的第一缕朝霞刚出现，教堂里便传出斧头砍木料和锯子锯木材的声音，直到最后一线晚霞逝去才停止。教堂是移民们为上帝建造的一座丰碑，因为有了上帝的指引，他们才能历尽无数的艰险，安全抵达这片乐土。

① monument ['mɔnjumənt] *n.* 纪念碑；纪念性建筑

两位迷途者，也就是约翰·费里厄和那位小姑娘，她与前者同甘共苦，并且做了他的养女，跟随着摩门教徒们到达这次伟大朝圣之旅的终点。一路上，小露茜·费里厄一直待在斯坦格森长老的篷车上，挺舒心惬意的。同车的还有摩门教长老的三位妻子和他那位执拗任性的十二岁的儿子。儿童的适应性很强，小姑娘从丧母之痛中恢复过来之后，很快就成了篷车上的女人们的宝贝疙瘩了，同时也适应了在这个帆布覆盖着的移动家庭中的新生活。与此同时，费里厄也从极度虚弱的身体状态中恢复了过来，成了一名作用巨大的向导和不知疲倦的猎手，很快赢得了新伙伴们的尊重。当他们到达旅途的终点时，大家一致同意，除了杨百翰本人和斯坦格森、坎博尔、约翰斯顿和德雷伯四位长老外，费里厄应该同其他任何居民一样，分配同样大小、同样肥沃的土地。

② retreat [ri'tri:t] *n.* 静居处

③ headstrong ['hedˌstrɔ:ŋ] *a.* 任性的

④ elasticity[ˌelæs'tisiti] *n.* 顺应性

⑤ reconcile ['rekənsail] *v.* 使…和谐

⑥ indefatigable [ˌindi'fætigəbl] *a.* 不屈不挠的

⑦ unanimously [ju'nænimәsli] *ad.* 全体一致地

约翰·费里厄分得土地之后，替自己建造了一幢结实的木屋。木屋在接下来的岁月中不断扩建，最后变成了一幢宽敞的别墅。他是个讲求实际的人，处事精明，手艺高超，还有一副铁打的身子骨。每天起早摸黑地在地里劳作，因此，辛勤的劳作有了好的回报，农田里丰收了，一切都兴旺了。三年之后，他日子比其他邻居过得更加殷实。六年之后，他富有了。九年之后，他成富人了。十二年之后，整座盐湖城，能与他匹敌的只有五六个人了。从这片浩瀚的内陆海到遥远的瓦萨奇山脉，约翰·费里厄的知名度无人可比。

⑧ substantial [səb'stænʃəl] *a.* 结实的

There was one way and only one in which he offended the **susceptibilities**① of his co-religionists. No argument or persuasion could ever **induce**② him to set up a female establishment after the manner of his companions. He never gave reasons for this persistent refusal, but contented himself by resolutely and inflexibly **adhering**③ to his determination. There were some who accused him of lukewarmness in his adopted religion, and others who put it down to greed of wealth and **reluctance**④ to incur expense. Others, again, spoke of some early love affair, and of a fair-haired girl who had pined away on the shores of the Atlantic. Whatever the reason, Ferrier remained strictly **celibate**⑤. In every other respect he conformed to the religion of the young settlement, and gained the name of being an **orthodox**⑥ and straight-walking man.

Lucy Ferrier grew up within the log-house, and assisted her adopted father in all his undertakings. The keen air of the mountains and the **balsamic**⑦ odour of the pine trees took the place of nurse and mother to the young girl. As year succeeded to year she grew taller and stronger, her cheek more rudy, and her step more elastic. Many a wayfarer upon the high road which ran by Ferrier's farm felt long-forgotten thoughts revive in their mind as they watched her lithe girlish figure tripping through the wheatfields, or met her mounted upon her father's **mustang**⑧, and managing it with all the ease and grace of a true child of the West. So the bud blossomed into a flower, and the year which saw her father the richest of the farmers left her as fair a **specimen**⑨ of American girlhood as could be found in the whole Pacific slope.

It was not the father, however, who first discovered that the child had developed into the woman. It seldom is in such cases. That mysterious change is too subtle and too gradual to be measured by dates. Least of all does the maiden herself know it until the tone of a voice or the touch of a hand sets her heart thrilling within her, and she learns, with a mixture of pride and of fear, that a new and a larger nature has awoken within her. There are few who cannot recall that day and remember the one little incident which **heralded**⑩ the dawn of a new life. In the case of Lucy Ferrier the occasion was serious

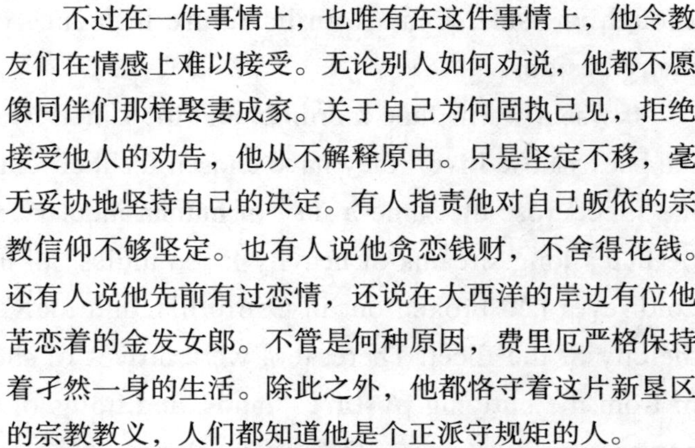

不过在一件事情上，也唯有在这件事情上，他令教友们在情感上难以接受。无论别人如何劝说，他都不愿像同伴们那样娶妻成家。关于自己为何固执己见，拒绝接受他人的劝告，他从不解释原由。只是坚定不移，毫无妥协地坚持自己的决定。有人指责他对自己皈依的宗教信仰不够坚定。也有人说他贪恋钱财，不舍得花钱。还有人说他先前有过恋情，还说在大西洋的岸边有位他苦恋着的金发女郎。不管是何种原因，费里厄严格保持着孑然一身的生活。除此之外，他都恪守着这片新垦区的宗教教义，人们都知道他是个正派守规矩的人。

露茜·费里厄就在木屋中长大成人，帮着养父料理一切。山区清新的空气，松树树脂的芬芳代替了保姆和母亲的位置，抚育着小姑娘成长。年复一年，她的个子越来越高，身体越来越结实，脸颊越来越红润，步态越来越轻盈。有许多游人从费里厄的农庄旁的大路上走过。每当他们目睹了姑娘轻盈曼妙的身影款款穿过麦地，或者遇上她骑在父亲的野马背上，显出西部之女策马前行时轻松优雅的姿态，他们的心中会有一种久违的情怀油然而生。就这样，花蕾绽放了，等到她父亲成为农民中最富有的人时，她也成了整个太平洋坡地内美国少女的典范。

然而，头一位发现小姑娘已经长大了的人并不是她父亲。对于这种情况，做父亲的往往极少会注意到。这种神秘的变化非常微妙，非常缓慢，无法用具体的日期来标识。最最浑然不觉的是少女自己，直到有一天，某一种说话的腔调或者某一只手的触碰令她砰然心动时，她才半是骄傲半是恐惧地意识到，某种崭新而又更加强烈的天性在自己的体内苏醒了。很少有人会忘记那个日子，会忘记那件预示着一种新生活开始的小小事件。就露西·费里厄而言，事情本身是够严重的，除了影响到她自己未来的命运之外，还影响了许多旁人的命运。

① susceptibility [sə,septə'biliti] *n.* 感情
② induce [in'dju:s] *v.* 劝导
③ adhere [əd'hiə] *v.* 坚持
④ reluctance[ri'lʌktəns] *n.* 不情愿
⑤ celibate ['selibit] *n.* 独身者
⑥ orthodox ['ɔ:θədɔks] *a.* 规矩的
⑦ balsamic [bɔ:l'sæmik] *a.* 如香脂般的
⑧ mustang ['mʌstæŋ] *n.* 野马
⑨ specimen ['spesimən] *n.* 典范
⑩ herald ['herəld] *v.* 预示

enough in itself, apart from its future influence on her destiny and that of many besides.

It was a warm June morning, and the **Latter Day Saints**① were as busy as the bees whose **hive**② they have chosen for their **emblem**③. In the fields and in the streets rose the same **hum**④ of human industry. Down the dusty high roads **defiled**⑤ long streams of heavily-laden mules, all heading to the west, for the gold fever had broken out in California, and the Overland Route lay through the city of the Elect. There, too, were droves of sheep and **bullocks**⑥ coming in from the outlying **pasture**⑦ lands, and trains of tired immigrants, men and horses equally weary of their **interminable**⑧ journey. Through all this motley **assemblage**⑨, threading her way with the skill of an accomplished rider, there galloped Lucy Ferrier, her fair face flushed with the exercise and her long chestnut hair floating out behind her. She had a commission from her father in the city, and was dashing in as she had done many a time before, with all the fearlessness of youth, thinking only of her task and how it was to be performed. The travel-stained adventurers gazed after her in astonishment, and even the unemotional Indians, journeying in with their **peltries**⑩ relaxed their accustomed **stoicism**⑪ as they marvelled at the beauty of the pale-faced maiden.

She had reached the **outskirts**⑫ of the city when she found the road blocked by a great drove of cattle, driven by a half-dozen wild-looking herdsmen from the plains. In her impatience she endeavoured to pass this obstacle by pushing her horse into what appeared to be a gap. Scarcely had she got fairly into it, however, before the beasts closed in behind her, and she found herself completely imbedded in the moving stream of fierce-eyed, long-horned bullocks. Accustomed as she was to deal with cattle, she was not alarmed at her situation, but took advantage of every opportunity to urge her horse on in the hopes of pushing her way through the **cavalcade**⑬. Unfortunately the horns of one of the creatures, either by accident or design, came in violent contact with the flank of the mustang, and excited it to madness. In an instant it reared up upon its hind legs with a snort of rage, and **pranced**⑭ and **tossed**⑮ in a way

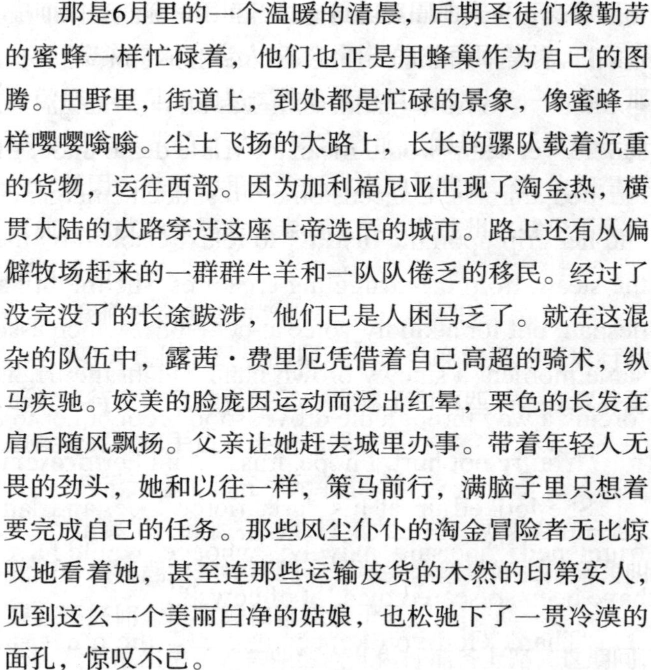

那是6月里的一个温暖的清晨，后期圣徒们像勤劳的蜜蜂一样忙碌着，他们也正是用蜂巢作为自己的图腾。田野里，街道上，到处都是忙碌的景象，像蜜蜂一样嘤嘤嗡嗡。尘土飞扬的大路上，长长的骡队载着沉重的货物，运往西部。因为加利福尼亚出现了淘金热，横贯大陆的大路穿过这座上帝选民的城市。路上还有从偏僻牧场赶来的一群群牛羊和一队队倦乏的移民。经过了没完没了的长途跋涉，他们已是人困马乏了。就在这混杂的队伍中，露茜·费里厄凭借着自己高超的骑术，纵马疾驰。姣美的脸庞因运动而泛出红晕，栗色的长发在肩后随风飘扬。父亲让她赶去城里办事。带着年轻人无畏的劲头，她和以往一样，策马前行，满脑子里只想着要完成自己的任务。那些风尘仆仆的淘金冒险者无比惊叹地看着她，甚至连那些运输皮货的木然的印第安人，见到这么一个美丽白净的姑娘，也松驰下了一贯冷漠的面孔，惊叹不已。

① the Latter Day Saint 后期圣徒，即美国摩门教徒
② hive [haiv] *n.* 蜂巢
③ emblem ['embləm] *n.* 标记
④ hum [hʌm] *n.* 嗡嗡声
⑤ defile [di'fail] *v.* 纵列行进
⑥ bullock ['bulək] *n.* 小公牛
⑦ pasture ['pɑ:stʃə] *n.* 牧场
⑧ interminable [in'tə:minəbl] *a.* 没有尽头的
⑨ assemblage [ə'semblidʒ] *n.* 聚集
⑩ peltry ['peltri] *n.* 生皮；毛皮
⑪ stoicism ['stəuiˌsizəm] *n.* 淡漠
⑫ outskirts ['autskə:ts] *n.* 郊外

露茜到达城外时，发现道路被一大群牛给堵住了，六个外貌彪悍的平原牧人赶着牛群。她情急之下扬鞭策马，插入一个空隙，企图突破前方的障碍。然而，她刚一挤进牛群，后面的牛就围了上来，完全陷入了流动的牛群中，周围全是目光凶狠、牛角高翘的公牛。她经常与牛打交道，所以落入重围也毫不慌乱，不停地寻找空隙继续策马向前，想方设法要冲出牛群。不幸的是，不知是有意还是无意，其中有头牛的角猛地顶在马肚子上，马受惊了。随即，狂怒地喷着鼻息，高扬起前蹄，踢踏乱跳。若非骑术精湛，马鞍上的人早被甩到了地上。当时情况万分危急。受惊后的马每次跳跃，都会反复地顶到牛角，这便使马越发地疯狂起来。在这种情况下，露茜只能紧紧贴在马鞍上。如果不小心掉到地上，就会被受惊失控的牲畜践踏而死。面对这种突如其来的紧急状况，她不知所措，眼前天旋地转，拽着缰绳的手

⑬ cavalcade [ˌka:vəl'keid] *n.* 队，这里指牛群
⑭ prance [pra:ns] *v.* 腾跃
⑮ toss [tɔs] *v.* 抛；猛倾；颠簸

that would have unseated any but a most skilful rider. The situation was full of **peril**[①]. Every plunge of the excited horse brought it against the horns again, and **goaded**[②] it to fresh madness. It was all that the girl could do to keep herself in the saddle, yet a slip would mean a terrible death under the hoofs of the unwieldy and terrified animals. Unaccustomed to sudden emergencies, her head began to swim, and her grip upon the **bridle**[③] to relax. Choked by the rising cloud of dust and by the steam from the struggling creatures, she might have abandoned her efforts in despair, but for a kindly voice at her elbow which assured her of assistance. At the same moment a sinewy brown hand caught the frightened horse by the curb, and forcing a way through the drove, soon brought her to the outskirts.

"You're not hurt, I hope, miss," said her **preserver**[④], respectfully.

She looked up at his dark, fierce face, and laughed **saucily**[⑤]. "I'm awful frightened," she said, naively; "whoever would have thought that Poncho would have been so scared by a lot of cows?"

"Thank God you kept your seat," the other said earnestly. He was a tall, savage-looking young fellow, mounted on a powerful roan horse, and clad in the rough dress of a hunter, with a long rifle slung over his shoulders. "I guess you are the daughter of John Ferrier," he remarked, "I saw you ride down from his house. When you see him, ask him if he remembers the Jefferson Hopes of St. Louis. If he's the same Ferrier, my father and he were pretty thick."

"Hadn't you better come and ask yourself?" she asked, **demurely**[⑥].

The young fellow seemed pleased at the suggestion, and his dark eyes sparkled with pleasure. "I'll do so," he said, "we've been in the mountains for two months, and are not over and above in visiting condition. He must take us as he finds us."

"He has a good deal to thank you for, and so have I," she answered, "he's awful fond of me. If those cows had jumped on me he'd have never got over it."

"Neither would I," said her companion.

"You! Well, I don't see that it would make much matter to you, anyhow. You ain't even a friend of ours."

① peril ['peril] *n.* 极大的危险
② goad [gəud] *v.* 刺激
③ bridle ['braidl] *n.* 马笼头
④ preserver [pri'zə:və] *n.* 保护者
⑤ saucily ['sɔsili] *ad.* 调皮地
⑥ demurely [di'mjuəli] *ad.* 故作庄重地

也控制不住了。扬起的尘埃和挤在一起的牲口散发出的恶臭几乎令她窒息。她已陷入绝望，几乎支持不住了。突然，耳畔响起一个亲切的声音，有人来救她了。此时，一只强壮有力的棕色大手抓住惊马的嚼环，从牛群中强行挤出一条道，迅速把她带离牛群。

“但愿您没有伤着吧，小姐，”救她的人说，态度毕恭毕敬。

露茜抬起头看了看他黝黑粗犷的面孔，爽朗地笑了起来。“可把我给吓坏了，”她说着，语气显得很天真，“骑士面对一大群牛会吓成这个样子，谁想得到啊？”

“感谢上帝，您没有从马鞍上掉下来。”对方语气真诚地说。他是个年轻人，身材高大，相貌粗狂，骑着一匹沙毛大马，穿着猎人的粗布装，肩上斜挎着一支长枪。“我猜，您是约翰·费里厄先生的女儿吧，”他说，“我看到您从他家骑马过来，您见到他时问一问，他是否还记得圣路易斯的杰弗逊·霍普。如果他是同一个约翰·费里厄的话，我父亲和他过去交往甚密。”

“您亲自去问一问不是更好吗？”她说，态度显得故作严肃。

年轻人听后显得很高兴，黑色的眼睛闪烁着喜悦的光芒。“我会这样做的，”他说，“我们在山区逗留了两个月了，并不大适合于上门做客。他看到我们的样子，准会把我们给逮起来的。”

“他谢您都谢不过来呢，我也是一样的，”她回应说，“他可疼爱我啦，如果那些牛把我给踩踏了，他可是会受不了的。”

“我也会受不了的。”年轻人说。

“您？啊！我不明白，我可看不出，这事同您有什么关系。您连我们的朋友都算不上。”

年轻的猎人听到这句话之后显得很郁闷，露茜不禁哈哈大笑起来。

The young hunter's dark face grew so gloomy over this remark that Lucy Ferrier laughed aloud.

"There, I didn't mean that," she said; "of course, you are a friend now. You must come and see us. Now I must push along, or father won't trust me with his business any more. Good-bye!"

"Good-bye," he answered, raising his broad **sombrero**[①], and bending over her little hand. She wheeled her mustang round, gave it a cut with her riding-whip, and darted away down the broad road in a rolling cloud of dust.

Young Jefferson Hope rode on with his companions, gloomy and **taciturn**[②]. He and they had been among the Nevada Mountains **prospecting**[③] for silver, and were returning to Salt Lake City in the hope of raising capital enough to work some lodes which they had discovered. He had been as keen as any of them upon the business until this sudden incident had drawn his thoughts into another channel. The sight of the fair young girl, as frank and **wholesome**[④] as the Sierra breezes, had stirred his volcanic, **untamed**[⑤] heart to its very depths. When she had vanished from his sight, he realized that a crisis had come in his life, and that neither silver **speculations**[⑥] nor any other questions could ever be of such importance to him as this new and all-absorbing one. The love which had sprung up in his heart was not the sudden, changeable fancy of a boy, but rather the wild, fierce passion of a man of strong will and **imperious**[⑦] temper. He had been accustomed to succeed in all that he undertook. He swore in his heart that he would not fail in this if human effort and human perseverance could render him successful.

He called on John Ferrier that night, and many times again, until his face was a familiar one at the farm-house. John, cooped up in the valley, and absorbed in his work, had had little chance of learning the news of the outside world during the last twelve years. All this Jefferson Hope was able to tell him, and in a style which interested Lucy as well as her father. He had been a pioneer in California, and could narrate many a strange tale of fortunes made and fortunes lost in those wild, **halcyon**[⑧] days. He had been a **scout**[⑨] too, and a **trapper**[⑩], a

“噢，我不是那个意思呢，”她说，“当然，你现在是朋友啦。你可一定要去看我们啊。我现在得赶路了，要不，父亲以后不会再放心让我替他办事情了。再见！”

“再见，”他回答说，举起了头上那顶宽沿帽，俯身吻了一下她的小手。露茜掉转马头，鞭子一扬，策马离去了，卷起一阵尘烟。

年轻的杰弗逊·霍普和他的同伴们一道继续策马前行，显得闷闷不乐，沉默寡言。他和同伴们一直在内华达山区跋涉着，寻找银矿，这时要回盐湖城去，筹集足够的资金开采已探明的银矿。本来，对于开采银矿的事情，他和其他人一样信心满满，但这个突然出现的情况，令他的思绪转向了。美丽的姑娘犹如山里的清风，爽朗怡人，见到了她之后，他的内心躁动了起来，按耐不住，像火山一样要爆发了。当她从自己的视线中消失时，他意识到，自己的人生到达了一个紧要关头。刚才出现的情况让他整个人都陷进去了，银矿生意也好，别的问题也罢，对他而言都已经不重要了。他内心迸发出的爱意，不是一个小伙子的一时兴起，也不是暂时的迷恋，而是一个意志坚定、性格刚毅的男人所具有的那种原始炙热的情感。他想要做的事，就从来没有失败过。他心中暗暗发誓：如果凭着个人的努力和执着能够使他成功的话，他就决不会在这件事情上失败。

他当晚就去拜访了约翰·费里厄，后来也登门了许多次，这样便成了这个家庭的常客。过去的十二年来，约翰深居峡谷之中，全部精力投入到了劳作中，几乎没有机会了解外面的情况。杰弗逊·霍普把峡谷外面的情况全部讲给他听，说得有声有色，露茜和她父亲听得津津有味。由于霍普很早就到加利福尼亚去淘金，能讲很多新奇的故事。讲的都是那些疯狂而又繁荣的日子里如何发财接着又破产的故事。他做过侦察者、猎手、银矿探寻者和牧场工。哪儿盛行了什么冒险的活动，杰弗

① sombrero [sɔm'brɛərəu] *n.* 宽边帽

② taciturn ['tæsi,tə:n] *a.* 沉默寡言的

③ prospect ['prɔspekt] *v.* 勘探

④ wholesome ['həulsəm] *a.* 对身心有意的，这里指清新的

⑤ untamed [ʌn'teimd] *a.* 未被驯服的

⑥ speculation [,spekju'leiʃən] *n.* 投机买卖

⑦ imperious [im'piəriəs] *a.* 不随意的

⑧ halcyon ['hælsiən] *a.* 平静的

⑨ scout [skaut] *n.* 侦查员

⑩ trapper ['træpə] *n.* 捕兽人

silver explorer, and a **ranchman**①. Wherever stirring adventures were to be had, Jefferson Hope had been there in search of them. He soon became a favourite with the old farmer, who spoke **eloquently**② of his **virtues**③. On such occasions, Lucy was silent, but her blushing cheek and her bright, happy eyes, showed only too clearly that her young heart was no longer her own. Her honest father may not have observed these symptoms, but they were assuredly not thrown away upon the man who had won her affections.

It was a summer evening when he came galloping down the road and pulled up at the gate. She was at the doorway, and came down to meet him. He threw the bridle over the fence and strode up the pathway.

"I am off, Lucy," he said, taking her two hands in his, and gazing tenderly down into her face; "I won't ask you to come with me now, but will you be ready to come when I am here again?"

"And when will that be?" she asked, blushing and laughing.

"A couple of months at the outside. I will come and claim you then, my darling. There's no one who can stand between us."

"And how about father?" she asked.

"He has given his **consent**④, provided we get these mines working all right. I have no fear on that head."

"Oh, well; of course, if you and father have arranged it all, there's no more to be said," she whispered, with her cheek against his broad breast.

"Thank God!" he said, **hoarsely**⑤, stooping and kissing her. "It is settled, then. The longer I stay, the harder it will be to go. They are waiting for me at the canon. Good-bye, my own darling—good-bye. In two months you shall see me."

He tore himself from her as he spoke, and, **flinging**⑥ himself upon his horse, galloped furiously away, never even looking round, as though afraid that his resolution might fail him if he took one glance at what he was leaving. She stood at the gate, gazing after him until he vanished from her sight. Then she walked back into the house, the happiest girl in all Utah.

① ranchman [ˈrɑːntʃmæn] *n.* 牧场工人

② eloquently [ˈeləkwəntli] *ad.* 能说会道地

③ virtue [ˈvəːtjuː] *n.* 优点

④ consent [kənˈsent] *n.* 允许

⑤ hoarsely [ˈhɔːsli] *ad.* 嘶哑地

⑥ fling [fliŋ] *v.* 抛，掷，使投身，这里指跃

逊·霍普就前往哪儿。他很快就赢得了年迈的农场主的喜爱。农场主对年轻人赞不绝口。每当这种时候，露茜就会缄口不言，但脸上会泛起红晕，眼睛里闪烁着明亮喜悦的光芒，这再清楚不过了，她年轻的心已不再属于自己的了。她忠厚诚恳的父亲可能看不出什么苗头，但赢得她的芳心的那个人是肯定心领神会的。

夏天里的一个傍晚，霍普顺着大路一路策马奔腾，然后在门口停了下来。露茜站立在门口，走下台阶迎接他。他把缰绳往栅栏上一扔，大步向前。

“我要走了，露茜，”他说，双手握住了她的手，神情温柔地盯着她的脸看，“我不会要求你现在同我一道走，但是，等我下一回过来时，你愿意同我一道走吗？”

“那下回是什么时候啊？”她说，脸上绯得通红，哈哈笑了起来。

“在外面就待两个月，到时我就来向你求婚，亲爱的。没人阻拦得了我们。”

“你父亲是什么态度呢？”她问。

“他已经同意了，只要我们的银矿正常运转起来了就行。那方面的事情我一点都不担心。”

“噢，那行。当然，如果你和你父亲把一切都安排妥当了，那就没有什么可多说的了。”她低声说，脸贴在他宽阔的胸膛上。

“感谢上帝啊！”他说，声音嘶哑，低头吻了她，“那就这么说定了。我要是再待下去，就越难离开了。他们都在峡谷那儿等着我呢。再见啦，亲爱的——再见，再过两个月就又可以看到我啦。”

他一边说着，一边依依不舍地离开了她，跃身上了马，狂奔而去了，连头都没有回一下，好像担心，如果回眸一望，那身后的情形就会令他改变主意。她伫立在门口，目不转睛地看着他，直到他在视线中消失了。她这才转身回到室内，成了整个犹他州最最幸福的姑娘。

Chapter 3 John Ferrier Talks with the Prophet

Three weeks had passed since Jefferson Hope and his comrades had departed from Salt Lake City. John Ferrier's heart was sore within him when he thought of the young man's return, and of the **impending**① loss of his adopted child. Yet her bright and happy face reconciled him to the arrangement more than any argument could have done. He had always determined, deep down in his **resolute**② heart, that nothing would ever induce him to allow his daughter to wed a Mormon. Such a marriage he regarded as no marriage at all, but as a shame and a disgrace. Whatever he might think of the Mormon doctrines, upon that one point he was **inflexible**③. He had to seal his mouth on the subject, however, for to express an **unorthodox**④ opinion was a dangerous matter in those days in the Land of the Saints.

Yes, a dangerous matter—so dangerous that even the most saintly dared only whisper their religious opinions with bated breath, lest something which fell from their lips might be misconstrued, and bring down a swift **retribution**⑤ upon them. The victims of **persecution**⑥ had now turned **persecutors**⑦ on their own account, and persecutors of the most terrible description. Not the Inquisition of Seville, nor the German Vehm-gericht, nor the Secret Societies of Italy, were ever able to put a more formidable machinery in motion than that

第三章 约翰·费里厄同先知的交谈

自从杰弗逊·霍普和他的同伴们离开盐湖城，已经过去三个星期的时间了。约翰·费里厄想到那个年轻人一回来自己就要失去养女，内心就很不是滋味。不过，看到养女那洋溢着喜悦的面容，他就释然了，这种安排比任何说辞都更加有说服力。他意志坚定，早就下定了决心，无论如何，他都不会同意让自己的女儿嫁给一个摩门教徒的。在他看来，与摩门教徒的婚姻压根儿就不是什么婚姻，而是一种羞耻和耻辱。不管他对于摩门教教义有些什么样的看法，但他在这一点上是决不会改变的。然而，他却不得不缄口不言，因为这个时候，在这样一片属于圣徒们的土地上，散布有悖教义的言论是件危险的事情。

对啊，是件危险的事情——非常危险，即便是那些圣徒中的圣徒也都只敢低声屏气地表达自己对宗教看法，唯恐什么话说出口了，结果被人误解，那样就会立刻招致惩罚。曾经遭受迫害的教徒现在已经演变成了迫害别人的人了，其迫害手段之残忍简直难以形容。摩门教徒在犹他州所布下的天罗地网非常可怕，相比之下，塞维利亚的宗教法庭，德国的秘密刑事法庭，意大利秘

① impending [im'pendiŋ] *a.* 即将发生的

② resolute ['rezəlu:t] *a.* 坚决的

③ inflexible [in'fleksəbl] *a.* 坚定不移的

④ unorthodox [ʌn'ɔ:θəˌdɔks] *a.* 异端的

⑤ retribution [ˌretri'bju:ʃən] *n.* 应得的惩罚

⑥ persecution [ˌpə:si'kju:ʃən] *n.* 迫害

⑦ persecutor ['pə:sikju:tə] *n.* 迫害者

which cast a cloud over the State of Utah.

Its invisibility, and the mystery which was attached to it, made this organization doubly terrible. It appeared to be **omniscient**[①] and **omnipotent**[②], and yet was neither seen nor heard. The man who held out against the Church vanished away, and none knew whither he had gone or what had befallen him. His wife and his children awaited him at home, but no father ever returned to tell them how he had fared at the hands of his secret judges. A rash word or a hasty act was followed by **annihilation**[③], and yet none knew what the nature might be of this terrible power which was suspended over them. No wonder that men went about in fear and trembling, and that even in the heart of the wilderness they dared not whisper the doubts which oppressed them.

At first this vague and terrible power was exercised only upon the **recalcitrants**[④] who, having embraced the Mormon faith, wished afterwards to pervert or to abandon it. Soon, however, it took a wider range. The supply of adult women was running short, and **polygamy**[⑤] without a female population on which to draw was a barren doctrine indeed. Strange rumours began to be bandied about—rumours of murdered immigrants and rifled camps in regions where Indians had never been seen. Fresh women appeared in the **harems**[⑥] of the Elders—women who pined and wept, and bore upon their faces the traces of an **unextinguishable**[⑦] horror. Belated wanderers upon the mountains spoke of gangs of armed men, masked, **stealthy**[⑧], and noiseless, who flitted by them in the darkness. These tales and rumours took substance and shape, and were corroborated and re-corroborated, until they resolved themselves into a definite name. To this day, in the lonely ranches of the West, the name of the Danite Band, or the Avenging Angels, is a sinister and an ill-omened one.

Fuller knowledge of the organization which produced such terrible results served to increase rather than to lessen the horror which it inspired in the minds of men. None knew who belonged to this ruthless society. The names of the

密社团，全都无法与之匹敌。

这个组织无影无踪，再加上神秘莫测，这就令它显得加倍地恐怖。它似乎无所不知，无所不能，但其行动人们看不见也听不着。如果有人站出来反对教会，他就会立刻失踪，没有人知道他去哪儿了，也没有人知道其境遇如何。妻儿在家中等待着他，但做父亲的却一去不返，没有人告诉她们他在那些秘密法官的手里遭遇到了什么。不当的言论和不慎的行为都有可能招致灭顶之灾，但却没人知道这种笼罩在头顶上的可怕势力究竟是什么性质的。因此，人人都生活在诚惶诚恐之中，即使在荒郊野外，他们也不敢对压在他们头上的势力低声吐露半点疑虑。

刚开始的时候，这种看不见的恐怖势力只针对叛教者，因为他们先前已经皈依了摩门教，但后来又打算背叛或者放弃摩门教。不过，很快，该组织便扩大了惩处的范围。由于成年妇女数量越来越少，没有可资利用的女性人口，一夫多妻制的教义就形同虚设了。种种怪异的谣言开始四处流传开了——说什么在没有印第安人涉足的区域里出现了遇害的移民和遭到洗劫的营地。长老们的后房里出现了新面孔的女人——她们面容憔悴，哭哭啼啼，脸上惊恐的神色挥之不去。那些在山区里跋涉晚归的人说到，黑暗之中，看见多伙全副武装的人，那些人全都蒙着脸，行动诡秘，悄无声息，从他们的身边一掠而过。这些故事和传言说得有模有样，还经过人们一而再再而三地确认，最后，有了个确切的名字。直到今日，在荒凉的西部大草原上，“丹奈特帮”或者“复仇天使”这个名字仍然是罪恶和不详的代名词。

人们对这样一个酿成恐怖后果的组织有了更加充分的了解之后，在心中激发起的恐怖感只会增加，而不会减少。没有人知道，谁是属于这个残忍无情的团体的。打着宗教的旗号，制造血腥和暴力的事件，其参加者的

① omniscient [ɔm'nisiənt] *a.* 无所不知的
② omnipotent [ɔm'nipətənt] *a.* 全能的
③ annihilation [ə,naiə'leiʃən] *n.* 灭绝
④ recalcitrant [ri'kælsitrənt] *a.* 拒不服从的
⑤ polygamy [pə'ligəmi] *n.* 一夫多妻
⑥ harem ['hɑ:ri:m] *n.* 后宫
⑦ unextinguishable [ʌn,iks'tiŋgwiʃəbl] *a.* 挥之不去的
⑧ stealthy ['stelθi] *a.* 悄悄的

participators in the deeds of blood and violence done under the name of religion were kept profoundly secret. The very friend to whom you communicated your misgivings as to the Prophet and his mission, might be one of those who would come forth at night with fire and sword to exact a terrible **reparation**① . Hence every man feared his neighbour, and none spoke of the things which were nearest his heart.

One fine morning, John Ferrier was about to set out to his wheatfields, when he heard the click of the latch, and, looking through the window, saw a stout, sandy-haired, middle-aged man coming up the pathway. His heart leapt to his mouth, for this was none other than the great Brigham Young himself. Full of **trepidation**② —for he knew that such a visit boded him little good—Ferrier ran to the door to greet the Mormon chief. The latter, however, received his **salutations**③ coldly, and followed him with a stern face into the sitting-room.

"Brother Ferrier," he said, taking a seat, and eyeing the farmer keenly from under his light-coloured **eyelashes**④ , "the true believers have been good friends to you. We picked you up when you were starving in the desert, we shared our food with you, led you safe to the Chosen Valley, gave you a goodly share of land, and allowed you to wax rich under our protection. Is not this so?"

"It is so," answered John Ferrier.

"In return for all this we asked but one condition: that was, that you should embrace the true faith, and conform in every way to its usages. This you promised to do, and this, if common report says truly, you have neglected."

"And how have I neglected it?" asked Ferrier, throwing out his hands in **expostulation**⑤ . "Have I not given to the common fund? Have I not attended at the Temple? Have I not——?"

"Where are your wives?" asked Young, looking round him. "Call them in, that I may greet them."

"It is true that I have not married," Ferrier answered. "But women were

姓名是严格保密的。一旦你向某个朋友表露了自己对先知和其使命的疑虑，夜间可能就有人举着火把和刀剑对你实施惩处，而那个朋友可能在其中。因此，所有人都害怕自己的邻居，谁都不会吐露自己的心声。

① reparation [ˌrepəˈreiʃən] *n.* 惩罚

一个晴朗的早晨，约翰·费里厄正要打算去自己的麦地里，突然听到了门闩咔哒的声音，透过窗户朝外一看，只见一个身体结实、头发淡黄的中年男子顺着小路走过来。他的心提到了嗓子眼了，因为来者不是别人，正是大人物杨百翰本人。费里厄心里充满了惶恐——因为他知道，这样一位头领上门不会是什么好事情——于是，急忙跑到门口去迎接这位摩门教的头领。然而，后者却表现出一副不理不睬的样子，铁青着脸随他走进了客厅。

② trepidation [ˌtrepiˈdeiʃən] *n.* 害怕；颤抖

③ salutation [ˌsæljuˈteiʃən] *n.* 招呼

"费里厄兄弟，"他说着，坐了下来，淡色的睫毛下一双锐利的眼睛盯着对方看，"真诚的信徒们一直把你当朋友看。你在沙漠里忍受着饥饿时，我们收留了你，把我们的食物分给了你，把你安全地带到这个上帝赐予的峡谷，分配给了你一大片土地，还让你在我们的庇护之下慢慢富裕起来了。是不是这么回事？"

④ eyelash [ˈailæʃ] *n.* 睫毛

"是这么回事。"费里厄回答说。

"作为对所有这一切的回报，我们只提了一个条件，那就是，你要皈依真正的宗教信仰，而且身体力行教规。你答应了这么做，而如果人们报告的情况属实的话，你可是忽略这一点了。"

"我怎么忽略了呢？"费里厄问了一声，伸出双手表示争辩，"我没有缴纳公共基金吗？我没有去圣殿朝拜吗？我没有——？"

⑤ expostulation [ikˌspɔstjuˈleiʃən] *n.* 劝告

"你的妻子们在哪儿呢？"扬问，环顾了一下四周，"把她们叫来吧，我要问候她们一声呢。"

"我没有结婚，这是事实，"费里厄回答说，"但是，女人的数量本来就很少，而且许多人比我更有权力娶她

few, and there were many who had better claims than I. I was not a lonely man: I had my daughter to attend to my wants."

"It is of that daughter that I would speak to you," said the leader of the Mormons. "She has grown to be the flower of Utah, and has found favour in the eyes of many who are high in the land."

John Ferrier **groaned**① internally.

"There are stories of her which I would fain disbelieve—stories that she is sealed to some Gentile. This must be the gossip of idle tongues. What is the thirteenth rule in the code of the sainted Joseph Smith? 'Let every maiden of the true faith marry one of the elect; for if she wed a Gentile, she commits a **grievous**② sin.' This being so, it is impossible that you, who profess the holy creed, should suffer your daughter to violate it."

John Ferrier made no answer, but he played nervously with his riding-whip.

"Upon this one point your whole faith shall be tested—so it has been decided in the Sacred Council of Four. The girl is young, and we would not have her wed grey hairs, neither would we **deprive**③ her of all choice. We Elders have many **heifers**④, but our children must also be provided. Stangerson has a son, and Drebber has a son, and either of them would gladly welcome your daughter to their house. Let her choose between them. They are young and rich, and of the true faith. What say you to that?"

Ferrier remained silent for some little time with his brows knitted.

"You will give us time," he said at last. "My daughter is very young—she is **scarce**⑤ of an age to marry."

"She shall have a month to choose," said Young, rising from his seat. "At the end of that time she shall give her answer."

He was passing through the door, when he turned, with flushed face and flashing eyes. "It were better for you, John Ferrier," he thundered, "that you and she were now lying blanched skeletons upon the Sierra Blanco, than that you

们。我并不是孑然一身的人，我有个女儿伺候着我呢。”

“我要来对你说的就是你女儿的事，”摩门教的头领说，“她已长大了，成了犹他之花。有许多身份地位都很高的人看上她啦。”

约翰·费里厄心中暗暗叫苦。

“有关于她的传言，我对此宁可不相信来着——说她同某个异教徒订立了婚约。这一定是那些闲着没事的人生出来的流言蜚语。圣徒约瑟夫·史密斯订立的教规里第十三条是怎么说的？‘每一个具备真正信仰的摩门教未婚女要嫁给上帝的选民。如果她与异教徒通婚，那就犯下了大罪。’上面就是这么说的，你既然信奉这神圣的教义，你就不会容忍你的女儿来亵渎它的。”

约翰·费里厄没有吭声，摆弄着手里的马鞭。

“在这一点上，你的整个信仰都将受到考验——四圣会就是这么决定的。姑娘还很年轻，我们不会让她嫁给头发灰白的老者，也不会剥夺她的全部选择权。我们四位长老已有许多小女子了，但是，我们的孩子们必须要娶妻啊。斯坦格森有个儿子，德雷伯也有个儿子。他们两个人都想把你的女儿娶进门，就让她在他们两个人之间挑选吧。他们既年轻又富有，而且信仰真挚。你觉得怎么样？”

费里厄依沉默了片刻，眉头紧锁。

“您要给我们时间啊，”他最后开口说，“我女儿还很小——她还不到结婚嫁人的年龄呢。”

“给她一个月时间做出选择吧，”扬说着，从坐着的椅子上站起身，“一个月结束时，她可要给出答案啊。”

他正要走出门口，突然转过身来，满脸通红，眼睛闪烁着凶光。“我可告诉你，约翰·费里厄，”他大声吼着，“你和你女儿如果不量力地对抗四圣的命令，还不如当初就躺在布兰科山上，成为两堆白骨的好！”

他用手做了个威胁的动作，转身走了。费里厄只听

① groan [grəun] *v.* 发牢骚

② grievous ['gri:vəs] *a.* 严重的

③ deprive [di'praiv] *v.* 剥夺

④ heifer ['hefə] *n.* 小母牛；（贬）指年轻漂亮的女子

⑤ scarce [skεəs] *a.* 不足的

should put your weak wills against the orders of the Holy Four!"

With a threatening gesture of his hand, he turned from the door, and Ferrier heard his heavy step **scrunching**[①] along the shingly path.

He was still sitting with his elbows upon his knees, considering how he should broach the matter to his daughter, when a soft hand was laid upon his, and looking up, he saw her standing beside him. One glance at her pale, frightened face showed him that she had heard what had passed.

"I could not help it," she said, in answer to his look. "His voice rang through the house. Oh, father, father, what shall we do?"

"Don't you scare yourself," he answered, drawing her to him, and passing his broad, rough hand **caressingly**[②] over her **chestnut**[③] hair. "We'll fix it up somehow or another. You don't find your fancy kind o' lessening for this chap, do you?"

A sob and a squeeze of his hand was her only answer.

"No; of course not. I shouldn't care to hear you say you did. He's a likely lad, and he's a Christian, which is more than these folk here, in spite o' all their praying and **preaching**[④]. There's a party starting for Nevada to-morrow, and I'll manage to send him a message letting him know the hole we are in. If I know anything o' that young man, he'll be back here with a speed that would whip electro-telegraphs."

Lucy laughed through her tears at her father's description.

"When he comes, he will advise us for the best. But it is for you that I am frightened, dear. One hears—one hears such dreadful stories about those who oppose the Prophet: something terrible always happens to them."

"But we haven't opposed him yet," her father answered. "It will be time to look out for **squalls**[⑤] when we do. We have a clear month before us; at the end of that, I guess we had best **shin**[⑥] out of Utah."

"Leave Utah!"

"That's about the size of it."

① scrunch [skrʌntʃ] *v.* 发出咯咯声

② caressingly [kə'resiŋli] *ad.* 爱抚地

③ chestnut ['tʃesnʌt] *a.* 栗色的

④ preaching ['pri:tʃiŋ] *n.* 讲道

⑤ squall [skwɔ:l] *n.* 麻烦事

⑥ shin [ʃin] *v.* 快步走

见他那沉重的脚步踩在砂石路上的咯吱声。

费里厄双肘支在膝头上，呆呆地坐着，心里在思忖着，自己如何开口向女儿说这件事。这时，一只柔软的手搭在了他的手上。他抬起头，看见女儿站立在自己身边。瞥一眼她那苍白而又惊恐的面容，他便知道了，女儿已经听到了刚才说的事情。

"我不听都不行啊，"她说，回应着父亲的注视，"他说话的声音整幢房子都听得见。噢，父亲，父亲，我们该怎么办啊？"

"可别自己吓自己，"他回答说，一边把她拉到自己身边，粗糙的大手抚摸着女儿的栗色头发，"我们总会有办法解决这件事情的。你对那个年轻人的感情不会冷淡，对吧？"

露茜没有回答，不停地抽泣，紧紧地捏住父亲的手。

"对，当然不会。我也不想听到你说会冷淡。他是个招人喜爱的年轻人，还是个基督徒。比起这儿的那些人可强多了，尽管他们又是祈祷又是布道的。明天有一群人要动身去内华达州，我会设法给捎个信儿去，让他知道我们面临的处境。如果我对那个年轻人还有所了解的话，他会快速赶回来，比电报的速度还要快呢。"

露茜听到父亲这么一说，立刻破涕为笑了。

"等到他返回之后，他会拿出最好的办法来的。但是，我担心的是您啊，亲爱的父亲。人们听说过——人们听说过那些有关同先知作对的人的可怕遭遇。发生在他们身上的事情总是令人感到可怕。"

"但是，我们还没有同他作对啊，"她父亲回答说，"我们要那么办，那也得小心谨慎才是。我们还有整整一个月的时间，到一个月结束的时候，我看我们最好逃离犹他。"

"离开犹他！"

"But the farm?"

"We will raise as much as we can in money, and let the rest go. To tell the truth, Lucy, it isn't the first time I have thought of doing it. I don't care about **knuckling**① under to any man, as these folk do to their darned prophet. I'm a free-born American, and it's all new to me. Guess I'm too old to learn. If he comes browsing about this farm, he might chance to run up against a charge of **buckshot**② travelling in the opposite direction."

"But they won't let us leave," his daughter objected.

"Wait till Jefferson comes, and we'll soon manage that. In the meantime, don't you **fret**③ yourself, my dearie, and don't get your eyes swelled up, else he'll be walking into me when he sees you. There's nothing to be afeared about, and there's no danger at all."

John Ferrier uttered these consoling remarks in a very confident tone, but she could not help observing that he paid unusual care to the fastening of the doors that night, and that he carefully cleaned and loaded the rusty old shotgun which hung upon the wall of his bedroom.

“也只能这么办了。”

“那农场呢？”

“我们尽可能变换成现钱，其余的就不管了。实话对你说吧，露茜，我已经不是头一回想到要这样做了。那些人对那个该死的先知卑躬屈膝，但我不想对任何人低三下四。我是个生而自由的美国人，这样的情况从未见过。估计是我年岁太大了，也学不来。如果他再到这个农场到处荡来荡去，没准迎面向他飞来的就是一颗大号枪子儿呢。”

“但是，他们不会放我们走的。”女儿争辩说。

“等杰弗逊回来，我们很快就可以安排这事。这段时间里，你就不用烦心劳神了，宝贝儿，可别把眼睛哭肿了，不然的话，等他回来见你这模样，可是会找我算账的。没什么好担心的，没事的。”

约翰·费里厄对女儿说这些安慰的话时，语气中充满了自信。但就在那天夜里，她注意到父亲的举动显得不同寻常了。他谨慎小心地拴紧了所有的门，把卧室墙上那支生锈的猎枪仔仔细细地擦拭一新，装上了子弹。

① knuckle ['nʌkl] *v.* 屈服

② buckshot ['bʌkʃɔt] *n.* 大铅弹

③ fret [fret] *v.* 使焦急

Chapter 4 A Flight for Life

On the morning which followed his interview with the Mormon Prophet, John Ferrier went in to Salt Lake City, and having found his acquaintance, who was **bound**[①] for the Nevada Mountains, he entrusted him with his message to Jefferson Hope. In it he told the young man of the **imminent**[②] danger which threatened them, and how necessary it was that he should return. Having done thus he felt easier in his mind, and returned home with a lighter heart.

As he approached his farm, he was surprised to see a horse hitched to each of the posts of the gate. Still more surprised was he on entering to find two young men in possession of his sitting-room. One, with a long pale face, was leaning back in the rocking-chair, with his feet cocked up upon the stove. The other, a bull-necked youth with coarse **bloated**[③] features, was standing in front of the window with his hands in his pocket, whistling a popular hymn. Both of them nodded to Ferrier as he entered, and the one in the rocking-chair commenced the conversation.

"Maybe you don't know us," he said. "This here is the son of Elder Drebber, and I'm Joseph Stangerson, who travelled with you in the desert when the Lord stretched out His hand and gathered you into the true fold."

"As He will all the nations in His own good time," said the other in a **nasal**[④] voice; "He grindeth slowly but exceeding small."

第四章　启程逃亡

同摩门教先知见面后的第二天早晨，约翰·费里厄便出发去了盐湖城。他找到那个马上要出发去内华达山区的熟人之后，便托他给杰弗逊·霍普带封信过去。他在信中告诉年轻人，他们正危险临头，他必须要赶回来。办妥了这件事之后，他心里感到轻松了些，心情愉快地回了家。

① bound [baund] *a.* 打算前往的

② imminent ['iminənt] *a.* 迫在眉睫的

就在他快要到达自己的农庄时，他突然惊讶地看到，大门口的两个柱子上各拴着一匹马。进到室内后，更加令他感到惊讶的是，客厅里面坐着两个年轻人。一个长着一张长而苍白的脸，身子斜靠在摇椅里，两只脚翘起来搁在火炉上。另一个长着像牛一样的粗脖子，五官粗糙臃肿，站立在窗户前，双手插在衣服口袋里，嘴里吹着流行的圣歌。两个人看见费里厄进门便朝着他点了点头。坐在摇椅上的那位先开口说话。

③ bloated ['bləutid] *a.* 浮肿的

"您可能还不认识我们，"他说，"这位是德雷伯长老的儿子，我是约瑟夫·斯坦格森。当上帝伸手把你们引入这个真正的教会时，我曾经和你们一道在沙漠里跋涉来着。"

"上帝将会按照他自己选择的佳期把所有民族引入真正的教会，"另一个说，鼻音很重，"他行动速度虽然缓慢，但特别细致。"

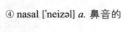

④ nasal ['neizəl] *a.* 鼻音的

John Ferrier bowed coldly. He had guessed who his visitors were.

"We have come," continued Stangerson, "at the advice of our fathers to **solicit**[①] the hand of your daughter for whichever of us may seem good to you and to her. As I have but four wives and Brother Drebber here has seven, it appears to me that my claim is the stronger one."

"Nay, nay, Brother Stangerson," cried the other; "the question is not how many wives we have, but how many we can keep. My father has now given over his mills to me, and I am the richer man."

"But my prospects are better," said the other, warmly. "When the Lord removes my father, I shall have his **tanning**[②] yard and his leather factory. Then I am your elder, and am higher in the Church."

"It will be for the maiden to decide," rejoined young Drebber, **smirking**[③] at his own reflection in the glass. "We will leave it all to her decision."

During this dialogue, John Ferrier had stood fuming in the doorway, hardly able to keep his riding-whip from the backs of his two visitors.

"Look here," he said at last, striding up to them, "when my daughter summons you, you can come, but until then I don't want to see your faces again."

The two young Mormons stared at him in amazement. In their eyes this competition between them for the maiden's hand was the highest of honours both to her and her father.

"There are two ways out of the room," cried Ferrier; "there is the door, and there is the window. Which do you care to use?"

His brown face looked so **savage**[④], and his gaunt hands so threatening, that his visitors sprang to their feet and beat a hurried **retreat**[⑤]. The old farmer followed them to the door.

"Let me know when you have settled which it is to be," he said, sardonically.

"You shall smart for this!" Stangerson cried, white with rage. "You have defied the Prophet and the Council of Four. You shall **rue**[⑥] it to the end of your

约翰·费里厄冷漠地鞠了一躬，因为已经猜出他的客人是什么人了。

“我们来到这儿，”斯坦格森接着说，“是奉了我们父亲的命，向您女儿求婚的，看看您和她觉得我们中哪一位更加合意。由于我只有四位妻子，这位德雷伯兄弟已经有七位了，看起来，我求婚的理由更加充分一些。”

“不对，不对，斯坦格森兄弟，”另一个大声说，“问题的关键不在于我们有多少位妻子，而在于我们能够养得起多少位。我父亲已经把他的多座磨坊交给我了，所以，我是个更加富有的人。”

“但是，我的前景更加美好，”斯坦格森说着，情绪激动起来了，“等到上帝把我父亲召唤去了之后，我将拥有他的鞣皮工场和制革工厂。还有就是，我资格比你老，在教会的地位比你高”

“那要看姑娘怎么决定，”小德雷伯接话说，对着玻璃上映照出的自己的形象傻笑起来，“我们还是让她自己来决定吧。”

两位一来一去说着这些话的当儿，约翰·费里厄站在门口，非常气愤，好不容易才克制住了自己，没有用手上的鞭子往客人身上抽。

“听好啦，”他最后说，大步朝他们走过去，“我女儿招呼你们来，你们才可以来，但是，在那之前，我不想再看到你们的面孔。”

两个年轻的摩门教徒惊愕地盯住他看。在他们的眼中，他们这样争着来向姑娘求婚，对她和她父亲都是至高无上的荣耀。

“离开这间房子有两种途径可供选择，”费里厄大声说，“一种是从门口走出去，一种是从窗户被扔出去，你们选择哪一种？”

他棕褐色的脸庞显得非常凶狠，瘦骨嶙峋的双手显得很有攻击力，两个客人见状一跃站起身来，拔腿就

① solicit [sə'lisit] *v.* 恳求

② tanning ['tæniŋ] *n.* 制革

③ smirk [smə:k] *v.* 傻笑

④ savage ['sævidʒ] *a.* 凶猛的

⑤ retreat [ri'tri:t] *n.* 后退

⑥ rue [ru:] *v.* 对…感到后悔

days."

"The hand of the Lord shall be heavy upon you," cried young Drebber; "He will arise and **smite**[①] you!"

"Then I'll start the smiting," exclaimed Ferrier furiously, and would have rushed upstairs for his gun had not Lucy seized him by the arm and restrained him. Before he could escape from her, the **clatter**[②] of horses' hoofs told him that they were beyond his reach.

"The young canting **rascals**[③]!" he exclaimed, wiping the perspiration from his forehead; "I would sooner see you in your grave, my girl, than the wife of either of them."

"And so should I, father," she answered, with spirit; "but Jefferson will soon be here."

"Yes. It will not be long before he comes. The sooner the better, for we do not know what their next move may be."

It was, indeed, high time that someone capable of giving advice and help should come to the aid of the **sturdy**[④] old farmer and his adopted daughter. In the whole history of the settlement there had never been such a case of rank **disobedience**[⑤] to the authority of the Elders. If minor errors were punished so sternly, what would be the fate of this arch rebel? Ferrier knew that his wealth and position would be of no avail to him. Others as well known and as rich as himself had been spirited away before now, and their goods given over to the Church. He was a brave man, but he trembled at the vague, shadowy terrors which hung over him. Any known danger he could face with a firm lip, but this suspense was **unnerving**.[⑥] He **concealed**[⑦] his fears from his daughter, however, and affected to make light of the whole matter, though she, with the keen eye of love, saw plainly that he was ill at ease.

He expected that he would receive some message or **remonstrance**[⑧] from Young as to his conduct, and he was not mistaken, though it came in an

跑。老农跟随他们到了门口。

“你们决定了哪一种，请告诉我一声，”他用揶揄的口吻说。

“你会因此而付出代价的！”斯坦格森大声说，气得脸色煞白的，“你公然藐视先知和四圣会，会后悔一辈子的！”

“上帝会对你下很手的，”小德雷伯大声说，“他会现身把你给灭了！”

“那就让我先开始灭了你们吧，”费里厄情绪激动，大声吼着，若不是露茜一把拽住了他的胳膊，把他给拦住了，他准会冲上楼去拿枪了。等他从露茜的手中挣脱出来，只听得马蹄声，知道他们已走远了，追不上了。

“两个满嘴伪善言辞的小无赖！”他一边情绪激动地说，一边擦着额头上的汗珠，“女儿啊，我宁可看见你死去，也不愿让看到你嫁给他们中的任何一个。”

“我也宁可这样，父亲，”她说着，语气坚定，“不过，杰弗逊很快就会到这儿来了。”

“是啊，他过不了多久就会到。越快越好啊，因为我们不知道他们下一步会采取什么样的行动。”

确实，在眼下这个节骨眼上，性格坚毅的老农和他的养女需要有人能够出主意，提供帮助。这个居民点有史以来，还从未出现过这样的公然藐视长老权威的事情。如果说连微不足道的小过失都要受到严厉的惩罚，那这种大逆不道的冒犯还不知道将要面临什么样的命运呢？费里厄心里清楚，他的财富和地位帮不上任何忙。先前另外一些像他拥有同样的声望和同样的财富的人就被神不知鬼不觉地带走了，其财产收缴给了教会。他是个勇敢无畏的人，但当这种朦胧未知的恐怖悬在头顶上时，也会感到不寒而栗。对于任何出现在明处的危险，他可以坚定面对，但这种提心吊胆的状况却令他非常不安。尽管他不想让女儿知道自己内心的恐惧，极力装出

① smite [smait] *v.* 毁灭

② clatter ['klætə] *n.* （马蹄的）嘚嘚声

③ rascal ['rɑ:skl] *n.* 流氓

④ sturdy ['stə:di] *a.* 强壮的

⑤ disobedience [ˌdisə'bi:diəns] *n.* 违背

⑥ unnerving [ˌʌn'nə:viŋ] *a.* 使人紧张不安的

⑦ conceal [kən'si:l] *v.* 隐藏

⑧ remonstrance [ri'mɔnstrəns] *n.* 抗议；告诫

unlooked-for manner. Upon rising next morning he found, to his surprise, a small square of paper pinned on to the **coverlet**① of his bed just over his chest. On it was printed, in bold straggling letters:—

"Twenty-nine days are given you for amendment, and then——"

The dash was more fear-inspiring than any threat could have been. How this warning came into his room puzzled John Ferrier sorely, for his servants slept in an **outhouse**②, and the doors and windows had all been secured. He **crumpled**③ the paper up and said nothing to his daughter, but the incident struck a chill into his heart. The twenty-nine days were evidently the balance of the month which Young had promised. What strength or courage could avail against an enemy armed with such mysterious powers? The hand which fastened that pin might have struck him to the heart, and he could never have known who had slain him.

Still more shaken was he next morning. They had sat down to their breakfast when Lucy with a cry of surprise pointed upwards. In the centre of the ceiling was scrawled, with a burned stick apparently, the number 28. To his daughter it was unintelligible, and he did not enlighten her. That night he sat up with his gun and kept watch and ward. He saw and he heard nothing, and yet in the morning a great 27 had been painted upon the outside of his door.

Thus day followed day; and as sure as morning came he found that his unseen enemies had kept their register, and had marked up in some conspicuous position how many days were still left to him out of the month of grace. Sometimes the fatal numbers appeared upon the walls, sometimes upon the floors, occasionally they were on small placards stuck upon the garden gate or the railings. With all his **vigilance**④ John Ferrier could not discover whence these daily warnings proceeded. A horror which was almost superstitious came upon him at the sight of them. He became **haggard**⑤ and restless, and his eyes

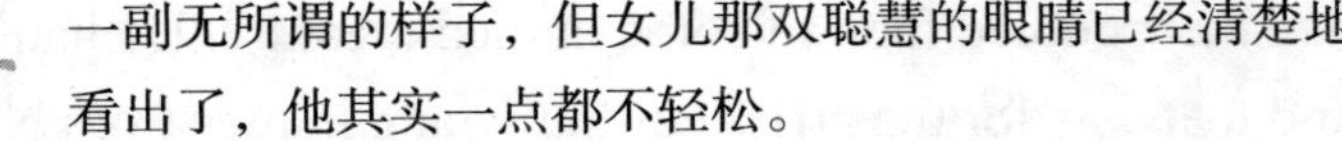

一副无所谓的样子，但女儿那双聪慧的眼睛已经清楚地看出了，他其实一点都不轻松。

他知道，针对自己的这样行为，扬百翰定会传来某种信息或者警示。他的看法没有错，只不过其方式方法出乎了他的想象。翌日早晨，他刚一起床就惊讶地发现，他胸口位置的被子上钉着一张方形小纸条，上面歪歪扭扭地用黑体写着这样一些字：

限二十九天之内改邪归正，否则——

这个破折号比任何威胁都更加令人毛骨悚然。警示是如何放进房间的呢？约翰·费里厄百思不得其解。他的佣人全都睡在外室，全部门窗都关得严严的。他把纸条揉成一团，没有对女儿吭一声，但这事使他胆战心惊。二十九天显然就是给予的最后期限。需要怎样的力量和勇气才能对付得了这样一个拥有神秘力量的敌人呢？那只手可以把纸条扎在被褥上，也完全可以扎进他的心脏，而他却根本就不会知道谋杀自己的人是谁。

接下来的那个早晨，他更加感到胆战心惊了。他们坐下来用早餐，突然，露茜惊叫了起来，手向上指着。天花板的中间潦潦草草地写着“二十八”这个数字，显然是用燃烧过的木棒写的。女儿不明白这个数字是什么意思，他并没有向她点破。当晚，他拿着枪守了一夜，但既没听见也没看见什么异常的情况。而翌日清晨，他家的门上却写着大大的“二十七”这个数字。

就这样，日子一天连着一天过去了。就像早晨一定会到来一样，他发现，自己看不见的敌人一直不停地在数着日子，而且会在某个显眼的地方标示，给他宽限的一个月还剩下多少天。命运攸关的数字有时候出现在墙壁上，有时候出现在地板上，偶尔还会用小字条贴在花

① coverlet ['kʌvəlit] *n.* 床罩

② outhouse ['authaus] *n.* 外屋

③ crumple ['krʌmpl] *v.* 弄皱

④ vigilance ['vidʒiləns] *n.* 警觉

⑤ haggard ['hægəd] *a.* 憔悴的

had the troubled look of some hunted creature. He had but one hope in life now, and that was for the arrival of the young hunter from Nevada.

Twenty had changed to fifteen and fifteen to ten, but there was no news of the absentee. One by one the numbers **dwindled**[①] down, and still there came no sign of him. Whenever a horseman clattered down the road, or a driver shouted at his team, the old farmer hurried to the gate, thinking that help had arrived at last. At last, when he saw five give way to four and that again to three, he lost heart, and abandoned all hope of escape. Singlehanded, and with his limited knowledge of the mountains which surrounded the settlement, he knew that he was powerless. The more-frequented roads were strictly watched and guarded, and none could pass along them without an order from the Council. Turn which way he would, there appeared to be no avoiding the blow which hung over him. Yet the old man never wavered in his resolution to part with life itself before he consented to what he regarded as his daughter's **dishonour**[②].

He was sitting alone one evening pondering deeply over his troubles, and searching **vainly**[③] for some way out of them. That morning had shown the figure 2 upon the wall of his house, and the next day would be the last of the allotted time. What was to happen then? All manner of vague and terrible fancies filled his imagination. And his daughter—what was to become of her after he was gone? Was there no escape from the invisible network which was drawn all round them? He sank his head upon the table and sobbed at the thought of his own **impotence**[④].

What was that? In the silence he heard a gentle scratching sound—low, but very distinct in the quiet of the night. It came from the door of the house. Ferrier crept into the hall and listened intently. There was a pause for a few moments, and then the low **insidious**[⑤] sound was repeated. Someone was evidently tapping very gently upon one of the panels of the door. Was it some midnight assassin who had come to carry out the murderous orders of the secret **tribunal**[⑥]? Or was it some agent who was marking up that the last day of grace had arrived? John Ferrier felt that instant death would be better than the

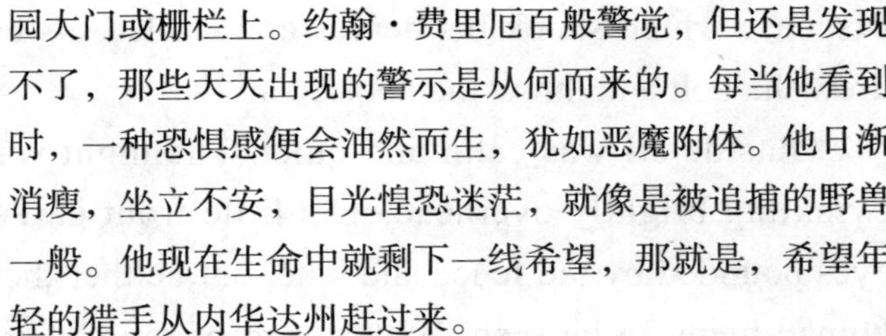

园大门或栅栏上。约翰·费里厄百般警觉，但还是发现不了，那些天天出现的警示是从何而来的。每当他看到时，一种恐惧感便会油然而生，犹如恶魔附体。他日渐消瘦，坐立不安，目光惶恐迷茫，就像是被追捕的野兽一般。他现在生命中就剩下一线希望，那就是，希望年轻的猎手从内华达州赶过来。

二十天变成了十五天，十五天变成了十天，但迟迟未到的人依旧杳无音信。数字一天比一天更小，但还是不见他的影子。每当有人骑着马在大路上发出嘚嘚的马蹄声，或者赶车人冲着牲口大声吆喝，老农就会赶紧跑到门口张望，以为救兵终于到来了。最后，他看到日子五天变成四天，然后又变成三天，这时候，他心灰意冷了，几乎放弃了逃跑的希望了。一个人单枪匹马的，又不熟悉居民点周围山区的情况，他知道自己是跑不掉的。平常走的大路肯定被严密监视和把守着，没有“四圣会”的命令，谁都过不去。无论他想什么办法，都无法躲过临头的灾祸。然而，老人矢志不移，即便丢失掉性命，也决不会同意让自己的女儿蒙受耻辱。

一天傍晚，他独自一人坐着，满脑子想着自己的麻烦事，绞尽了脑汁也没有想出一个解决问题的办法来。当天早晨，他家房屋的墙壁上出现了数字“二”。次日就是宽限时间的最后一天了。到时会出现什么情况啊？他的思绪中充满了各种各样的模糊不清而又恐怖可怕的情景。而他的女儿——如果自己死了，她会怎么样呢？难道就毫无办法逃脱笼罩在他们身上的这张无形的网吗？想到自己无能为力，他把头伏在桌子上，哭泣了起来。

什么声音？寂静之中，他听见一阵轻柔的刮擦声——声音微弱，但是，在万籁寂静的夜晚，显得很清晰。声音是从房门边传来的。费里厄蹑手蹑脚走到厅堂，凝神静听。微弱可怕的声音停顿了片刻，然后又响了起来。很显然，有人在轻轻地敲击门板，难道是刺客

① dwindle ['dwindl] *v.* 减少

② dishonor [dis'ɔnə] *n.* 不名誉的事

③ vainly ['veinli] *ad.* 徒劳地

④ impotence['impətəns] *n.* 无能为力

⑤ insidious [in'sidiəs] *a.* 潜伏的

⑥ tribunal [trai'bju:nəl] *n.* 特别法庭

suspense which shook his nerves and chilled his heart. Springing forward he drew the bolt and threw the door open.

Outside all was calm and quiet. The night was fine, and the stars were twinkling brightly overhead. The little front garden lay before the farmer's eyes bounded by the fence and gate, but neither there nor on the road was any human being to be seen. With a sigh of relief, Ferrier looked to right and to left, until, happening to glance straight down at his own feet, he saw to his astonishment a man lying flat upon his face upon the ground, with arms and legs all asprawl.

So unnerved was he at the sight that he leaned up against the wall with his hand to his throat to **stifle**① his **inclination**② to call out. His first thought was that the **prostrate**③ figure was that of some wounded or dying man, but as he watched it he saw it **writhe**④ along the ground and into the hall with the rapidity and noiselessness of a serpent. Once within the house the man sprang to his feet, closed the door, and revealed to the astonished farmer the fierce face and resolute expression of Jefferson Hope.

"Good God!" gasped John Ferrier. "How you scared me! Whatever made you come in like that."

"Give me food," the other said, **hoarsely**⑤. "I have had no time for bite or sup for eight-and-forty hours." He flung himself upon the cold meat and bread which were still lying upon the table from his host's supper, and **devoured**⑥ it **voraciously**⑦. "Does Lucy bear up well?" he asked, when he had satisfied his hunger.

"Yes. She does not know the danger," her father answered.

"That is well. The house is watched on every side. That is why I crawled my way up to it. They may be darned sharp, but they're not quite sharp enough to catch a Washoe hunter."

John Ferrier felt a different man now that he realized that he had a devoted ally. He seized the young man's leathery hand and wrung it cordially. "You're a man to be proud of," he said. "There are not many who would come to share

半夜前来执行秘密法庭的暗杀指令吗？还是那人又来写那限期规定的最后一个天数呢？约翰·费里厄觉得，整天提心吊胆，神经受折磨，心里发毛，还不如痛快地死了好。他一跃身子向前，拉开了门闩，猛然打开了门。

门外悄无声息，一片宁静。夜空晴好，群星闪烁。门前的小花园呈现在老农的眼前，他看得清周围的栅栏和大门，但无论是花园里还是大路上都没有出现一个人影儿。费里厄舒了一口气，左右打量了一番，最后眼睛不经意地瞥了一下自己的脚下，令他大吃了一惊，因为他看到有个人趴在地上，四肢张开。

眼前的情景令他失魂落魄，他不由得把身子斜靠在了墙上，一只手扼住自己的喉咙，以免叫喊出声音来。他心中闪过的第一个念头是，眼前趴在地上的人可能受了伤，或者奄奄一息了。但是，在他注目看时，他看到那人匍匐着向前爬，像蛇一样迅速悄无声息地爬进了厅堂。一进到屋里，他就站了起来，关上了门。老农很是惊讶，出现在眼前的一张粗狂的脸庞和一副坚毅刚强的神态，原来是杰弗逊·霍普。

① stifle ['staifl] *v.* 遏制
② inclination [ˌinkli'neiʃən] *n.* 倾向
③ prostate ['prɔstreit] *a.* 卧倒的
④ writhe [raið] *v.* 扭动

“天哪！”约翰·费里厄喘着粗气说，“看你把我给吓得！你怎么会这样进来？”

“给我点吃的，”对方说，嗓门嘶哑，“我已经四十八个小时没吃没喝了。”他看见主人的晚餐还摆放在餐桌上，便扑到了那些冷肉和面包面前，狼吞虎咽地吃了起来。“露茜还好吗？”他吃饱了之后问。

⑤ hoarsely [hɔːsli] *ad.* 嘶哑的
⑥ devour [di'vauə] *v.* 狼吞虎咽
⑦ voraciously [və'reiʃəsli] *ad.* 贪婪地

“还好，她不知道这些危险。”做父亲的回答说。

“那就好。这幢房子四面八方都被人监视起来了，所以我要匍匐着爬过来。他们或许精明过人，但想要逮住一位瓦休的猎手，还差了点儿。”

约翰·费里厄意识到自己有了忠实的帮手了，所以觉得像是换了个人似的，热情洋溢地握住年轻人粗糙的手，久久不放。“你真是个了不起的人啊，”他说，“我

our danger and our troubles."

"You've hit it there, pard," the young hunter answered. "I have a respect for you, but if you were alone in this business I'd think twice before I put my head into such a **hornet's**[①] nest. It's Lucy that brings me here, and before harm comes on her I guess there will be one less o' the Hope family in Utah."

"What are we to do?"

"To-morrow is your last day, and unless you act to-night you are lost. I have a mule and two horses waiting in the Eagle Ravine. How much money have you?"

"Two thousand dollars in gold, and five in notes."

"That will do. I have as much more to add to it. We must push for Carson City through the mountains. You had best wake Lucy. It is as well that the servants do not sleep in the house."

While Ferrier was absent, preparing his daughter for the approaching journey, Jefferson Hope packed all the eatables that he could find into a small parcel, and filled a **stoneware**[②] jar with water, for he knew by experience that the mountain wells were few and far between. He had hardly completed his arrangements before the farmer returned with his daughter all dressed and ready for a start. The greeting between the lovers was warm, but brief, for minutes were precious, and there was much to be done.

"We must make our start at once," said Jefferson Hope, speaking in a low but resolute voice, like one who realizes the greatness of the peril, but has steeled his heart to meet it. "The front and back entrances are watched, but with caution we may get away through the side window and across the fields. Once on the road we are only two miles from the Ravine where the horses are waiting. By daybreak we should be half-way through the mountains."

"What if we are stopped?" asked Ferrier.

Hope slapped the revolver **butt**[③] which protruded from the front of his tunic. "If they are too many for us, we shall take two or three of them with us,"

们面临着危险和困境，过来分担解围的人可不多啊。”

“您说得对，老人家，”年轻的猎手回答说，“我很崇敬您，但是，如果这件事情就只涉及到您一个人，那在我把头钻进这个大黄蜂窝之前，倒是再三思量一番的。是因为有露茜我这才赶过来的，我看，在他们得手以前，我就能和露茜远走高飞了，尤他州也就少了一户姓霍普的人家。”

① hornet ['hɔ:nit] *n.*大黄蜂

“我们现在怎么办？”

“明天是你们最后的期限了，今晚如果不采取行动那就不行了。我准备好了一头骡子和两匹马，在鹰谷那边候着呢。您手边有多少现钱？”

“两千元金币和五千元纸币。”

“足够了，我拥有的数目更大一些，可以合在一起。我们必须得翻山越岭赶到卡森城去。您最好去把露茜叫醒。还好佣人没有睡在这幢房子里。”

费里厄出去了，去叫醒女儿做好准备上路，这期间，杰弗逊·霍普把室内能找到的全部食物包成一个小包裹，还把一个粗陶罐装满了水。因为根据经验，他知道，山区水井极少，而且水井与水井之间距离遥远。他刚刚把这些东西收拾妥当，老农便就领着女儿出现了，穿戴好了，准备出发。两个恋人见面后相互间亲切问候，但只是短短几句话，分分秒秒都弥足珍贵，要做的事情还很多。

② stoneware ['stəun,wεə] *n.* 石器

“我们必须立刻出发，”杰弗逊·霍普说，说话的声音很低沉，但语气坚定，就好像是意识到了危险重重，但铁了心要去面对，“前门和后门都有人监视，但如果小心谨慎的话，我们可以从旁边的窗户出去，然后穿过田地。一旦到了大路上，只需要再走两英里路程，我们就可以到达鹰谷了，马匹在那儿等待着呢。到天亮时，我们应该走过了一半山路。”

“如果有人阻拦，那怎么办？”费里厄问。

③ butt [bʌt] *n.* 枪柄

霍普拍了拍从上衣前面露出来的手枪枪柄。“如果

he said with a sinister smile.

The lights inside the house had all been extinguished, and from the darkened window Ferrier peered over the fields which had been his own, and which he was now about to abandon forever. He had long nerved himself to the sacrifice, however, and the thought of the honour and happiness of his daughter outweighed any regret at his ruined fortunes. All looked so peaceful and happy, the **rustling**① trees and the broad silent **stretch**② of grain-land, that it was difficult to realize that the spirit of murder lurked through it all. Yet the white face and set expression of the young hunter showed that in his approach to the house he had seen enough to satisfy him upon that head.

Ferrier carried the bag of gold and notes, Jefferson Hope had the **scanty**③ provisions and water, while Lucy had a small bundle containing a few of her more valued possessions. Opening the window very slowly and carefully, they waited until a dark cloud had somewhat obscured the night, and then one by one passed through into the little garden. With bated breath and crouching figures they stumbled across it, and gained the shelter of the hedge, which they skirted until they came to the gap which opened into the cornfields. They had just reached this point when the young man seized his two companions and dragged them down into the shadow, where they lay silent and **trembling**④.

It was as well that his **prairie**⑤ training had given Jefferson Hope the ears of a lynx. He and his friends had hardly crouched down before the melancholy hooting of a mountain owl was heard within a few yards of them, which was immediately answered by another hoot at a small distance. At the same moment a vague shadowy figure emerged from the gap for which they had been making, and uttered the **plaintive**⑥ signal cry again, on which a second man appeared out of the obscurity.

"To-morrow at midnight," said the first, who appeared to be in authority. "When the Whip-poor-Will calls three times."

"It is well," returned the other. "Shall I tell Brother Drebber?"

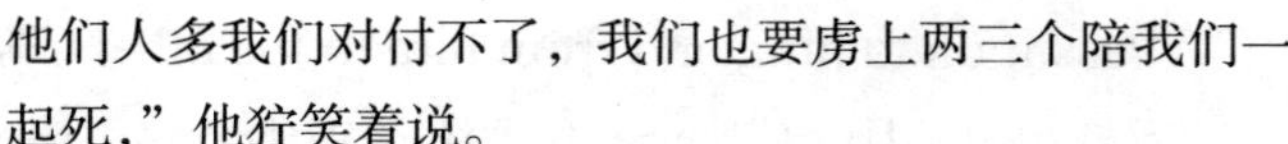

他们人多我们对付不了，我们也要虏上两三个陪我们一起死，”他狞笑着说。

室内的灯光全部熄灭了，透过黑暗的窗户口，费里厄张望着外面的田地，眼前的田地曾经是属于他的，但现在就要永远舍弃了。不过，他早就鼓足了勇气，做好了舍弃的准备。一想到自己女儿的名誉和福祉，失去财产的事，也就没有什么好遗憾的了。一切都显得如此平静祥和，树影婆娑，宽阔的田地一片静谧，很难想象，杀戮的幽灵竟然潜藏在一切的背后。然而，年轻猎手惨白的面容和凝重的表情表明，他在接近这幢住宅时，已经见识够多了，这里的险恶情况，心里面已经有底了。

费里厄提着装满金币和钞票的钱袋，杰弗逊·霍普拿着很少的一点食物和水，而露茜则提着一个小包，里面装着她的一些比较值钱的物品。他们动作缓慢，小心翼翼，把窗户打开了，等待着，直到有一片乌云遮蔽住了夜空，这才一个接着一个地爬出窗户，进入到小花园里。他们屏住呼吸，猫着身子，跌跌撞撞地走过了花园，隐身树篱边，紧贴着树篱向前走，最后到达了一个缺口，通向玉米地。他们刚刚到了缺口处，突然，年轻人猛然抓住自己的两个同伴，把他们拽到了阴暗处，待在那儿默不作声，浑身颤抖。

还算好，杰弗逊·霍普在大草原经受了训练，有了山猫一样灵敏的耳朵。他和两个同伴刚刚蹲下身子，离他们几码远的地方便传来了一只山鸮枭凄厉的鸣叫声，紧接着，不远处传来另一个应和的鸣叫声。同一时刻，一个朦胧的身影出现在他们刚才准备穿过的缺口，又一次发出了那种作为信号的凄厉鸣叫声，声音响过之后，另一个人从黑暗中走了出来。

“明天半夜时分，”第一个人说，他似乎是个领头的，“三声夜鹰鸣叫三声为号。”

“那好，”另一人回答说，“我要跟德雷伯兄弟说一

① rustle ['rʌsl] *v.* 发出沙沙的声音

② stretch [stretʃ] *n.* 延亘，连绵

③ scanty ['skænti] *a.* 勉强够的

④ trembling ['trembliŋ] *a.* 发抖的

⑤ prairie ['preəri] *n.* 大草原

⑥ plaintive ['pleintiv] *a.* 哀怨的

"Pass it on to him, and from him to the others. Nine to seven!"

"Seven to five!" repeated the other; and the two figures flitted away in different directions. Their concluding words had evidently been some form of sign and **countersign**[①]. The instant that their footsteps had died away in the distance, Jefferson Hope sprang to his feet, and helping his companions through the gap, led the way across the fields at the top of his speed, supporting and half-carrying the girl when her strength appeared to fail her.

"Hurry on! hurry on!" he gasped from time to time. "We are through the line of **sentinels**[②]. Everything depends on speed. Hurry on!"

Once on the high road, they made rapid progress. Only once did they meet anyone, and then they managed to slip into a field, and so avoid recognition. Before reaching the town the hunter branched away into a rugged and narrow footpath which led to the mountains. Two dark, jagged peaks loomed above them through the darkness, and the **defile**[③] which led between them was the Eagle Canon in which the horses were awaiting them. With unerring instinct Jefferson Hope picked his way among the great boulders and along the bed of a dried-up watercourse, until he came to the retired corner, screened with rocks, where the faithful animals had been **picketed**[④]. The girl was placed upon the mule, and old Ferrier upon one of the horses, with his money-bag, while Jefferson Hope led the other along the **precipitous**[⑤] and dangerous path.

It was a bewildering route for anyone who was not accustomed to face Nature in her wildest moods. On the one side a great crag towered up a thousand feet or more, black, stern, and menacing, with long **basaltic**[⑥] columns upon its rugged surface like the ribs of some petrified monster. On the other hand a wild chaos of boulders and **debris**[⑦] made all advance impossible. Between the two ran the irregular track, so narrow in places that they had to travel in Indian file, and so rough that only practised riders could have traversed it at all. Yet in spite of all dangers and difficulties, the hearts of the **fugitives**[⑧]

声吗？”

“把这个传给他，再由他传给其他人。七点差九分！”

“五点差七分！”另一个回应了一声，然后两个人朝着不同的方向离开了。他们最后说的话显然是一种问答式的暗号。他们的脚步声刚刚消失在远处的一瞬间，杰弗逊·霍普一跃身子站了起来，搀扶着他的两位同伴穿过缺口。领着他们以最快的速度穿过麦地，看到姑娘似乎有点支撑不住时，便半扶半拽着她。

“快点！快点！”他时不时地喘着粗气说，“我们已经穿过警戒线了，一切都取决于我们的速度啦，快点！”

到了大路之后，他们行进的速度很快。他们只遇到过一次人，当时设法躲闪进了一块地里，所以没有被人发现。到达城镇前夕，年轻的猎手拐进了一条通向山里的狭窄崎岖的小路。透过夜幕，他们的眼前耸立着两座黑压压的嶙峋山峰，中间那条狭窄的山道通向鹰谷，马匹就在那儿等候着。杰弗逊·霍普凭着准确无误的本能，在巨石从中，顺着一条干涸的河床，选择了一条路前行，终于到达了一个巨石遮蔽的僻静处，那儿匹忠实的牲口就拴在此地。姑娘被扶上了骡子，老费里厄被扶上两匹马中的一匹，装钱的口袋由他拿着，杰弗逊·霍普则骑上了另一匹马，沿着陡峻险恶的小路前行。

对任何人而言，如果他不熟悉大自然狂野不羁的习性，这条路会令他眼花缭乱。山路的一侧耸立着一堵上千英尺的悬崖峭壁，昏暗黑压，巍峨陡峻，气势汹汹。参差嶙峋的表面耸立着一根根玄武长柱，犹如某种成了化石的巨型怪兽的肋骨。山路的另一侧乱石嶙峋，根本无法通行。中间隐约可见的小道非常狭窄，很多地方只能一前一后纵身前行。山路非常颠簸，没有高超的骑术根本无法通行。然而，尽管有这么多的危险和困难，但

① countersign ['kauntəsain] n. 口令

② sentinel ['sentinəl] n. 岗哨

③ defile [di'fail] n. 峡谷

④ picket ['pikit] v. （把马等）系在桩上

⑤ precipitous [pri'sipitəs] a. 险峻的

⑥ basaltic [bə'sɔ:ltik] a. 玄武岩的

⑦ debris [də'bri:] n. 岩石

⑧ fugitive ['fju:dʒitiv] n. 逃命者

were light within them, for every step increased the distance between them and the terrible despotism from which they were flying.

They soon had a proof, however, that they were still within the jurisdiction of the Saints. They had reached the very wildest and most **desolate**[①] portion of the pass when the girl gave a **startled**[②] cry, and pointed upwards. On a rock which overlooked the track, showing out dark and plain against the sky, there stood a solitary **sentinel**[③]. He saw them as soon as they perceived him, and his military challenge of "Who goes there?" rang through the silent ravine.

"Travellers for Nevada," said Jefferson Hope, with his hand upon the rifle which hung by his saddle.

They could see the lonely watcher fingering his gun, and peering down at them as if dissatisfied at their reply.

"By whose permission?" he asked.

"The Holy Four," answered Ferrier. His Mormon experiences had taught him that that was the highest authority to which he could refer.

"Nine from seven," cried the sentinel.

"Seven from five," returned Jefferson Hope promptly, remembering the countersign which he had heard in the garden.

"Pass, and the Lord go with you," said the voice from above. Beyond his post the path broadened out, and the horses were able to break into a trot. Looking back, they could see the solitary watcher leaning upon his gun, and knew that they had passed the **outlying**[④] post of the chosen people, and that freedom lay before them.

这几个逃亡者的内心却很愉快，因为每前进一步，他们就离那可怕的暴政之地就远了一步。

然而，他们很快就发现他们仍然处在魔门圣徒们的势力范围内。他们到达了隘口最最荒凉和最最偏僻的地段，突然，姑娘惊恐地大叫了一声，并且用手向上指了指。小路的上方有一块的巨石，在夜空的映衬下，显得黝黑而又单调，上面孤零零地站着一个哨兵。他们刚一发现他，他也看见了他们。“那儿什么人？”寂静的山谷里响起了哨兵的吆喝声。

“去往内华达的游客，”杰弗逊·霍普说，一只手摸着挂在马鞍上的步枪。

他们看见，那个孤零零的哨兵手指扣着扳机，朝下注视着他们，好像对他们的回答并不感到满意。

“经过谁批准的？”他问。

“四圣会，”费里厄回答说，他在摩门教会中的经历告诉他，四圣会是他能够提及的最高权力机构。

“七点差九分，”哨兵大声说。

“五点差七分，”杰弗逊·霍普想起了自己在花园里听到的口令，便立刻应答了一声。

“过去吧，愿上帝与你们同在，”上面的声音说。过了这个哨位，道路宽阔了许多，马匹也可以小跑着前进了。回首望去，只见那个孤寂的哨兵倚着枪站立。他们知道，已经闯过了摩门教区的最后一道关卡，自由就在眼前了。

① desolate ['desələt] *a.* 凄凉的

② startle ['stɑːtld] *a.* 受惊吓的

③ sentinel ['sentinəl] *n.* 哨兵

④ outlying ['aut,laiiŋ] *a.* 偏远的

Chapter 5 The Avenging Angels

All night their course lay through intricate defiles and over irregular and rock-strewn paths. More than once they lost their way, but Hope's intimate knowledge of the mountains enabled them to regain the track once more. When morning broke, a scene of marvellous though savage beauty lay before them. In every direction the great snow-capped peaks **hemmed**① them in, peeping over each other's shoulders to the far horizon. So steep were the rocky banks on either side of them, that the **larch**② and the pine seemed to be suspended over their heads, and to need only a gust of wind to come hurtling down upon them. Nor was the fear entirely an illusion, for the barren valley was thickly strewn with trees and boulders which had fallen in a similar manner. Even as they passed, a great rock came thundering down with a hoarse rattle which woke the echoes in the silent gorges, and startled the weary horses into a **gallop**③.

As the sun rose slowly above the eastern horizon, the caps of the great mountains lit up one after the other, like lamps at a festival, until they were all ruddy and glowing. The magnificent **spectacle**④ cheered the hearts of the three fugitives and gave them fresh energy. At a wild torrent which swept out of a ravine they called a halt and watered their horses, while they partook of a hasty breakfast. Lucy and her father would fain have rested longer, but Jefferson Hope was **inexorable**⑤. "They will be upon our track by this time," he said. "Everything depends upon our speed. Once safe in Carson we may rest for the remainder of our lives."

第五章　复仇天使

整个夜间，他们都在地形复杂的峡谷和乱石堆积的小路上行进。不止一次迷了路，但霍普谙熟山区情况，他们这才又找回了正路。黎明时分，展现在他们眼前的是一派荒蛮但却瑰丽的景色。四方八面全是积雪皑皑的巨大山峰，层峦叠嶂，绵延到天边。两旁山岩陡立，上面生长的松树好像是悬在头顶上，似乎一阵风刮过，它们就会砸落下来。这种担心并不是多余的，荒凉的山谷中，四处堆满了从上方滚落的树木和巨石。甚至就在他们经过时，一块巨石轰隆隆地滚落了下来，雷鸣般的巨响在寂静的山谷中回荡，疲惫不堪的马匹吓得狂奔起来。

太阳从东方地平线上冉冉升起，朝霞照亮了一座座山峰，犹如节日里的盏盏彩灯，最后，所有山峰一片红色，熠熠生辉，活力四射。眼前壮丽的景象令三个逃亡者内心充满了欢乐，顿时神清气爽了起来。行至峡谷中的一处湍急的水流旁时，他们停了下来，让马饮水，他们自己则将就着用了点早餐。露茜和父亲本想多休息一会，但杰弗逊·霍普态度坚决。“这个时候，他们会在后面追赶我们了，”他说，“一切全都取决于我们的速度。一旦平安抵达了卡森城，我们想要休息一辈子都可以。”

① hem [hem] *v.* 包围

② larch [lɑːtʃ] *n.* 落叶松

③ gallop [ˈɡæləp] *n.* 疾驰

④ spectacle [ˈspektəkl] *n.* 景象

⑤ inexorably [inˈeksərəbl] *a.* 无情的，毫不宽容的

During the whole of that day they struggled on through the defiles, and by evening they calculated that they were more than thirty miles from their enemies. At night-time they chose the base of a beetling crag, where the rocks offered some protection from the chill wind, and there, huddled together for warmth, they enjoyed a few hours' sleep. Before daybreak, however, they were up and on their way once more. They had seen no signs of any pursuers, and Jefferson Hope began to think that they were fairly out of the reach of the terrible organization whose **enmity**① they had incurred. He little knew how far that iron grasp could reach, or how soon it was to close upon them and crush them.

About the middle of the second day of their flight their scanty store of provisions began to run out. This gave the hunter little uneasiness, however, for there was game to be had among the mountains, and he had frequently before had to depend upon his rifle for the needs of life. Choosing a sheltered nook, he piled together a few dried branches and made a blazing fire, at which his companions might warm themselves, for they were now nearly five thousand feet above the sea level, and the air was bitter and keen. Having tethered the horses, and bade Lucy adieu, he threw his gun over his shoulder, and set out in search of whatever chance might throw in his way. Looking back, he saw the old man and the young girl crouching over the blazing fire, while the three animals stood **motionless**② in the back-ground. Then the intervening rocks hid them from his view.

He walked for a couple of miles through one ravine after another without success, though, from the marks upon the bark of the trees, and other indications, he judged that there were numerous bears in the **vicinity**③. At last, after two or three hours' fruitless search, he was thinking of turning back in despair, when casting his eyes upwards he saw a sight which sent a thrill of pleasure through his heart. On the edge of a jutting **pinnacle**④, three or four hundred feet above him, there stood a creature somewhat **resembling**⑤ a sheep in appearance, but armed with a pair of **gigantic**⑥ horns. The big-horn—for so it is called—was acting, probably, as a guardian over a flock which were

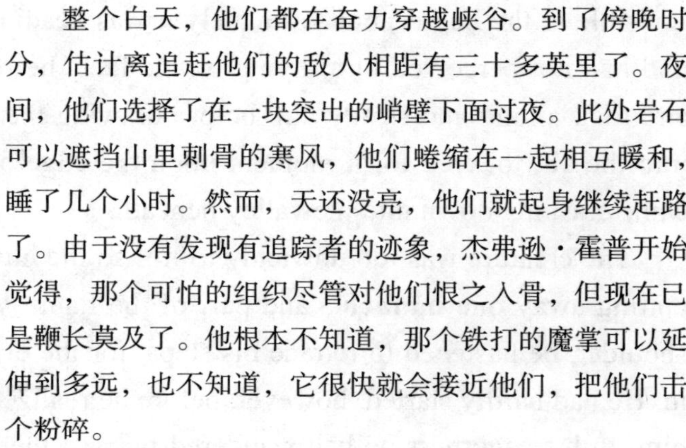

整个白天，他们都在奋力穿越峡谷。到了傍晚时分，估计离追赶他们的敌人相距有三十多英里了。夜间，他们选择了在一块突出的峭壁下面过夜。此处岩石可以遮挡山里刺骨的寒风，他们蜷缩在一起相互暖和，睡了几个小时。然而，天还没亮，他们就起身继续赶路了。由于没有发现有追踪者的迹象，杰弗逊·霍普开始觉得，那个可怕的组织尽管对他们恨之入骨，但现在已是鞭长莫及了。他根本不知道，那个铁打的魔掌可以延伸到多远，也不知道，它很快就会接近他们，把他们击个粉碎。

① enmity ['enməti] *n.* 敌对的状态

大概在他们出逃后的次日中午，他们仅有的一点粮食就要吃光了。然而，年轻猎手对此并不是很着急，山里到处是猎物，他以往就常常靠枪来获取不可或缺的食物。他找到了一个隐蔽的角落，堆起枯枝生火，让两个同伴暖和一下身子。他们此时已是在海拔五千英尺的高山上，天气冰冷彻骨。他把几匹骡马拴好后，对露茜道别了一声，便把枪背在了肩膀上，出发寻找猎物去了。回头望了一眼，看见老人和姑娘正蹲在熊熊燃烧的火边，三四牲口一动不动地站立在他们身后。再往前走，交错的岩石挡住了视线，看不见他们了。

② motionless ['məuʃənləs] *a.* 静止的

他穿过了一个又一个峡谷，走了有两英里路程，但一无所获。不过，根据在树干皮上留下的痕迹，还有其他一些迹象，他断定，附近有大量的熊出没。最后，经过了两三个小时搜寻毫无所获，他失望之极，正打算返回。这时候，他向上看了一眼，看到的情形令他心花怒放。在离他头顶三四百英尺高的地方，有一处突出的悬崖，悬崖边上站立着一只野兽，看上去像头绵羊，但长着一对大盘角。大盘羊——它其实就是叫这个名字——或许是给一群羊放哨，羊群处在猎手的视线之外。但幸运的是，它刚好背对着霍普所在的方向，没有看到他。霍普卧倒在地，把枪架在一块

③ vicinity [vi'sinəti] *n.* 附近

④ pinnacle ['pinəkl] *n.* 顶峰

⑤ resemble [ri'zembl] *v.* 类似于

⑥ gigantic [dʒai'gæntik] *a.* 巨大的

invisible to the hunter; but fortunately it was heading in the opposite direction, and had not perceived him. Lying on his face, he rested his rifle upon a rock, and took a long and steady aim before drawing the trigger. The animal sprang into the air, tottered for a moment upon the edge of the **precipice**[①], and then came crashing down into the valley beneath.

The creature was too unwieldy to lift, so the hunter contented himself with cutting away one **haunch**[②] and part of the flank. With this **trophy**[③] over his shoulder, he hastened to retrace his steps, for the evening was already drawing in. He had hardly started, however, before he realized the difficulty which faced him. In his eagerness he had wandered far past the ravines which were known to him, and it was no easy matter to pick out the path which he had taken. The valley in which he found himself divided and sub-divided into many gorges, which were so like each other that it was impossible to distinguish one from the other. He followed one for a mile or more until he came to a mountain **torrent**[④] which he was sure that he had never seen before. Convinced that he had taken the wrong turn, he tried another, but with the same result. Night was coming on rapidly, and it was almost dark before he at last found himself in a defile which was familiar to him. Even then it was no easy matter to keep to the right track, for the moon had not yet risen, and the high cliffs on either side made the obscurity more profound. Weighed down with his burden, and weary from his exertions, he stumbled along, keeping up his heart by the reflection that every step brought him nearer to Lucy, and that he carried with him enough to ensure them food for the remainder of their journey.

He had now come to the mouth of the very defile in which he had left them. Even in the darkness he could recognize the outline of the cliffs which bounded it. They must, he reflected, be awaiting him anxiously, for he had been absent nearly five hours. In the gladness of his heart he put his hands to his mouth and made the glen **reecho**[⑤] to a loud **halloo**[⑥] as a signal that he was coming. He paused and listened for an answer. None came save his own cry, which clattered up the dreary, silent ravines, and was borne back to his ears in countless

岩石上，不慌不忙地瞄准目标后，扣动扳机。猎物突地向上跳了一下，在悬崖边上晃了晃，就跌落到了峡谷底了。

猎物十分沉重，根本背不起来。所以，猎手决定，割下一条后腿，再从腹部切下一部分。他把战利品扛到肩上，匆匆忙忙往回赶路，因为夜幕已经开始降临了。然而，他刚要出发，便就意识到自己面临着困境。由于自己心急火燎地寻找猎物，已经走了很远的路程了，离那些熟悉的峡谷已经很远了，很难寻找到他来时的小路了。他眼下所处的这道峡谷分成了许多沟沟壑壑，看上去都差不多，很难分辨清楚。他沿着一条沟壑走了一英里多，最后到达了一个山涧，他肯定来时并没有看到过这条山涧。他坚信，自己走错路了，于是换了另外一条路线，结果还是错了。夜幕很快笼罩了下来，等到最后找到那条自己熟悉的峡谷时，天差不多已经全黑了。虽然他找到了这条熟路，沿着正确的路线走也不是件容易的事情，因为月亮还没有升起，两边高耸的悬崖更加深了昏暗的气氛。他肩上扛着东西，长途跋涉后感到疲惫不堪了，于是踉踉跄跄地前行着，振作精神，心里怀着一种念想，自己每前进一步，就离露茜近了一步。还有就是，自己肩上扛着的东西足够他们在后面的旅途中吃了。

他现在终于回到了同他们分别的那个峡谷的谷口了。尽管在黑暗中，他还是辨认出了周围峭壁的轮廓。他想到，他们一定等他等得很焦虑了，因为自己离开了将近五个小时。高兴之余，他把自己的两只手放到嘴边，大“嘿”了一声，声音在峡谷中回荡，作为信号，表明他回来了。他停了下来，听听有没有人回应。毫无反应，只有自己的呼声在阴郁寂静的峡谷中回荡，一次次传回自己的耳朵。他又叫喊了一声，声音比先前的更加响亮，但是，还是没有听到他的同伴们半点微弱的回

① precipice ['presipis] *n.* 悬崖

② haunch [hɔ:ntʃ] *n.* 腰腿

③ trophy ['trəufi] *n.* 战利品

④ torrent ['tɔrənt] *n.* 急流

⑤ reecho ['ri:'ekəu] *n.* 回响

⑥ hallo [hə'lu:] *n.* 狩猎时招呼猎犬的喊声

repetitions. Again he shouted, even louder than before, and again no whisper came back from the friends whom he had left such a short time ago. A vague, nameless dread came over him, and he hurried onwards frantically, dropping the precious food in his agitation.

When he turned the corner, he came full in sight of the spot where the fire had been lit. There was still a glowing pile of wood ashes there, but it had evidently not been tended since his departure. The same dead silence still **reigned**[①] all round. With his fears all changed to **convictions**[②], he hurried on. There was no living creature near the remains of the fire: animals, man, maiden, all were gone. It was only too clear that some sudden and terrible disaster had occurred during his absence—a disaster which had embraced them all, and yet had left no traces behind it.

Bewildered and stunned by this blow, Jefferson Hope felt his head spin round, and had to lean upon his rifle to save himself from falling. He was essentially a man of action, however, and speedily recovered from his temporary **impotence**[③]. Seizing a half-consumed piece of wood from the smouldering fire, he blew it into a flame, and proceeded with its help to examine the little camp. The ground was all stamped down by the feet of horses, showing that a large party of mounted men had overtaken the fugitives, and the direction of their tracks proved that they had afterwards turned back to Salt Lake City. Had they carried back both of his companions with them? Jefferson Hope had almost persuaded himself that they must have done so, when his eye fell upon an object which made every nerve of his body tingle within him. A little way on one side of the camp was a low-lying heap of reddish soil, which had assuredly not been there before. There was no mistaking it for anything but a newlydug grave. As the young hunter approached it, he perceived that a stick had been planted on it, with a sheet of paper stuck in the **cleft**[④] fork of it. The **inscription**[⑤] upon the paper was brief, but to the point:

JOHN FERRIER,

FORMERLY OF SALT LAKE CITY,

Died August 4th, 1860.

声，不久前他可是还同他们在一起的啊。一种朦胧莫名的恐惧感袭上了心头。于是，他疯狂地急忙向前跑，慌乱中，那来之不易的食物掉到了地上。

他转过崖壁之后，前面的情形看得很清楚了，就是先前生火的地点。还有一堆闷烧着的木柴灰烬，但很显然，从他离开之后，就再没有人照管过，周围也同样是一片死寂。他的担心演化成了现实，他快步走上前。火堆的余烬附近再没有活着的生命了，牲口，老人，姑娘，全都消失了。情况再清楚不过了，他不在的这段时间里，某个突如其来的可怕灾难降临了——灾难瞬间毁灭了他们，而且还没有留下半点痕迹。

① reign [rein] v. 统治
② conviction [kən'vikʃən] n. 确信

面对这个突如其来的打击，杰弗逊·霍普不知所措，目瞪口呆，只觉得天旋地转，只得用枪支撑着身子才没有倒下去。但是，他终归是个行动敏捷的人，很快就消除了一时的无力感。他从闷烧着火堆里抓起一根烧了一半的木柴，把木柴吹出火苗，借着火把的光亮仔细地查看了一遍。地面上到处是马蹄印，说明有一大群骑马的人袭击了两个逃亡的人。马蹄印表明的方向证明了，他们随后返回到盐湖城去了。他们把他的两个同伴都一道带回去了吗？杰弗逊·霍普几乎说服自己了，即他们一定那样做了。突然，他的眼睛落到了一样东西上，不禁全身的每一根神经都感到刺痛。营地一侧的不远处，有个低矮的红土堆，毫无疑问，先前是没有的。这不可能是别的东西，一定是一座新坟。年轻猎人走到近处，只见上面插了根木棍，在木棍的枝桠处夹了张纸。纸条上的文字很简略，但意思很清楚：

③ impotence ['impətəns] n. 无能为力

约翰·费里厄

盐湖城人

死于1860年8月4日

④ cleft [kleft] n. 裂缝
⑤ inscription [in'skripʃən] n. 文字

The sturdy old man, whom he had left so short a time before, was gone, then, and this was all his **epitaph**①. Jefferson Hope looked wildly round to see if there was a second grave, but there was no sign of one. Lucy had been carried back by their terrible pursuers to fulfil her original destiny, by becoming one of the harem of the Elder's son. As the young fellow realized the certainty of her fate, and his own powerlessness to prevent it, he wished that he, too, was lying with the old farmer in his last silent resting-place.

Again, however, his active spirit shook off the **lethargy**② which springs from despair. If there was nothing else left to him, he could at least devote his life to revenge. With **indomitable**③ patience and perseverance, Jefferson Hope possessed also a power of sustained **vindictiveness**④, which he may have learned from the Indians amongst whom he had lived. As he stood by the desolate fire, he felt that the only one thing which could assuage his grief would be thorough and complete retribution, brought by his own hand upon his enemies. His strong will and untiring energy should, he determined, be devoted to that one end. With a grim, white face, he retraced his steps to where he had dropped the food, and having stirred up the smouldering fire, he cooked enough to last him for a few days. This he made up into a bundle, and, tired as he was, he set himself to walk back through the mountains upon the track of the Avenging Angels.

For five days he toiled footsore and weary through the defiles which he had already traversed on horseback. At night he flung himself down among the rocks, and **snatched**⑤ a few hours of sleep; but before daybreak he was always well on his way. On the sixth day, he reached the Eagle Canon, from which they had commenced their ill-fated flight. Thence he could look down upon the home of the Saints. Worn and exhausted, he leaned upon his rifle and shook his gaunt hand fiercely at the silent widespread city beneath him. As he looked at it, he observed that there were flags in some of the principal streets, and other signs of **festivity**⑥. He was still speculating as to what this might mean when he heard the clatter of horse's hoofs, and saw a mounted man riding towards him.

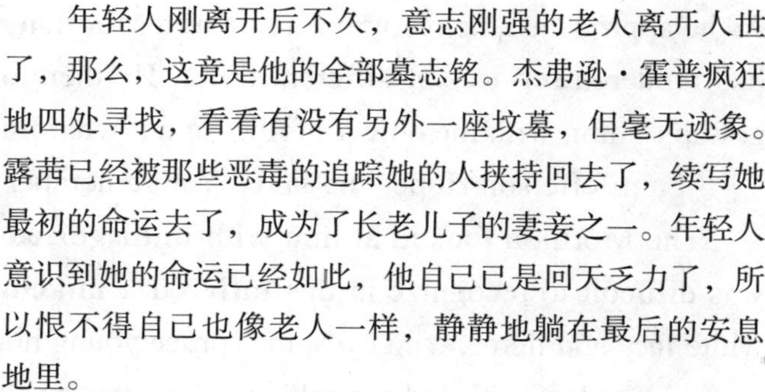

年轻人刚离开后不久，意志刚强的老人离开人世了，那么，这竟是他的全部墓志铭。杰弗逊·霍普疯狂地四处寻找，看看有没有另外一座坟墓，但毫无迹象。露茜已经被那些恶毒的追踪她的人挟持回去了，续写她最初的命运去了，成为了长老儿子的妻妾之一。年轻人意识到她的命运已经如此，他自己已是回天乏力了，所以恨不得自己也像老人一样，静静地躺在最后的安息地里。

① epitaph ['epitɑ:f] *n.* 墓志铭

② lethargy ['leθədʒi] *n.* 没精打采

然而，他积极进取的精神使他又一次摆脱了因绝望而致的萎靡消沉的状态。即便没有任何别的东西了，他至少可以用自己毕生的精力来报仇雪恨。杰弗逊·霍普除了拥有百折不饶的耐心和毅力之外，还有着无穷的复仇力量。这可能是他在同印第安人朝夕相处的过程中受到的影响。他伫立在被遗弃的火堆旁，心里感觉到，唯一能够减轻自己内心悲伤的事情是，亲手完全彻底地报仇。他下定了决心，把自己坚定的意志和不竭的精力全部倾注在这个目标上。他表情凝重，脸色苍白，返回到自己掉落食物的地方去。拨旺了闷烧的火堆，烤好了够几天吃的羊肉。他把烤好的肉包了起来之后，尽管很疲倦了，还是出发往回走，翻山越岭，踏上了复仇天使们走过的路。

③ indomitable [in'dɔmitəbl] *a.* 不屈服的

④ vindictiveness [vin'diktivnəs] *n.* 复仇

他先前骑着马跨过了一座座峡谷，现在徒步行走，整整走了五天，艰难跋涉，身心疲惫。夜间，躺卧在乱石丛中，将就着睡上几个小时，但是，天还没有亮，他就已经踏上旅途了。到了第六天时，他到达了鹰谷。当时就是在这样一处地方，他们开始了自己命运悲惨的逃亡之路，由此可以看到摩门教徒们的家园。他尽管已经精疲力竭了，但身子仍然倚靠着枪身，朝着下方那座寂静宽广的城市恶狠狠地挥舞着一只干瘦的手。望着城市的时候，他注意到了，一些主要的街道上挂起了旗帜，还有别的节日装饰。他正琢磨着这是怎么回事，突然听

⑤ snatch [snætʃ] *v.* 夺取；抓住机会做

⑥ festivity [fes'tivəti] *n.* 喜庆日

As he approached, he recognized him as a Mormon named Cowper, to whom he had rendered services at different times. He therefore **accosted**[①] him when he got up to him, with the object of finding out what Lucy Ferrier's fate had been.

"I am Jefferson Hope," he said. "You remember me."

The Mormon looked at him with **undisguised**[②] astonishment—indeed, it was difficult to recognize in this **tattered**[③], **unkempt**[④] wanderer, with ghastly white face and fierce, wild eyes, the spruce young hunter of former days. Having, however, at last, satisfied himself as to his identity, the man's surprise changed to **consternation**[⑤].

"You are mad to come here," he cried. "It is as much as my own life is worth to be seen talking with you. There is a warrant against you from the Holy Four for assisting the Ferriers away."

"I don't fear them, or their warrant," Hope said, earnestly. "You must know something of this matter, Cowper. I conjure you by everything you hold dear to answer a few questions. We have always been friends. For God's sake, don't refuse to answer me."

"What is it?" the Mormon asked, uneasily. "Be quick. The very rocks have ears and the trees eyes."

"What has become of Lucy Ferrier?"

"She was married yesterday to young Drebber. Hold up, man, hold up; you have no life left in you."

"Don't mind me," said Hope faintly. He was white to the very lips, and had sunk down on the stone against which he had been leaning. "Married, you say?"

"Married yesterday—that's what those flags are for on the Endowment House. There was some words between young Drebber and young Stangerson as to which was to have her. They'd both been in the party that followed them, and Stangerson had shot her father, which seemed to give him the best claim; but when they argued it out in council, Drebber's party was the stronger, so the Prophet gave her over to him. No one won't have her very long though, for I

① accost [ə'kɔst] *v.* 走过去跟…说话

② undisguised [ˌʌndis'gaizd] *a.* 不加掩饰的

③ tattered ['tætəd] *a.* 衣衫褴褛的

④ unkempt [ˌʌn'kempt] *a.* 邋遢的

⑤ consternation [ˌkɔnstə'neiʃən] *n.* 惊慌失措

到一阵奔腾的马蹄声，看见一个人骑着马朝他的方向奔驰而来。等到靠近时，他认出了来者，是一个名叫考珀的摩门教徒。霍普曾帮过他几次忙。所以，当他出现在跟前时，霍普向他打了声招呼，想探听一下露茜的境遇如何。

"我是杰弗逊·霍普，"他说，"你应该有印象的。"

摩门教徒一脸惊诧地看着霍普——确实，眼前这个流浪者衣衫褴褛，蓬头垢面，脸色惨白，目光狰狞，很难把他同那个曾经年轻英俊的猎手联系起来。然而，当他好不容易辨认出眼前站着的是杰弗逊·霍普时，惊诧变成了惶恐。

"你简直疯了，竟然还跑到这儿来，"他大声说，"如果有人看见我同你说话，我的命就搭上去啦！由于你帮助费里厄父女出逃，四圣会已经下令通缉你了！"

"我不怕他们，也不怕他们通缉，"霍普说，语气迫切，"关于这件事，你一定知道些情况。考珀，我想向你打听一下，请你务必回答。我一直把你当朋友的。看在上帝的份上，请不要拒绝我。"

"什么事？"摩门教徒问，心神不宁，"快说吧，这儿的石头都长了耳朵，树木都长了眼睛啊。"

"露茜·费里厄怎样了？"

"她昨天嫁给小德雷伯了。挺住啊，朋友，挺住。你好像是丢了魂魄似的。"

"我没有事，"霍普有气无力地说，连嘴唇都是惨白的，瘫坐在刚才倚靠着那块石头上，"你说已经嫁了？"

"昨天嫁的——赐福堂就是因为这个挂起了旗帜的。为了争夺谁有权娶到她，小德雷伯和小斯坦格森之间还吵闹起来了呢。他们两个人都加入到了追踪他们的队伍，但斯坦格森打死了那位父亲，所以，他似乎有了优先权。但是，他们两个人把事情闹到四圣会上时，德雷

saw death in her face yesterday. She is more like a ghost than a woman. Are you off, then?"

"Yes, I am off," said Jefferson Hope, who had risen from his seat. His face might have been **chiselled**[①] out of marble, so hard and set was its expression, while its eyes glowed with a **baleful**[②] light.

"Where are you going?"

"Never mind," he answered; and, slinging his weapon over his shoulder, strode off down the gorge and so away into the heart of the mountains to the haunts of the wild beasts. Amongst them all there was none so fierce and so dangerous as himself.

The prediction of the Mormon was only too well fulfilled. Whether it was the terrible death of her father or the effects of the hateful marriage into which she had been forced, poor Lucy never held up her head again, but pined away and died within a month. Her **sottish**[③] husband, who had married her **principally**[④] for the sake of John Ferrier's property, did not affect any great grief at his **bereavement**[⑤]; but his other wives mourned over her, and sat up with her the night before the burial, as is the Mormon custom. They were grouped round the bier in the early hours of the morning, when, to their inexpressible fear and astonishment, the door was flung open, and a savage-looking, weather-beaten man in tattered garments strode into the room. Without a glance or a word to the cowering women, he walked up to the white silent figure which had once contained the pure soul of Lucy Ferrier. Stooping over her, he pressed his lips reverently to her cold forehead, and then, snatching up her hand, he took the wedding-ring from her finger. "She shall not be buried in that," he cried with a fierce snarl, and before an alarm could be raised sprang down the stairs and was gone. So strange and so brief was the episode, that the watchers might have found it hard to believe it themselves or persuade other people of it, had it not been for the undeniable fact that the **circlet**[⑥] of gold which marked her as having been a bride had disappeared.

For some months Jefferson Hope lingered among the mountains, leading a

伯一方势力更加强大，所以先知就把露茜许配给了德雷伯。不过，不管是谁得到了她，那都不会长久的，因为我昨天从她的脸上看到了死亡的迹象。她不像个女人，简直就像个鬼。怎么，你要走了吗？”

① chiselled ['tʃizld] *a.* 凿过的
② baleful ['beilful] *a.* 凶恶的

“是啊，我要走了，”杰弗逊·霍普说，已经从坐着的地方站立了起来，面部五官就像是大理石雕刻成的，表情冷酷阴沉，眼睛里闪着凶光。

“你要去哪儿？”

“这你别管，”他回答说，把枪挎在了肩上，大步走下山谷，走进了大山深处野兽出没的地方。野兽群中他成了最凶狠和最危险的成员。

③ sottish [sɔtiʃ] *a.* 酗酒的
④ principally ['prinsipli] *ad.* 主要的
⑤ bereavement [bi'ri:vmənt] *n.* 丧亲之痛

摩门教徒的预言完全应验了。不知道是因为父亲惨遭杀害，还是因为被迫接受了这桩充满了仇恨的婚姻，可怜的露茜再也没有扬起过头来，形容枯槁，不到一个月就去世了。她那酒鬼丈夫之所以要娶她，主要看中的是约翰·费里厄的财产，所以，对于她的离世，他并没有表露什么悲哀之情，倒是他的另外几个妻子在为她哀悼。她们按照摩门教的风俗，葬礼之前整夜为她守灵。次日凌晨，她们围着灵柩坐着，突然间，令她们感到莫名的恐惧和震惊的是，房门猛然扇开，闯进了一个衣衫褴褛的男人，只见他样貌粗野，饱经风霜。他毫不理会几个吓得瑟瑟发抖的女人，没有看她们一眼，也没有吭一声，径直走向那毫无声息的躯体。躯体中曾经有露茜·费里厄纯洁的灵魂。他躬下身子对着她，虔诚地在她冰冷的额头上亲吻了一下，然后一把抓起她的手，取下手指上的结婚戒指。“她不能戴着这个下葬！”他怒吼着。还没没等周围的人反应过来，他就飞身下楼走了。如果不是标志着她当了新娘的金戒指确实不见了，这件事情离奇突兀得连在场的几个女人都难以置信，当然也很难令别人相信。

⑥ circlet ['sə:klət] *n.* 环形饰品，这里指戒指

几个月的时间里，杰弗逊·霍普在群山之中颠沛流

strange, wild life, and nursing in his heart the fierce desire for vengeance which possessed him. Tales were told in the City of the weird figure which was seen **prowling**[①] about the suburbs, and which haunted the lonely mountain gorges. Once a bullet whistled through Stangerson's window and flattened itself upon the wall within a foot of him. On another occasion, as Drebber passed under a cliff a great boulder crashed down on him, and he only escaped a terrible death by throwing himself upon his face. The two young Mormons were not long in discovering the reason of these attempts upon their lives, and led repeated expeditions into the mountains in the hope of capturing or killing their enemy, but always without success. Then they adopted the **precaution**[②] of never going out alone or after nightfall, and of having their houses guarded. After a time they were able to relax these measures, for nothing was either heard or seen of their opponent, and they hoped that time had cooled his vindictiveness.

Far from doing so, it had, if anything, augmented it. The hunter's mind was of a hard, unyielding nature, and the **predominant**[③] idea of revenge had taken such complete possession of it that there was no room for any other emotion. He was, however, above all things, practical. He soon realized that even his iron constitution could not stand the **incessant**[④] strain which he was putting upon it. Exposure and want of wholesome food were wearing him out. If he died like a dog among the mountains, what was to become of his revenge then? And yet such a death was sure to overtake him if he persisted. He felt that that was to play his enemy's game, so he reluctantly returned to the old Nevada mines, there to recruit his health and to **amass**[⑤] money enough to allow him to pursue his object without privation.

His intention had been to be absent a year at the most, but a combination of unforeseen circumstances prevented his leaving the mines for nearly five. At the end of that time, however, his memory of his wrongs and his craving for revenge were quite as keen as on that memorable night when he had stood by John Ferrier's grave. Disguised, and under an assumed name, he returned to Salt Lake City, careless what became of his own life, as long as he obtained

离，过着怪异野蛮的生活，要报仇雪恨的欲望在心中不断滋长，越来越强烈。城里面盛传着各种各样的说法，说有人看见有个怪异人物行踪诡秘，徘徊在荒郊野外，出没在深山峡谷。有一次，一颗子弹嗖地一声穿过了斯坦格森家的窗户，击在离他不到一英尺的墙壁上。另有一次，德雷伯在一处悬崖下面经过时，一块巨石从上面朝着他滚落下来，他纵身脸朝下扑到在地，这才逃过了死亡的悲惨命运。两位年轻的摩门教徒不久发现了，有人企图谋杀他们的原由。于是，一再领着队伍进山搜索，指望着抓捕或者击毙他们的敌手，但总是未能成功。后来，他们采取了预防措施，决不单独或者夜间外出，同时派人在他们的住宅加强警戒。过了一段时间之后，他们开始放松这些戒备措施，因为没有听到有关他们对手的消息，也没有看见其踪影。他们希望，随着时间的流逝，他的复仇斗志逐渐减弱了。

情况并非如此。如果说随着时间流逝，有什么变化的话，那就是，他的复仇斗志增强了。猎手生性意志坚强，不屈不饶，如今一门心思想着的就是报仇雪恨，再也容不下别的情感了。然而，他最最显著的品格还是讲求实际。他很快就意识到，如果自己没完没了地饱受折磨，即便是铁打的身子骨也承受不了。风吹日晒，缺少有益于健康的食物，他的身体日渐垮下去。如果他像条狗似的死在荒山野岭之间，那他报仇雪恨的事怎么办呢？然而，如果他继续硬撑下去，那死亡的事在所难免。他感觉到，这样做正中他的敌人的下怀，于是，他勉强回到了昔日的内华达矿区。到那儿让自己的身体得到恢复，积攒足够的钱，以便自己能够实现复仇的目标，而又不至于挨饿受穷。

他原本计划离开最多一年，但由于出了些意外，一直无法从矿上脱身，结果耽搁了将近五年。然而，在过了五年之后，他对自己冤屈的记忆和对复仇的渴望，还

① prowl [praul] v. 徘徊

② precaution [pri'kɔːʃən] n. 警惕

③ predominant [pri'dɔminənt] a. 占主导地位的

④ incessant [in'sesənt] a. 不停的

⑤ amass [ə'mæs] v. 积累

what he knew to be justice. There he found evil tidings awaiting him. There had been a **schism**① among the Chosen People a few months before, some of the younger members of the Church having rebelled against the authority of the Elders, and the result had been the secession of a certain number of the **malcontents**②, who had left Utah and become Gentiles. Among these had been Drebber and Stangerson; and no one knew whither they had gone. Rumour reported that Drebber had managed to convert a large part of his property into money, and that he had departed a wealthy man, while his companion, Stangerson, was comparatively poor. There was no clue at all, however, as to their **whereabouts**③.

Many a man, however vindictive, would have abandoned all thought of revenge in the face of such a difficulty, but Jefferson Hope never faltered for a moment. With the small competence he possessed, eked out by such employment as he could pick up, he travelled from town to town through the United States in quest of his enemies. Year passed into year, his black hair turned **grizzled**④, but still he wandered on, a human bloodhound, with his mind wholly set upon the one object upon which he had devoted his life. At last his perseverance was rewarded. It was but a glance of a face in a window, but that one glance told him that Cleveland in Ohio possessed the men whom he was in pursuit of. He returned to his miserable lodgings with his plan of vengeance all arranged. It chanced, however, that Drebber, looking from his window, had recognized the **vagrant**⑤ in the street, and had read murder in his eyes. He hurried before a justice of the peace accompanied by Stangerson, who had become his private secretary, and represented to him that they were in danger of their lives from the jealousy and hatred of an old rival. That evening Jefferson Hope was taken into custody, and not being able to find **sureties**⑥, was detained for some weeks. When at last he was liberated it was only to find that Drebber's house was deserted, and that he and his secretary had departed for Europe.

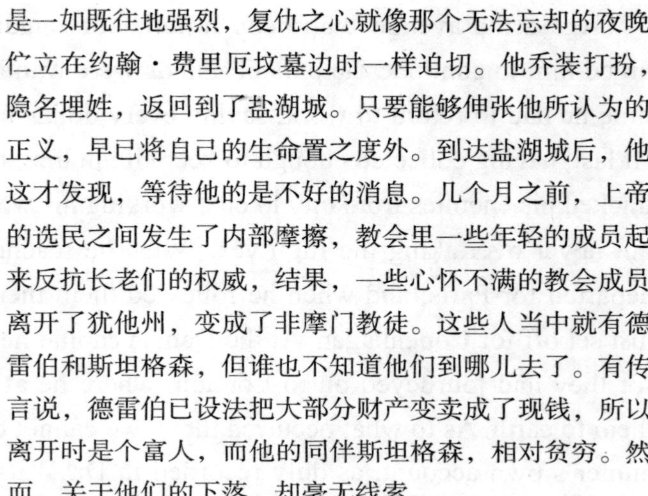

是一如既往地强烈，复仇之心就像那个无法忘却的夜晚伫立在约翰·费里厄坟墓边时一样迫切。他乔装打扮，隐名埋姓，返回到了盐湖城。只要能够伸张他所认为的正义，早已将自己的生命置之度外。到达盐湖城后，他这才发现，等待他的是不好的消息。几个月之前，上帝的选民之间发生了内部摩擦，教会里一些年轻的成员起来反抗长老们的权威，结果，一些心怀不满的教会成员离开了犹他州，变成了非摩门教徒。这些人当中就有德雷伯和斯坦格森，但谁也不知道他们到哪儿去了。有传言说，德雷伯已设法把大部分财产变卖成了现钱，所以离开时是个富人，而他的同伴斯坦格森，相对贫穷。然而，关于他们的下落，却毫无线索。

不管人们报仇雪恨的决心有多么坚定，但许多人面对如此困境都会完全打消报仇的念头。但是，杰弗逊·霍普却从未动摇过。他依靠自己很有限的一点收入，另外做点零工给予补贴，从一座城镇辗转到另一座，走遍了整个美国，寻找仇人的下落。年复一年，他的黑发变得灰白了，但他仍然像一只猎犬一样四处寻觅着，把自己全部的精力和心思都贯注在复仇上了。最后，他锲而不舍的精神终于有了回报。回报只不过是从一扇窗户里瞥见了一张面孔而已，但这一瞥让他明白了，自己追踪的人就在俄亥俄州的克利夫兰市。他回到了自己那破败不堪的住处，谋划好了整个复仇计划。但是，事情凑巧的是，德雷伯刚好从窗户往外看，认出了街上的那个流浪汉，而且看出了对方的目光中充满了杀气。因此，他在已成为自己私人秘书的斯坦格森的陪同下，匆匆忙忙来到了一位治安法官的面前，向他报告说，有个昔日的情敌心怀着嫉妒和仇恨，找上门来了，他们的生命面临着危险。当晚，杰弗逊·霍普被拘捕了，由于找不到担保人，被关押了几个星期。等到被释放的时候，他发现德雷伯的住处已是人去楼空，他带着秘书去了欧洲。

① schism ['sizəm] *n.* 教会分裂

② malcontent ['mælkən,tent] *n.* 不满者

③ whereabouts ['hwεərə'bauts] *n.* 行踪

④ grizzled ['grizld] *a.* 头发斑白的

⑤ vagrant ['veigrənt] *n.* 流浪者

⑥ surety ['ʃuəti] *n.* 保证人

Again the avenger had been **foiled**①, and again his concentrated hatred urged him to continue the pursuit. Funds were wanting, however, and for some time he had to return to work, saving every dollar for his approaching journey. At last, having collected enough to keep life in him, he departed for Europe, and tracked his enemies from city to city, working his way in any **menial**② capacity, but never overtaking the fugitives. When he reached St. Petersburg they had departed for Paris; and when he followed them there he learned that they had just set off for Copenhagen. At the Danish capital he was again a few days late, for they had journeyed on to London, where he at last succeeded in running them to earth. As to what occurred there, we cannot do better than quote the old hunter's own account, as duly recorded in Dr. Watson's Journal, to which we are already under such **obligations**③.

① foil [fɔi] *v.* 挫败

② menial ['mi:niəl] *a.* （指工作）不体面的

③ obligation [ˌɔbli'geiʃən] *n.* 义务

复仇者又一次遭受了挫折，但心头的积恨再一次使他鼓起了勇气，继续追踪仇敌。然而，因为没有路费，他只得回去先干一段时间活，把每一分钱都存起来，为日后踏上追踪之旅做好准备。最后，他总算攒够了足够的费用，随即动身前往欧洲，从一座城市辗转到另外一座，寻找敌人的行踪。一路上干着又苦又累的活儿。可是，一直没有追寻到那两个逃亡者。当他到达圣彼得堡时，他们已离开去了巴黎，而当他一路追踪到巴黎时，又得知他们去了哥本哈根。到了丹麦的首都，他又晚到了几天，他们已经启程去伦敦了。最后，他总算在伦敦追上了他们。至于在伦敦所发生的一切，我们最好还是引用老猎手自己的叙述。华生医生在他的日记中一字不落地记录了下了这一切。我们所知道的情况全都记录在那本回忆录中。

Chapter 6 A Continuation of the Reminiscences of John Watson, M.D.

Our prisoner's furious resistance did not apparently indicate any **ferocity**① in his **disposition**② towards ourselves, for on finding himself powerless, he smiled in an **affable**③ manner, and expressed his hopes that he had not hurt any of us in the **scuffle**④. "I guess you're going to take me to the police-station," he remarked to Sherlock Holmes. "My cab's at the door. If you'll loose my legs I'll walk down to it. I'm not so light to lift as I used to be."

Gregson and Lestrade exchanged glances as if they thought this **proposition**⑤ rather a **bold**⑥ one; but Holmes at once took the prisoner at his word, and loosened the towel which we had bound round his ankles. He rose and stretched his legs, as though to assure himself that they were free once more. I remember that I thought to myself, as I eyed him, that I had seldom seen a more powerfully built man; and his dark, sunburned face bore an expression of determination and energy which was as formidable as his personal strength.

"If there's a vacant place for a chief of the police, I reckon you are the man for it," he said, gazing with undisguised admiration at my fellow-lodger. "The way you kept on my trail was a caution."

"You had better come with me," said Holmes to the two detectives.

第六章 约翰·华生医生的回忆录续

① ferocity [fə'rɔsəti] *n.* 凶猛

② disposition [ˌdispə'ziʃən] *n.* 性情

③ affable ['æfəbl] *a.* 友善的

④ scuffle ['skʌfl] *n.* 扭打

⑤ proposition [ˌprɔpə'ziʃən] *n.* 建议

⑥ bold [bəuld] *a.* 大胆的

我们抓住的犯人虽然情绪暴怒，拼命进行了抵抗，但很显然，这并不表明他在情感上对我们怀有什么敌意，因为当他意识到反抗无效时，便态度和蔼地微笑了起来，并且表示，但愿在扭打过程中，他没有伤害到我们中任何一位。"我估计，您会把我送到警察局去，"他对夏洛克·福尔摩斯说，"我的马车就在门口。如果你们把我的腿松开，我可以自己下楼走到马车边去。我可不像过去那样轻了，抬不动的。"

格雷格森和莱斯特雷德交换了一下眼神，他们似乎觉得，这个提议有点过于胆大妄为，但是，福尔摩斯却立刻采用了犯人的提议，解开了绑在他脚踝上的毛巾。他站立了起来，舒展了一下双腿，好像是要让自己确认一下，双腿已经确实重获自由了。我记得，我当时看着他时，心里觉得，我还很少看到过比他更加强壮有力的人。还有他的那张被太阳晒得黝黑的脸上显露着坚定的神情，表现出充沛的精力，这都像他的体格力量一样令人畏惧。

"如果警察局缺个警长的话，我看您就是适合的人选，"他说，两眼注视着我的同室房客，钦佩之情溢于

"I can drive you," said Lestrade.

"Good! and Gregson can come inside with me. You too, Doctor, you have taken an interest in the case, and may as well stick to us."

I assented gladly, and we all descended together. Our prisoner made no attempt at escape, but stepped calmly into the cab which had been his, and we followed him. Lestrade mounted the box, whipped up the horse, and brought us in a very short time to our destination. We were ushered into a small chamber, where a police inspector noted down our prisoner's name and the names of the men with whose murder he had been charged. The official was a white-faced, unemotional man, who went through his duties in a dull mechanical way. "The prisoner will be put before the **magistrates**① in the course of the week," he said; "in the mean time, Mr. Jefferson Hope, have you anything that you wish to say? I must warn you that your words will be taken down, and may be used against you."

"I've got a good deal to say," our prisoner said slowly. "I want to tell you gentlemen all about it."

"Hadn't you better reserve that for your trial?" asked the inspector.

"I may never be tried," he answered. "You needn't look startled. It isn't suicide I am thinking of. Are you a Doctor?" He turned his fierce dark eyes upon me as he asked this last question.

"Yes; I am," I answered.

"Then put your hand here," he said, with a smile, motioning with his **manacled**② wrists towards his chest.

I did so; and became at once conscious of an extraordinary **throbbing**③ and **commotion**④ which was going on inside. The walls of his chest seemed to thrill and quiver as a **frail**⑤ building would do inside when some powerful engine was at work. In the silence of the room I could hear a dull humming and buzzing noise which proceeded from the same source.

"Why," I cried, "you have an **aortic**⑥ **aneurism**⑦!"

言表，“您追寻我的行踪的手段可真了得。”

“你们最好同我一道过去。”福尔摩斯对两位警探说。

“我来给你们驾车吧。”莱斯特雷德说。

“那好！格雷格森陪我坐到车里。你也来吧，华生。你既然对本案产生了兴趣，那就奉陪我们到底吧。”

我欣然同意了，我们所有人一同下了楼。我们的犯人再也没有要逃脱的意思了，而是平静地登上了他自己配好的马车，我们也跟着上了马车。莱斯特雷德坐在车夫的位置上，挥鞭催马，很快就把我们载到了目的地。我们被人领进了一个小房间，房间里有位警长记录下了我们带去犯人的姓名，还有那两个遇害者的姓名。警长是个脸色煞白、神情冷漠的人。他呆板而又机械地履行着自己的职责。“一个星期之内，犯人就会带上法庭接受审判的，”他说，“同时，杰弗逊·霍普先生，您有什么话要说吗？我必须提醒您，您所说的每一句话都将记录在案，并可能用作指控您的证据。”

“我有很多话要说，”犯人开口说，话说得很缓慢，“我想要把事情的经过原原本本地告诉你们各位先生。”

“等到审判您的时候再说，难道不更好吗？”警长说。

“我可能等不到审判的时候了，”他回答说，“你们不用紧张，我不会想到要自杀的。您是医生吧？”他最后提出这个问题时，充满了凶狠目光的黑眼睛看着我。

“对，我是医生，”我回答说。

“那就请您把手按着这里。”他笑着说，用戴着手铐的双腕朝胸口处指了指。

我把手按在他的胸部，立刻就感觉到，那里面的心脏跳动异常，十分紊乱，胸腔似乎在轻微地颤动，好比是一幢摇摇欲坠的房子，里面有一架功率强大的机器在运转。房间里面寂静无声，我都可以听见他胸膛里嗡嗡的杂音。

① magistrate ['mædʒistreit] *n.* 地方法官

② manacle ['mænəkl] *v.* 给…带上手铐

③ throbbing [θrɔbiŋ] *a.* 跳动的

④ commotion [kə'məuʃən] *n.* 混乱

⑤ frail [freil] *a.* 摇摇欲坠的

⑥ aortic [ei'ɔ:tik] *a.* 大动脉的

⑦ aneurism ['ænjuə,rizəm] *n.* 动脉瘤

"That's what they call it," he said, **placidly**[1]. "I went to a Doctor last week about it, and he told me that it is bound to burst before many days passed. It has been getting worse for years. I got it from overexposure and under-feeding among the Salt Lake Mountains. I've done my work now, and I don't care how soon I go, but I should like to leave some account of the business behind me. I don't want to be remembered as a common cut-throat."

The inspector and the two detectives had a hurried discussion as to the **advisability**[2] of allowing him to tell his story.

"Do you consider, Doctor, that there is immediate danger?" the former asked,

"Most certainly there is," I answered.

"In that case it is clearly our duty, in the interests of justice, to take his statement," said the inspector. "You are at liberty, sir, to give your account, which I again warn you will be taken down."

"I'll sit down, with your leave," the prisoner said, suiting the action to the word. "This aneurism of mine makes me easily tired, and the **tussle**[3] we had half an hour ago has not mended matters. I'm on the **brink**[4] of the grave, and I am not likely to lie to you. Every word I say is the absolute truth, and how you use it is a matter of no consequence to me."

With these words, Jefferson Hope leaned back in his chair and began the following remarkable statement. He spoke in a calm and methodical manner, as though the events which he narrated were commonplace enough. I can **vouch**[5] for the accuracy of the subjoined account, for I have had access to Lestrade's note-book, in which the prisoner's words were taken down exactly as they were uttered.

"It don't much matter to you why I hated these men," he said; "it's enough that they were guilty of the death of two human beings—a father and a daughter—and that they had, therefore, **forfeited**[6] their own lives. After the lapse of time that has passed since their crime, it was impossible for me to secure a conviction against them in any court. I knew of their guilt though, and I determined that I

① placidly [ˈplæsidli] *ad.* 平静地

② advisability [ədˌvaizəˈbiliti] *n.* 明智

③ tussle [ˈtʌsl] *n.* 扭打

④ brink [briŋk] *n.* 边缘

⑤ vouch [vautʃ] *v.* 担保

⑥ forfeit [ˈfɔːfit] *v.* 丧失

"怎么，"我大声说，"您得了主动脉血管瘤！"

"医生就是这么说的，"他态度平静地说，"上个星期，我就此去看过医生，医生告诉我说，过不了几天，血管瘤就会爆裂。我早就得了这种病，这些年里一直在恶化。自己之所以患上这种毛病，那是因为在盐湖城的山区，风吹日晒，忍饥挨饿。我现在完成了自己的使命了，所以不在乎死的日子来得有多快。但是，我想要把这件事交待明白，死后好有个记载。我不想以一个普通杀人犯的形象留在人们的记忆中。"

警长和两个警探急忙商议了一下，决定是否允许他讲述自己的经历。

"医生，您觉得他随时会有生命危险吗？"警长问。

"确实如此。"我回答说。

"既然如此，为了公正起见，我们显然有责任要取得他的供述，"警长说，"先生，您尽可以陈述自己的事情，不过，我要再次提醒一声，您的话会被记录下来的。"

"如果你们同意的话，我要坐下来说，"犯人说着，坐了下来，"动脉血管瘤病很容易使我疲惫。还有半小时前搏斗了一番，情况更糟了。我已经站到了坟墓的边缘上了，不可能在你们面前说谎的。我说的每一句话都千真万确，至于你们如何使用，对我无关紧要。"

说完这些，杰弗逊·霍普就倚靠在椅子上，开始了下面非同凡响的陈述。他说话时语气平静，有条不紊，仿佛他所说的是很平常的一件事情。我保证，每一条记录都准确无误，因为我参阅过莱斯特雷德的记录本，上面把犯人所叙述的情况一字不差地记录下来了。

"我为何要恨那两个人，这同你们没有什么关系，"他说，"但是，他们罪行累累，害死了两个人——一个父亲和女儿，因此，他们搭上了自己的性命，这就足够了。自从他们犯下了罪行以来，已经过去了那么长时

should be judge, jury, and **executioner**① all rolled into one. You'd have done the same, if you have any manhood in you, if you had been in my place.

"That girl that I spoke of was to have married me twenty years ago. She was forced into marrying that same Drebber, and broke her heart over it. I took the marriage ring from her dead finger, and I vowed that his dying eyes should rest upon that very ring, and that his last thoughts should be of the crime for which he was punished. I have carried it about with me, and have followed him and his **accomplice**② over two continents until I caught them. They thought to tire me out, but they could not do it. If I die to-morrow, as is likely enough, I die knowing that my work in this world is done, and well done. They have **perished**③, and by my hand. There is nothing left for me to hope for, or to desire.

"They were rich and I was poor, so that it was no easy matter for me to follow them. When I got to London my pocket was about empty, and I found that I must turn my hand to something for my living. Driving and riding are as natural to me as walking, so I applied at a cab owner's office, and soon got employment. I was to bring a certain sum a week to the owner, and whatever was over that I might keep for myself. There was seldom much over, but I managed to **scrape along**④ somehow. The hardest job was to learn my way about, for I reckon that of all the **mazes**⑤ that ever were **contrived**⑥, this city is the most confusing. I had a map beside me though, and when once I had spotted the principal hotels and stations, I got on pretty well.

"It was some time before I found out where my two gentlemen were living; but I inquired and inquired until at last I dropped across them. They were at a boarding-house at Camberwell, over on the other side of the river. When once I found them out I knew that I had them at my mercy. I had grown my beard, and there was no chance of their recognizing me. I would dog them and follow them until I saw my opportunity. I was determined that they should not escape me again.

"They were very near doing it for all that. Go where they would about London, I was always at their heels. Sometimes I followed them on my cab, and sometimes on foot, but the former was the best, for then they could not

① executioner [ˌeksi'kjuːʃənə] *n.* 行刑者

② accomplice [ə'kʌmplis] *n.* 共犯

③ perish ['periʃ] *v.* 丧生

④ scrape along 勉强活下去

⑤ maze [meiz] *n.* 迷宫

⑥ contrive [kən'traiv] *v.* 设计

间，我不可能在任何法庭告倒他们。我认定他们有罪，于是决定，法官、陪审团和行刑官全由我一个人来承担。如果你们有血性，如果你们处在我的位置上，那你们同样会这么干的。

“我所说的那位姑娘，本来二十年前就要嫁给我的。但是，却被逼嫁给了那个德雷伯，结果肝肠寸断，抑郁而终。我从她的遗体上把这枚婚戒指取了下来，当时发誓，要让德雷伯死前的目光落在这枚戒指上，让他意识到，他是因为犯下了罪才受到惩罚的。我带着这枚戒指浪迹天涯，跟踪着他和他的同伙跑遍了两个大洲，最后逮住了他们。他们想要把我累垮，但他们未能如愿。我即便是明天就死去——这很有可能，但我死亡时知道，自己在这个世界的任务已经完成了，而且还完成得很漂亮。他们死了，而且是我亲手杀死的。我再也没什么希望或渴求的东西了。

“他们很富有，而我却很贫穷，因此，要跟踪他们，这对我来说可不是件容易的事情。我到达伦敦之后，口袋里几乎一文不名。因此，我意识到，自己必须去干点零活儿，以便维持生计。驾车骑马对我而言就好比走路一样再平常不过了，于是，我到一家车行找工作，很快就有了差事了。我每个星期要向车行上缴一定数目的费用，余下的钱就归自己所有。虽然所剩无几，但还是千方百计挺过来了。对我来说，最大的困难是认路。我不得不说，虽然所有城市的街道都是星罗棋布的，但没有一个比伦敦城更像迷宫的。我身上一直都带着地图，等熟悉了一些大的旅馆和车站后，自己的活儿才干得顺当。

“过了一段时间，我才找到了自己要寻找的两位绅士的住处。我四处打听，最后才无意中遇上了他们。他们住在泰晤士河对面坎伯韦尔区的一幢公寓里。既然找到了他们，我便知道，他们的命运就已经掌握在我的手

get away from me. It was only early in the morning or late at night that I could earn anything, so that I began to get behind hand with my employer. I did not mind that, however, as long as I could lay my hand upon the men I wanted.

"They were very cunning, though. They must have thought that there was some chance of their being followed, for they would never go out alone, and never after nightfall. During two weeks I drove behind them every day, and never once saw them separate. Drebber himself was drunk half the time, but Stangerson was not to be caught **napping**①. I watched them late and early, but never saw the ghost of a chance; but I was not discouraged, for something told me that the hour had almost come. My only fear was that this thing in my chest might burst a little too soon and leave my work undone.

"At last, one evening I was driving up and down Torquay Terrace, as the street was called in which they boarded, when I saw a cab drive up to their door. Presently some luggage was brought out, and after a time Drebber and Stangerson followed it, and drove off. I whipped up my horse and kept within sight of them, feeling very ill at ease, for I feared that they were going to shift their **quarters**.② At Euston Station they got out, and I left a boy to hold my horse, and followed them on to the platform. I heard them ask for the Liverpool train, and the guard answer that one had just gone and there would not be another for some hours. Stangerson seemed to be put out at that, but Drebber was rather pleased than otherwise. I got so close to them in the **bustle**③ that I could hear every word that passed between them. Drebber said that he had a little business of his own to do, and that if the other would wait for him he would soon rejoin him. His companion **remonstrated**④ with him, and reminded him that they had resolved to stick together. Drebber answered that the matter was a delicate one, and that he must go alone. I could not catch what Stangerson said to that, but the other burst out swearing, and reminded him that he was nothing more than his paid servant, and that he must not **presume**⑤ to **dictate**⑥ to him. On that the Secretary gave it up as a bad job, and simply bargained with

心里了。我蓄了胡须，这样他们就认不出我了。我不停地跟踪他们，寻找机会下手。我下决心，无论如何不能再让他们跑掉。

“尽管这样，他们还是差点跑掉了。他们无论到伦敦的什么地方，我都紧跟其后。有时，我驾着马车跟在后面，有时步行。但是，前者是最好的办法，这样他们就没有办法逃掉。这样，我只有在凌晨或者深夜才能做生意，赚点钱。所以，我不能按时向车行缴费。但是，只要能亲手杀死这两个仇人，我什么都不在乎了。

“不过，他们非常狡猾，一定知道有可能会被人跟踪了，所以，从不单独出门，晚上也从不出门。整整两个星期，我每天驾着车跟在他们后面，从没见他们分开过。虽然德雷伯经常喝得烂醉，但斯坦格森一直都很警觉。我起早摸黑地监视着，但找不到一点机会下手。可我并没有泄气，因为有个声音告诉我，复仇的时刻就要来了。我唯一担心的就是，我胸口的动脉血管瘤可能过早破裂，这样我就没办法复仇了。

“结果，有一天傍晚，我驾着马车在托凯街转悠，因为他们就寄居在那条街。突然，有辆马车在他们门口停了下来。不一会儿，有人提了行李出来，随后德雷伯和斯坦格森也跟着出来，坐车离开。我策马驾车跟着他们。自己当时心里很紧张，担心他们又要换住处。他们在尤斯顿火车站下了马车。我找了个小孩帮我牵着马，随即跟着他们进了站台。我听到他们在打听去利物浦的火车。车站职员告诉他们刚开走了一趟车，下一趟车还要等几个小时。斯坦格森听了似乎有些不快，但德雷伯却相当高兴。我夹在人群中，离他们很近，他们两人的对话听得清清楚楚。德雷伯说他有点私事要去处理，如果斯坦格森愿意等他的话，他很快就会回来。斯坦格森不同意他这样做，还提醒说，他们说好不单独行动的。德雷伯回答说这件事非常私密，他必须自己一个人去。

① nap [næp] *v.* 疏忽

② quarters ['kwɔ:təs] *n.* 住处

③ bustle ['bʌsl] *n.* 喧闹

④ remonstrate ['remənstreit] *v.* 告诫

⑤ presume [pri'zju:m] *v.* 放肆

⑥ dictate [dik'teit] *v.* 命令；支配

him that if he missed the last train he should rejoin him at Halliday's Private Hotel; to which Drebber answered that he would be back on the platform before eleven, and made his way out of the station.

"The moment for which I had waited so long had at last come. I had my enemies within my power. Together they could protect each other, but singly they were at my mercy. I did not act, however, with undue **precipitation**①. My plans were already formed. There is no satisfaction in vengeance unless the offender has time to realize who it is that strikes him, and why retribution has come upon him. I had my plans arranged by which I should have the opportunity of making the man who had wronged me understand that his old sin had found him out. It chanced that some days before a gentleman who had been engaged in looking over some houses in the Brixton Road had dropped the key of one of them in my carriage. It was claimed that same evening, and returned; but in the **interval**② I had taken a **moulding**③ of it, and had a **duplicate**④ constructed. By means of this I had access to at least one spot in this great city where I could rely upon being free from **interruption**⑤. How to get Drebber to that house was the difficult problem which I had now to solve.

"He walked down the road and went into one or two liquor shops, staying for nearly half-an-hour in the last of them. When he came out he staggered in his walk, and was evidently pretty well on. There was a **hansom**⑥ just in front of me, and he hailed it. I followed it so close that the nose of my horse was within a yard of his driver the whole way. We rattled across Waterloo Bridge and through miles of streets, until, to my astonishment, we found ourselves back in the Terrace in which he had boarded. I could not imagine what his intention was in returning there; but I went on and pulled up my cab a hundred yards or so from the house. He entered it, and his hansom drove away. Give me a glass of water, if you please. My mouth gets dry with the talking."

I handed him the glass, and he drank it down.

我没听清斯坦格森又说了什么，但后者突然破口大骂，说对方只不过是他雇的佣人而已，无权对他说三道四的。听他这样一说，那位秘书也就不敢再多说什么，只是跟他商量说，如果他没赶上最后一趟车，就去哈利德私人旅馆找他。德雷伯答应十一点钟之前回到站台，接着就走出了车站。

“我等待已久的时刻终于到来了。我把仇人置于在我的掌控之中了。他们待在一块时，可以相互保护，但一旦分开，那就是由我说了算了。然而，我并没有仓促行事。我的计划是早就制定好了的。如果仇人来不及知道是谁对他下的手，他为何会遭此报应，那就毫无复仇的满足感可言。我先前就已经制定好了计划，一定要让加害过的那个人有机会知道，他昔日犯下的罪孽现在报应了。事情很巧，几天前，有位先生到布里克斯顿大街去看几幢房子，把其中一幢的钥匙落在了我的马车里。当天晚上，他就来取回了钥匙。只是在那期间，我获取了钥匙的模子，然后找人配了一把。这样一来，我在这样一座的偌大的城市里至少有了这么一处地方，可以在毫无干扰的情况下干自己的事情。我现在要解决的唯一难题就是如何才能把德雷伯带到那儿去。

“德雷伯沿着大街行走，进了一两家酒馆，并且在最后进的那家待了有半个小时。他走出酒馆时，走路跌跌撞撞的，显然喝了不少酒。我的前方正好有一辆双轮马车，他上了马车。我一路紧紧跟随，我的马的鼻子离他坐的马车的车夫还不到一码远。我们辘辘地驶过了滑铁卢桥，又在不同的街道上行进了几英里。最后，令我感到很吃惊的是，我们竟然回到了他原来住的地方。我不知道他返回到那儿去要干什么，但我还是要继续跟踪，把马车停在离住房大概一百码的地方。他进了房子，那辆双轮马车离开了。请给我一杯水好吗？我说得口都干了。”

我把水杯端给了他，他把水全喝了。

① precipitation [priˌsipiˈteiʃən] *n.* 仓促

② interval [ˈintəvəl] *n.* 间隔

③ moulding [ˈməuldiŋ] *n.* 模子

④ duplicate [ˈdjuːplikət] *a.* 复制的

⑤ interruption [ˌintəˈrʌpʃən] *n.* 打断

⑥ hansom [ˈhænsəm] *n.* 一马二轮的有盖双座小马车

"That's better," he said. "Well, I waited for a quarter of an hour, or more, when suddenly there came a noise like people struggling inside the house. Next moment the door was flung open and two men appeared, one of whom was Drebber, and the other was a young chap whom I had never seen before. This fellow had Drebber by the collar, and when they came to the head of the steps he gave him a shove and a kick which sent him half across the road. 'You hound,' he cried, shaking his stick at him; 'I'll teach you to insult an honest girl!' He was so hot that I think he would have **thrashed**① Drebber with his **cudgel**②, only that the cur **staggered**③ away down the road as fast as his legs would carry him. He ran as far as the corner, and then seeing my cab, he hailed me and jumped in. 'Drive me to Halliday's Private Hotel,' said he.

"When I had him fairly inside my cab, my heart jumped so with joy that I feared lest at this last moment my aneurism might go wrong. I drove along slowly, weighing in my own mind what it was best to do. I might take him right out into the country, and there in some deserted lane have my last interview with him. I had almost decided upon this, when he solved the problem for me. The craze for drink had seized him again, and he ordered me to pull up outside a **gin**④ palace. He went in, leaving word that I should wait for him. There he remained until closing time, and when he came out he was so far gone that I knew the game was in my own hands.

"Don't imagine that I intended to kill him in cold blood. It would only have been rigid justice if I had done so, but I could not bring myself to do it. I had long determined that he should have a show for his life if he chose to take advantage of it. Among the many **billets**⑤ which I have filled in America during my wandering life, I was once **janitor**⑥ and sweeper-out of the laboratory at York College. One day the professor was lecturing on poisions, and he showed his students some **alkaloid**⑦, as he called it, which he had **extracted**⑧ from some South American arrow poison, and which was so powerful that the least grain meant instant death. I spotted the bottle in which this preparation was kept, and when they were all gone, I helped

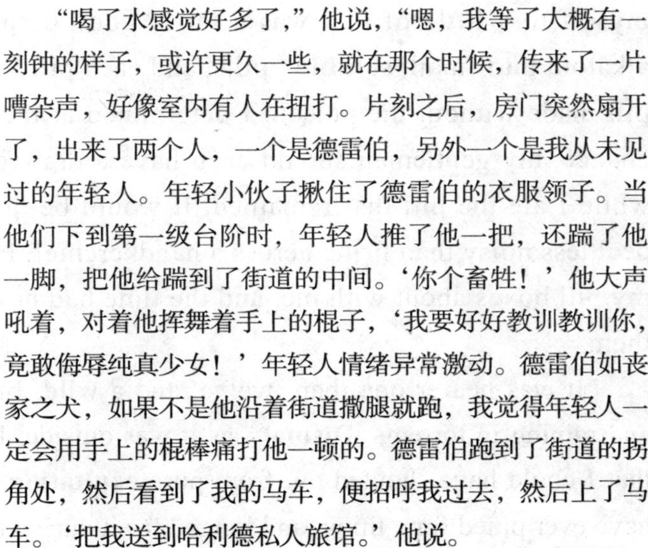

“喝了水感觉好多了，”他说，“嗯，我等了大概有一刻钟的样子，或许更久一些，就在那个时候，传来了一片嘈杂声，好像室内有人在扭打。片刻之后，房门突然扇开了，出来了两个人，一个是德雷伯，另外一个是我从未见过的年轻人。年轻小伙子揪住了德雷伯的衣服领子。当他们下到第一级台阶时，年轻人推了他一把，还踹了他一脚，把他给踹到了街道的中间。‘你个畜牲！’他大声吼着，对着他挥舞着手上的棍子，‘我要好好教训教训你，竟敢侮辱纯真少女！’年轻人情绪异常激动。德雷伯如丧家之犬，如果不是他沿着街道撒腿就跑，我觉得年轻人一定会用手上的棍棒痛打他一顿的。德雷伯跑到了街道的拐角处，然后看到了我的马车，便招呼我过去，然后上了马车。‘把我送到哈利德私人旅馆。’他说。

① thrash [θræʃ] *v.* 痛打
② cudgel [ˈkʌdʒl] *n.* 棍棒
③ stagger [ˈstægə] *v.* 蹒跚

“当我看到他确确实实地进了我的马车之后，我高兴不已，心跳得厉害，生怕到了这样一个关键的时刻，自己身上的血管瘤会出问题。我一路缓慢驾车前行，心里思忖着该怎么办才最妥当。我可以载着他直接出城到郊区去，找一处僻静的小径，最后跟他摊牌。我差不多要决定这样做了，突然，他替我解决了难题。他的酒瘾又上来了，吩咐我在一家奢华的大酒店外面停下。他进了酒店，要我在外面等着。他一直在里面待到了打烊才关门，出来时已经烂醉。我知道自己胜券在握了。

④ gin [dʒin] *n.* 杜松子酒

“不要以为，我会打算用冷血的手段杀死他。即便我那样做了，也是死板板地还以公道，但我不会那样做。我很早就已经决定了，只要他懂得如何利用，他应该拥有一个活命的机会。我在美国颠沛流离的日子里干过许多杂七杂八的活儿，其中有一件就是在约克学院的实验室当看门扫地的。有一天，教授给学生们讲授有关毒药的内容，给他们展示了一种他称之为生物碱的毒药，是他从南美土著人弓箭上的毒药中提取出来的，毒性很强，沾上一丁点儿就会立刻毙命。我记住了那只装

⑤ billet [ˈbilit] *n.* 工作职位
⑥ janitor [ˈdʒænitə] *n.* 看门人
⑦ alkaloid [ˈælkəlɔid] *n.* 生物碱
⑧ extract [ekˈstrækt] *v.* 提取

myself to a little of it. I was a fairly good **dispenser**①, so I worked this alkaloid into small, **soluble**② pills, and each pill I put in a box with a similar pill made without the poison. I determined at the time that when I had my chance, my gentlemen should each have a draw out of one of these boxes, while I ate the pill that remained. It would be quite as deadly, and a good deal less noisy than firing across a handkerchief. From that day I had always my pill boxes about with me, and the time had now come when I was to use them.

"It was nearer one than twelve, and a wild, **bleak**③ night, blowing hard and raining in torrents. **Dismal**④ as it was outside, I was glad within—so glad that I could have shouted out from pure **exultation**⑤. If any of you gentlemen have ever pined for a thing, and longed for it during twenty long years, and then suddenly found it within your reach, you would understand my feelings. I lit a cigar, and puffed at it to steady my nerves, but my hands were trembling and my temples throbbing with excitement. As I drove, I could see old John Ferrier and sweet Lucy looking at me out of the darkness and smiling at me, just as plain as I see you all in this room. All the way they were ahead of me, one on each side of the horse until I pulled up at the house in the Brixton Road.

"There was not a soul to be seen, nor a sound to be heard, except the **dripping**⑥ of the rain. When I looked in at the window, I found Drebber all **huddled**⑦ together in a drunken sleep. I shook him by the arm, 'It's time to get out,' I said.

"'All right, cabby,' said he.

"I suppose he thought we had come to the hotel that he had mentioned, for he got out without another word, and followed me down the garden. I had to walk beside him to keep him steady, for he was still a little top-heavy. When we came to the door, I opened it and led him into the front room. I give you my word that all the way, the father and the daughter were walking in front of us.

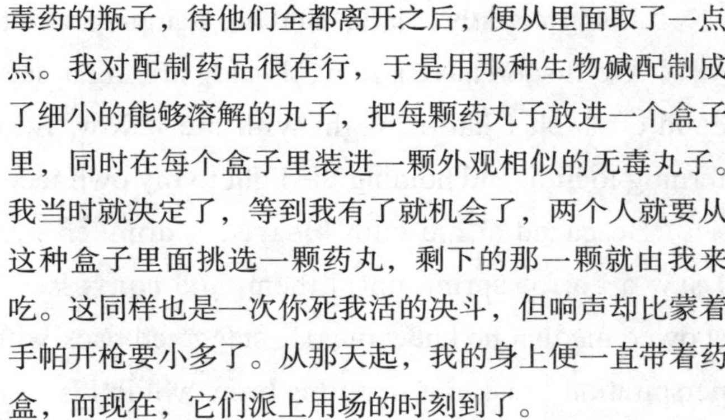

毒药的瓶子，待他们全都离开之后，便从里面取了一点点。我对配制药品很在行，于是用那种生物碱配制成了细小的能够溶解的丸子，把每颗药丸子放进一个盒子里，同时在每个盒子里装进一颗外观相似的无毒丸子。我当时就决定了，等到我有了就机会了，两个人就要从这种盒子里面挑选一颗药丸，剩下的那一颗就由我来吃。这同样也是一次你死我活的决斗，但响声却比蒙着手帕开枪要小多了。从那天起，我的身上便一直带着药盒，而现在，它们派上用场的时刻到了。

① dispenser [dis'pensə] *n.* 配药师

② soluble ['sɔljubl] *a.* 可溶的

“当晚快要接近一点钟了。这是个天气恶劣的夜晚，狂风大作，暴雨如注。虽然周围环境惨淡，但我的内心却充满了欣喜——高兴得都要放声欢叫起来了。如果你们哪位先生心里苦苦地挂念着一件事，而且等待了二十年，然后突然间发现自己触手可得了，那就能够理解我的心情了。我点了一支雪茄，抽了起来，以便使自己镇静下来，但是，我的双手还是不停地颤抖着，太阳穴也因为激动而突突直跳。我驾着马车的时候，看到了老约翰·费里厄和亲爱的露茜在黑暗中看着我，冲着我微笑，看得真真切切，就像看到你们大家在这个房间里一样。一路上，他们总是在我的前方，马匹两边一边一个，一直把我引到了布里克斯顿大街的那幢房子边停下。

③ bleak [bli:k] *a.* 寒冷的

④ dismal ['dizməl] *a.* 惨淡的

⑤ exultation [ˌegzʌl'teiʃən] *n.* 狂喜

“那儿看不到一个人影，听不见一丝声音，只有雨滴滴答答地下个不停。我透过车窗户朝着里面看了一眼，发现德雷伯蜷缩成一团，醉醺醺地睡着了。我拽着他的胳膊，把他摇醒了。‘该下车了。’我说。

⑥ dripping ['dripiŋ] *n.* 滴水声

⑦ huddle ['hʌdl] *v.* 蜷缩

“‘好的，车夫。’他说。

“我猜，他以为到达了他提到的那家旅馆，二话没说便下了车，跟着我走过房前的花园。他当时还有点头重脚轻，我只得在他身边搀扶着他，保持身体平衡。到达门边时，我打开了门，把他领到了前面的房间。我可以向你们保证，一路上，那位父亲和女儿一直在我们面

"'It's **infernally**[①] dark,' said he, stamping about.

"'We'll soon have a light,' I said, striking a match and putting it to a **wax**[②] candle which I had brought with me. 'Now, Enoch Drebber,' I continued, turning to him, and holding the light to my own face, 'who am I?'

"He gazed at me with **bleared**[③], drunken eyes for a moment, and then I saw a horror spring up in them, and **convulse**[④] his whole features, which showed me that he knew me. He staggered back with a livid face, and I saw the perspiration break out upon his brow, while his teeth chattered in his head. At the sight I leaned my back against the door and laughed loud and long. I had always known that vengeance would be sweet, but I had never hoped for the **contentment**[⑤] of soul which now possessed me.

"'You dog!' I said; 'I have hunted you from Salt Lake City to St. Petersburg, and you have always escaped me. Now, at last your wanderings have come to an end, for either you or I shall never see to-morrow's sun rise.' He **shrunk**[⑥] still further away as I spoke, and I could see on his face that he thought I was mad. So I was for the time. The pulses in my temples beat like **sledge-hammers**[⑦], and I believe I would have had a fit of some sort if the blood had not gushed from my nose and relieved me.

"'What do you think of Lucy Ferrier now?' I cried, locking the door, and shaking the key in his face. 'Punishment has been slow in coming, but it has overtaken you at last.' I saw his coward lips tremble as I spoke. He would have begged for his life, but he knew well that it was useless.

"'Would you murder me?' he stammered.

"'There is no murder,' I answered. 'Who talks of murdering a mad dog? What mercy had you upon my poor darling, when you dragged her from her **slaughtered**[⑧] father, and bore her away to your accursed and shameless harem.'

"'It was not I who killed her father,' he cried.

"'But it was you who broke her innocent heart,' I **shrieked**[①], **thrusting**[②]

前引着路呢。

① infernally [in'fəːnəli] *ad.* 地狱般地

"'简直跟地狱一样黑啊。'他一边说，一边跺着脚。

② wax [wæks] *n.* 蜡

"'马上就有灯光了，'我说着，擦了根火柴，点亮了我带来的一支蜡烛。'好啦，伊诺克·德雷伯，'我接着说，转身朝着他，用蜡烛照着我自己的脸庞，'知道我是谁吗？'

③ bleared [bliəd] *a.* 模糊的

④ convulse [kən'vʌls] *v.* 使抽搐

"他醉眼蒙胧地盯着我看了一会儿，然后我看到他的眼睛显露出惊恐的神色，五官抽搐了起来，我知道，他认出我来了。他面如土色，踉踉跄跄地往后退。我看见他的额头上冒着汗珠，牙齿则咯咯地响个不停。见此情形，我把身子靠到了后面的门上，哈哈大笑了好一阵子。我早就清楚了，复仇的感觉是甜蜜的，但自己从来都没有奢望过舒心惬意的感觉竟然会像此时这样占据着自己的整个身心。

⑤ contentment [kən'tentmənt] *n.* 满足

"'你个狗东西！'我骂了一声，'我从盐湖城一直追到圣彼得堡，每次你都逃脱掉了。现在，你的逃亡生涯结束了，因为我们当中一定有一个人看不见明天的太阳了。'我说话时，他还在往后退缩。他脸上的神情分明告诉我，他以为我疯了。那个时候，我的确跟疯了一样，太阳穴处的血管像挥动的铁锤一样狂跳不止。我相信，如果当时不是有鲜血从我的鼻孔里喷出来，缓解了一下的话，我的病当场就可能发作了。

⑥ shrink [ʃriŋk] *v.* 后退

⑦ sledge-hammer ['sledʒ,hæmə] *n.* 大锤

"'你现在对露茜·费里厄是怎么想的？'我大声吼着，锁上了门，朝着他的脸挥了挥钥匙，'惩罚姗姗来迟，但终究还是来了。'我说这话时，只见他的嘴唇在瑟瑟发抖。如果不是知道求饶无济于事，他可能会苦苦哀求我放过他一命。

"'你要谋杀我吗？'他结结巴巴地说。

"'不存在谋杀，"我回答说，"杀死一条疯狗，谁会说是谋杀呢？当年你把我可怜的心上人从她被杀害的父亲身边拖走，带到了你那该死的无耻的后宫，你可有过

⑧ slaughter ['slɔːtə] *v.* 屠杀

the box before him. 'Let the high God judge between us. Choose and eat. There is death in one and life in the other. I shall take what you leave. Let us see if there is justice upon the earth, or if we are ruled by chance.'

"He **cowered**③ away with wild cries and prayers for mercy, but I drew my knife and held it to his throat until he had obeyed me. Then I swallowed the other, and we stood facing one another in silence for a minute or more, waiting to see which was to live and which was to die. Shall I ever forget the look which came over his face when the first warning pangs told him that the poison was in his system? I laughed as I saw it, and held Lucy's marriage ring in front of his eyes. It was but for a moment, for the action of the alkaloid is rapid. A **spasm**④ of pain **contorted**⑤ his features; he threw his hands out in front of him, staggered, and then, with a hoarse cry, fell heavily upon the floor. I turned him over with my foot, and placed my hand upon his heart. There was no movement. He was dead!

"The blood had been streaming from my nose, but I had taken no notice of it. I don't know what it was that put it into my head to write upon the wall with it. Perhaps it was some **mischievous**⑥ idea of setting the police upon a wrong track, for I felt light-hearted and cheerful. I remembered a German being found in New York with RACHE written up above him, and it was argued at the time in the newspapers that the secret societies must have done it. I guessed that what puzzled the New Yorkers would puzzle the Londoners, so I dipped my finger in my own blood and printed it on a convenient place on the wall. Then I walked down to my cab and found that there was nobody about, and that the night was still very wild. I had driven some distance when I put my hand into the pocket in which I usually kept Lucy's ring, and found that it was not there. I was thunderstruck at this, for it was the only **memento**⑦ that I had of her. Thinking that I might have dropped it when I stooped over Drebber's body, I drove back, and leaving my cab in a side street, I went boldly up to the house—for I was

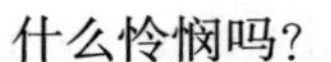

① shriek [ʃriːk] *v.* 尖叫
② thrust [θrʌst] *v.* 猛推

③ cower [ˈkauə] *v.* 畏缩

④ spasm [ˈspæzəm] *n.* 抽搐
⑤ contort [kənˈtɔːt] *v.* 扭曲

⑥ mischievous [ˈmistʃivəs] *a.* 恶作剧的

⑦ memento [məˈmentəu] *n.* 遗物；纪念物

什么怜悯吗？'

"'杀她父亲的人不是我。'他大声说。

"'但是，粉碎她那颗纯洁无暇的心的人是你，'我声嘶力竭地一边大吼着，一边把装了药的盒子亮到他的面前，'让至高无上的上帝在我们两个人中间做出裁决。选择一颗吃下去，一颗致死，另一颗获生。你挑剩下的那颗我来吃。让我们看看世界上是否还有公正可言，或者是全凭运气。'

"他发疯似地叫着，战战兢兢地往后缩，乞求我饶命。但是，我拔刀顶着他的喉咙，他不得已吃了一颗，我随后吞下了另一颗。我们面对面，一声不吭地站了一两分钟，看究竟谁生谁死。突如其来的剧痛让他明白，自己吞下的是毒药，他当时脸上的那副表情我怎么可能忘记呢？我看到他那副样子时，不禁哈哈大笑起来，同时把露茜的结婚戒指举到了他的眼前。只是片刻的功夫，因为生物碱发作很快。一阵剧痛使他五官痉挛变形了。他向前抬起双手，身体摇摇晃晃，接着惨叫一声，重重地倒在地板上。我用脚把他翻了身，把一只手按在他的胸口上，没有心跳，他死了！

"鲜血一直从我的鼻腔涌出来，但我根本就没有注意到。我都不知道，脑子里面会涌上这么一个念头，用鲜血在墙上写字。或许是自己当时心里觉得轻松愉快，所以想要搞点恶作剧，把警方引向错误的方向。我记得，曾经有个德国人在纽约被谋杀了，尸体上方就写着'RACHE'这个词。当时的报纸上都说，那一定是秘密社团干的。我估计，令纽约人迷惑不解的东西同样会令伦敦人迷惑不解。于是，我用自己的手指蘸着自己的鲜血，在墙上找了个合适的地方写下了这个词。然后，我走回到了马车停放处，周围没有一个人影儿，天气还是很恶劣。我驾着马车行进了一段路程，突然，我把手伸进了自己的衣服口袋，露茜的戒指一直是放在那

ready to dare anything rather than lose the ring. When I arrived there, I walked right into the arms of a police-officer who was coming out, and only managed to **disarm**[1] his suspicions by pretending to be hopelessly drunk.

"That was how Enoch Drebber came to his end. All I had to do then was to do as much for Stangerson, and so pay off John Ferrier's debt. I knew that he was staying at Halliday's Private Hotel, and I hung about all day, but he never came out. I fancy that he suspected something when Drebber failed to put in an appearance. He was cunning, was Stangerson, and always on his guard. If he thought he could keep me off by staying indoors he was very much mistaken. I soon found out which was the window of his bedroom, and early next morning I took advantage of some **ladders**[2] which were lying in the **lane**[3] behind the hotel, and so made my way into his room in the grey of the dawn. I woke him up and told him that the hour had come when he was to answer for the life he had taken so long before. I described Drebber's death to him, and I gave him the same choice of the poisoned pills. Instead of grasping at the chance of safety which that offered him, he sprang from his bed and flew at my throat. In self-defence I stabbed him to the heart. It would have been the same in any case, for Providence would never have allowed his guilty hand to pick out anything but the poison.

"I have little more to say, and it's as well, for I am about done up. I went on cabbing it for a day or so, intending to keep at it until I could save enough to take me back to America. I was standing in the yard when a ragged youngster asked if there was a cabby there called Jefferson Hope, and said that his cab was wanted by a gentleman at 221B, Baker Street. I went round, suspecting no harm, and the next thing I knew, this young man here had the **bracelets**[4] on my wrists, and as neatly **shackled**[5] as ever I saw in my life. That's the whole of my story, gentlemen. You may consider me to be a murderer; but I hold that I am just as much an officer of justice as you are."

So thrilling had the man's narrative been, and his manner was so impressive that we had sat silent and absorbed. Even the professional detectives, blase as

儿的，结果发现，戒指不见了。我像是遭到雷击了似的，因为那是我拥有的唯一一件她的纪念物。我想到，可能是在弯腰察看德雷伯的尸体时掉落了。于是赶着马车回去，把车停在附近的一条横街上，壮着胆子走向那幢房子——因为我宁可冒再大的风险，也不能丢失那枚戒指。一到门口，就跟一个刚从里面走出来的警察撞了个满怀。我只好装成一个酩酊大醉的酒鬼，以打消他的怀疑。

① disarm [dis'ɑːm] *v.* 消除

"这就是伊诺克·德雷伯死的过程。我接下来要办的事情就是，让斯坦格森遭受同样的下场，这样就偿还了他欠约翰·费里厄的债了。我知道他待在哈利德私人旅馆里，于是整个白天都徘徊在附近，但他压根儿就没有外出露过面。我估计，他一直不见德雷伯出现，可能觉得事情有点不妙。斯坦格森是个狡猾的家伙，一直小心提防着。如果他以为藏匿在旅馆不露面就可以躲避开我的话，那他就大错特错了。我很快就弄清楚了，哪扇是他卧室的窗户。第二天一大早，我利用了放在旅馆后面小巷子里的一张梯子，借着朦胧的晨光爬进了他的房间。我把他弄醒，告诉他，他很早以前欠下的人命现在该偿还了。我把德雷伯死亡的经过讲给他听，并同样给他机会在两颗药丸间做出选择。摆在他面前的机会他不好好把握，而是从床上跃起身子，想要扼住我的脖子。出于自卫，我一刀刺进了他的心脏。无论怎样，结果都一样。上帝无论如何都不会让他那罪恶之手挑中无毒药丸的。

② ladder ['lædə] *n.* 梯子

③ lane [lein] *n.* 小路；小巷

"我没有更多的情况要叙述的了，这样很好，因为我自己也快要不行了。我继续驾着马车走了一天，打算坚持下去，等到挣了足够的钱，可以返回到美国去。我站立在院子里，这时候，来了个衣服破烂的小伙子，打听是不是有个名叫杰弗逊·霍普的马车夫，并且说，贝克大街二百二十一号乙有位先生要雇辆马车。我没有怀疑就跟来了，后来在座的这位年轻人把手铐铐在我手腕

④ bracelets ['breislits] *n.* 手铐

⑤ shackle ['ʃækl] *n.* 给…带上手铐

they were in every detail of crime, appeared to be keenly interested in the man's story. When he finished, we sat for some minutes in a stillness which was only broken by the scratching of Lestrade's pencil as he gave the finishing touches to his **shorthand**① account.

"There is only one point on which I should like a little more information," Sherlock Holmes said at last. "Who was your accomplice who came for the ring which I advertised?"

The prisoner **winked**② at my friend **jocosely**③. "I can tell my own secrets," he said, "but I don't get other people into trouble. I saw your advertisement, and I thought it might be a plant, or it might be the ring which I wanted. My friend volunteered to go and see. I think you'll own he did it smartly."

"Not a doubt of that," said Holmes heartily.

"Now, gentlemen," the inspector remarked gravely, "the forms of the law must be complied with. On Thursday the prisoner will be brought before the magistrates, and your attendance will be required. Until then I will be responsible for him." He rang the bell as he spoke, and Jefferson Hope was led off by a couple of **warders**④, while my friend and I made our way out of the Station and took a cab back to Baker Street.

上，动作干脆利落，真是生平罕见！先生们，这就是整个事情的龙去脉。你们可以把我看做杀人犯，但我仍然觉得，我跟你们这些执法者一样，维护着公正。”

他叙述的事情令人惊心动魄，他叙述的方式令人印象深刻，我们全都坐着，缄默不语，全神贯注。连两位职业警探，尽管他们熟知案件的每一个细节，但他们都还是对霍普的叙述产生了浓厚的兴趣。在他讲完后，我们静静地坐了好一会儿，惟有莱斯特雷德的铅笔发出沙沙的声音，因为他要整理完成自己速记下来的内容。

“就剩下一点，我想要了解一下，”夏洛克·福尔摩斯最后说，“我登了招领启事后，帮助您前来领取那枚戒指的同伴是谁？”

犯人表情滑稽地朝着我的朋友眨了眨眼睛。“我可以把自己的种种秘密都讲述出来，”他说，“但是，我不能连累他人。我看见了你们登出的启事，但心里面觉得可能是个骗局，也可能是我想要的那枚戒指。我的朋友自告奋勇，要去看一看。我觉得，您会承认，他干得很漂亮。”

“毫无疑问。”福尔摩斯由衷地说。

“好啦，先生们，”警长神情严肃地说，“法律程序必须得遵循。星期四，犯人要带上法庭受审，诸位要悉数到场。上法庭之前，犯人由我来看管。”他说着，按响了铃，两名看守把杰弗逊·霍普带走了。我和我朋友走出了警察局，乘坐马车回到了贝克大街。

① shorthand [ˈʃɔːthænd] *a.* 速记法的

② wink [wiŋk] *v.* 眨眼

③ jocosely [dʒəuˈkəusli] *ad.* 滑稽地

④ warder [ˈwɔːdə] *n.* 监狱看守

Chapter 7 The Conclusion

We had all been warned to appear before the magistrates upon the Thursday; but when the Thursday came there was no occasion for our testimony. A higher Judge had taken the matter in hand, and Jefferson Hope had been summoned before a tribunal where strict justice would be **meted**[①] out to him. On the very night after his capture the aneurism burst, and he was found in the morning stretched upon the floor of the cell, with a **placid**[②] smile upon his face, as though he had been able in his dying moments to look back upon a useful life, and on work well done.

"Gregson and Lestrade will be wild about his death," Holmes remarked, as we chatted it over next evening. "Where will their **grand**[③] advertisement be now?"

"I don't see that they had very much to do with his capture," I answered.

"What you do in this world is a matter of no consequence," returned my companion, bitterly. "The question is, what can you make people believe that you have done? Never mind," he continued, more brightly, after a pause. "I would not have missed the investigation for anything. There has been no better case within my recollection. Simple as it was, there were several most **instructive**[④] points about it."

"Simple!" I ejaculated.

"Well, really, it can hardly be described as otherwise," said Sherlock

第七章　尾声

我们都接到通知，星期四必须到庭。但是，到了星期四，我们没有必要出庭作证。一位级别更高的法官接手了案件，杰弗逊·霍普被传唤到另一个法庭受审，说要给他最公正的审判。就在他被捕的当天晚上，他的动脉血管瘤破裂了，翌日早晨，人们发现他倒在监舍的地板上，四肢张开，脸上带着平静安详的笑容，看起来，他在弥留之际回首了自己充满了意义的人生，报仇大业已经如愿以偿了。

① mete [mi:t] *v.* 给予（处罚）

② placid ['plæsid] *a.* 平静的

“格雷格森和莱斯特雷德会因他的死而疯狂的，”翌日晚上，我们聊起这件事情时，福尔摩斯说，“他们现在到哪儿去四处炫耀啊？”

③ grand [grænd] *a.* 炫耀的

“我看吧，他们与他被捕的事情并没有多少关系啊。”我回答说。

“在这个世界上，你做了什么并不重要，”福尔摩斯回答说，语气显得尖刻，“问题是，你如何才能让人们相信你做过的事情？没有关系，”他停顿了一下，接着又语气轻松地说，“我不会因为任何情况而错过这次调查的。在我的记忆中，本案是最有意思的一桩。案情虽说简单，但其中有几处极具启发性的地方。”

④ instructive [in'strʌktiv] *a.* 教育性的

“简单！”我脱口而出。

“是啊，确实简单，很难用别的什么词来形容它，”

Holmes, smiling at my surprise. "The proof of its **intrinsic**① simplicity is, that without any help save a few very ordinary deductions I was able to lay my hand upon the criminal within three days."

"That is true," said I.

"I have already explained to you that what is out of the common is usually a guide rather than a **hindrance**②. In solving a problem of this sort, the grand thing is to be able to reason backwards. That is a very useful accomplishment, and a very easy one, but people do not practise it much. In the everyday affairs of life it is more useful to reason forwards, and so the other comes to be neglected. There are fifty who can reason **synthetically**③ for one who can reason **analytically**④."

"I confess," said I, "that I do not quite follow you."

"I hardly expected that you would. Let me see if I can make it clearer. Most people, if you describe a train of events to them, will tell you what the result would be. They can put those events together in their minds, and argue from them that something will come to pass. There are few people, however, who, if you told them a result, would be able to evolve from their own inner **consciousness**⑤ what the steps were which led up to that result. This power is what I mean when I talk of reasoning backwards, or analytically."

"I understand," said I.

"Now this was a case in which you were given the result and had to find everything else for yourself. Now let me endeavour to show you the different steps in my reasoning. To begin at the beginning. I approached the house, as you know, on foot, and with my mind entirely free from all impressions. I naturally began by examining the roadway, and there, as I have already explained to you, I saw clearly the marks of a cab, which, I **ascertained**⑥ by inquiry, must have been there during the night. I satisfied myself that it was a cab and not a private carriage by the narrow **gauge**⑦ of the wheels. The ordinary London **growler**⑧ is considerably less wide than a gentleman's **brougham**⑨.

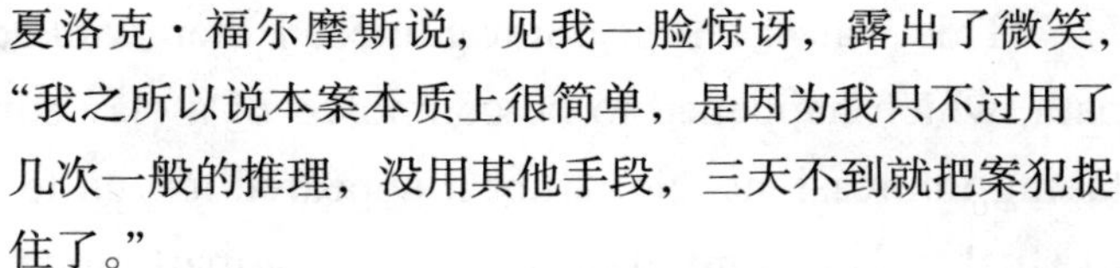

夏洛克·福尔摩斯说，见我一脸惊讶，露出了微笑，“我之所以说本案本质上很简单，是因为我只不过用了几次一般的推理，没用其他手段，三天不到就把案犯捉住了。”

“这倒也是。”我说。

“我已经向你解释过了，那些不同寻常的情况其实是破案的引指，而非障碍。要解决这类问题，最重要的是能够逆向推理。这个方法很管用，也很简单，可惜人们不大用。在日常生活中，顺向推理用得很普遍，而逆向推理往往被忽略。五十个能够进行综合推理的人中间，只有一个人能做逆向分析推理。”

“我承认，”我说，“我不大明白你说的意思。”

“我也没有指望你明白。让我看看能不能把事情解释得更加清晰一些。对于大多数人来说，如果你向他们描述一系列事件，他们都会指出事件的结果如何。他们可以在头脑中把那些事件糅合到一块儿，而且由此认定，会出现某种情况。然而，如果你告诉他们一个结果，却很少有人能通过内在的思维推理出导致这一结果的步骤是什么。这种能力就是我所讲的逆向推理，也可称之为分析推理。”

“我明白了。”我说。

“对啦，本案就是一个例证。你已经知道了结果，而其他情况则需要你自己去探寻。我现在就设法给你展示一下我推理过程中的各个不同步骤吧。从最开始讲起，我到达那幢住宅附近后——你知道，我是步行过去的——头脑里完全没有一点印象。自然而然，我首先查看的是路面。我已经向你解释过了，路上马车留下的车辙印清晰可见。通过询问，我确认，车辙印一定是夜间留下的。我断定，那是一辆出租马车，而非私人专用马车，因为其轮距比较狭窄。同绅士们的私家马车比起来，伦敦城里的那些日常用的出租马车轮子要窄很多。

① intrinsic [in'trinsik] *a.* 本质的

② hindrance ['hindrəns] *n.* 障碍

③ synthetically [sin'θetikəli] *ad.* 综合地

④ analytically [ˌænə'litikəli] *ad.* 分析地

⑤ consciousness ['kɔnʃəsnis] *n.* 意识

⑥ ascertain [ˌæsə'tein] *v.* 确认

⑦ gauge [geidʒ] *n.* 尺寸

⑧ growler ['graulə] *n.* 四轮出租马车

⑨ brougham ['bru:əm] *n.* 布鲁厄姆式马车

"This was the first point gained. I then walked slowly down the garden path, which happened to be composed of a clay soil, **peculiarly**[①] suitable for taking impressions. No doubt it appeared to you to be a mere **trampled**[②] line of **slush**[③], but to my trained eyes every mark upon its surface had a meaning. There is no branch of detective science which is so important and so much neglected as the art of tracing footsteps. Happily, I have always laid great stress upon it, and much practice has made it second nature to me. I saw the heavy footmarks of the constables, but I saw also the track of the two men who had first passed through the garden. It was easy to tell that they had been before the others, because in places their marks had been entirely obliterated by the others coming upon the top of them. In this way my second link was formed, which told me that the **nocturnal**[④] visitors were two in number, one remarkable for his height (as I calculated from the length of his stride), and the other fashionably dressed, to judge from the small and elegant impression left by his boots.

"On entering the house this last inference was confirmed. My well-booted man lay before me. The tall one, then, had done the murder, if murder there was. There was no wound upon the dead man's person, but the agitated expression upon his face assured me that he had foreseen his fate before it came upon him. Men who die from heart disease, or any sudden natural cause, never by any chance exhibit agitation upon their features. Having sniffed the dead man's lips I detected a slightly sour smell, and I came to the conclusion that he had had poison forced upon him. Again, I argued that it had been forced upon him from the hatred and fear expressed upon his face. By the method of **exclusion**[⑤], I had arrived at this result, for no other **hypothesis**[⑥] would meet the facts. Do not imagine that it was a very unheard-of idea. The forcible administration of poison is by no means a new thing in criminal annals. The cases of Dolsky in Odessa, and of Leturier in Montpellier, will occur at once to any **toxicologist**[⑦].

"And now came the great question as to the reason why. Robbery had

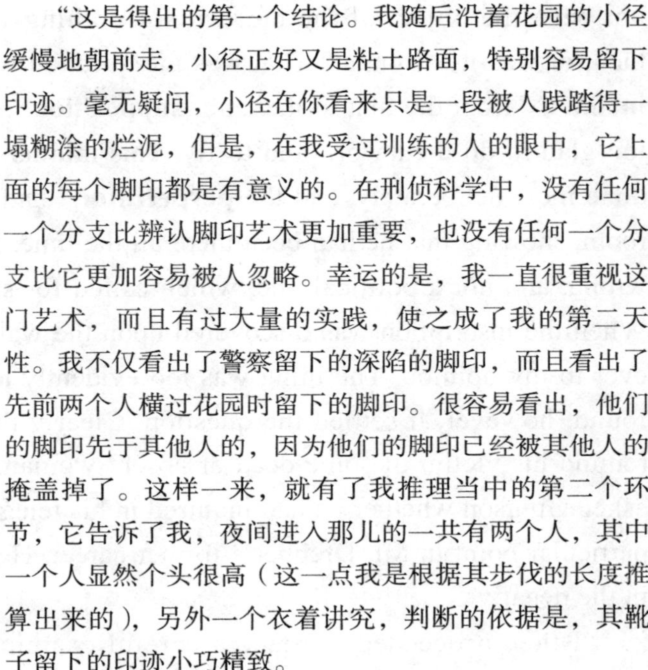

“这是得出的第一个结论。我随后沿着花园的小径缓慢地朝前走，小径正好又是粘土路面，特别容易留下印迹。毫无疑问，小径在你看来只是一段被人践踏得一塌糊涂的烂泥，但是，在我受过训练的人的眼中，它上面的每个脚印都是有意义的。在刑侦科学中，没有任何一个分支比辨认脚印艺术更加重要，也没有任何一个分支比它更加容易被人忽略。幸运的是，我一直很重视这门艺术，而且有过大量的实践，使之成了我的第二天性。我不仅看出了警察留下的深陷的脚印，而且看出了先前两个人横过花园时留下的脚印。很容易看出，他们的脚印先于其他人的，因为他们的脚印已经被其他人的掩盖掉了。这样一来，就有了我推理当中的第二个环节，它告诉了我，夜间进入那儿的一共有两个人，其中一个人显然个头很高（这一点我是根据其步伐的长度推算出来的），另外一个衣着讲究，判断的依据是，其靴子留下的印迹小巧精致。

“进入室内之后，刚才的推论就得到证实。我所说的那位脚穿精致靴子的人就躺在我的面前。如果此人死于谋杀的话，那便是那位高个子所为。死者的身上没有任何伤痕，但他脸上那种焦虑狂躁的表情令我确信，死亡的命运向他降临之前，他就已经预见到了。死于心脏疾病的人，或者死于其他突发原因的人，其脸部不可能出现焦虑狂躁的表情。我闻了闻死者的嘴唇，结果闻到了一股淡淡的酸味。于是，我得出了结论，他死前被迫服过毒。还有，我坚持认为他是被迫服毒的，那是因为他的脸上充满着仇恨和惊惧。通过使用排除法，我得出了这样一个结论，因为没有任何别的假设与这些事实相吻合。千万不要认为，这是个什么闻所未闻的看法。强迫他人服毒绝不会是犯罪史上的什么新鲜事。敖德萨的多尔斯基案和蒙彼利埃的勒蒂里埃案都是毒物学家立刻能联想起的案件。

① peculiarly [pi'kju:liəli] *ad.* 尤其地
② trample ['træmpl] *v.* 践踏
③ slush [slʌʃ] *n.* 烂泥
④ nocturnal [nɔk'tə:nəl] *a.* 夜间的
⑤ exclusion [ik'sklu:ʒən] *n.* 排除
⑥ hypothesis [hai'pɔθəsis] *n.* 假说
⑦ toxicologist [ˌtɔksi'kɔlədʒist] *n.* 毒物学家

not been the object of the murder, for nothing was taken. Was it politics, then, or was it a woman? That was the question which confronted me. I was **inclined**① from the first to the latter **supposition**②. Political assassins are only too glad to do their work and to fly. This murder had, on the contrary, been done most deliberately, and the **perpetrator**③ had left his tracks all over the room, showing that he had been there all the time. It must have been a private wrong, and not a political one, which called for such a methodical revenge. When the inscription was discovered upon the wall I was more inclined than ever to my opinion. The thing was too evidently a blind. When the ring was found, however, it settled the question. Clearly the murderer had used it to remind his victim of some dead or absent woman. It was at this point that I asked Gregson whether he had inquired in his telegram to Cleveland as to any particular point in Mr. Drebber's former career. He answered, you remember, in the negative.

"I then proceeded to make a careful examination of the room, which confirmed me in my opinion as to the murderer's height, and furnished me with the additional details as to the **Trichinopoly cigar**④ and the length of his nails. I had already come to the conclusion, since there were no signs of a struggle, that the blood which covered the floor had burst from the murderer's nose in his excitement. I could perceive that the track of blood coincided with the track of his feet. It is seldom that any man, unless he is very full-blooded, breaks out in this way through emotion, so I **hazarded**⑤ the opinion that the criminal was probably a robust and ruddy-faced man. Events proved that I had judged correctly.

"Having left the house, I proceeded to do what Gregson had neglected. I telegraphed to the head of the police at Cleveland, limiting my inquiry to the circumstances connected with the marriage of Enoch Drebber. The answer was **conclusive**⑥. It told me that Drebber had already applied for the protection of the law against an old rival in love, named Jefferson Hope, and that this same Hope was at present in Europe. I knew now that I held the clue to the mystery

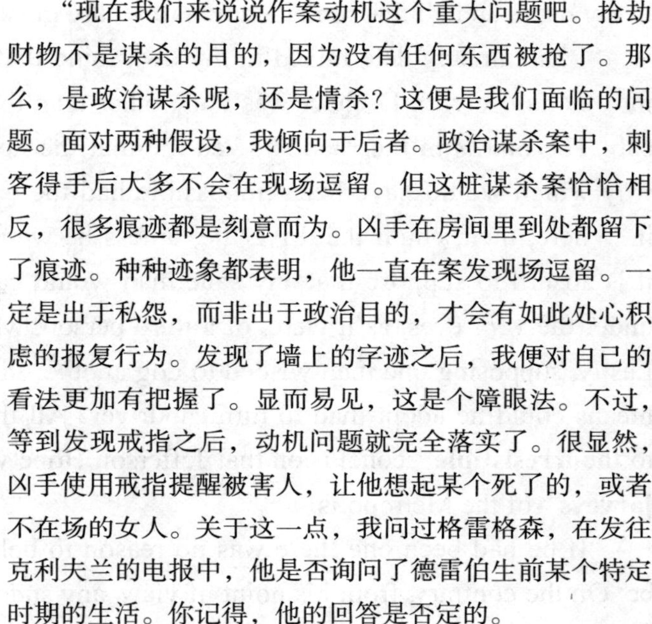

“现在我们来说说作案动机这个重大问题吧。抢劫财物不是谋杀的目的，因为没有任何东西被抢了。那么，是政治谋杀呢，还是情杀？这便是我们面临的问题。面对两种假设，我倾向于后者。政治谋杀案中，刺客得手后大多不会在现场逗留。但这桩谋杀案恰恰相反，很多痕迹都是刻意而为。凶手在房间里到处都留下了痕迹。种种迹象都表明，他一直在案发现场逗留。一定是出于私怨，而非出于政治目的，才会有如此处心积虑的报复行为。发现了墙上的字迹之后，我便对自己的看法更加有把握了。显而易见，这是个障眼法。不过，等到发现戒指之后，动机问题就完全落实了。很显然，凶手使用戒指提醒被害人，让他想起某个死了的，或者不在场的女人。关于这一点，我问过格雷格森，在发往克利夫兰的电报中，他是否询问了德雷伯生前某个特定时期的生活。你记得，他的回答是否定的。

“随后，我又对室内进行了仔细查看。查看的结果证实了我对凶手身高的判断，同时还给我提供另外一些细节，如特里其雪茄烟和凶手指甲的长度。既然没有发现搏斗的痕迹，证实了我先前就已经得出的结论，地板上的血是凶手因激动而流出的鼻血。我发现，血迹与足迹在方向上是一致的。一般人是不会这样的，只有血气过旺的人才会因情绪波动而出鼻血，因此我大胆推断：罪犯很可能是个身体健壮、脸色泛红的人。事实证明，我的判断是正确的。

“离开那幢住房之后，我接着做格雷格森忽略不做的事情，给克利夫兰的警察局长发了封电报，仅仅询问了一下伊诺克·德雷伯的婚姻状况。回电说得非常明确，德雷伯曾因昔日的情敌意图谋害他而请求法律保护。那个情敌的名字就叫杰弗逊·霍普，也就是眼下在欧洲的霍普。我这时已经明确了，自己手上已经掌握了谜案的线索，接下来要做的就是缉拿凶手了。

① incline [in'klain] *v.* 倾向于

② supposition [ˌsʌpə'ziʃən] *n.* 假定

③ perpetrator ['pə:pitreitə] *n.* 犯罪者

④ Trichinopoly cigar 特里奇雪茄烟（一种两端开口的印度雪茄烟）

⑤ hazard [hæzəd] *v.* 冒险作出

⑥ conclusive [kən'klu:siv] *a.* 确凿的

in my hand, and all that remained was to secure the murderer.

"I had already determined in my own mind that the man who had walked into the house with Drebber was none other than the man who had driven the cab. The marks in the road showed me that the horse had wandered on in a way which would have been impossible had there been anyone in charge of it. Where, then, could the driver be, unless he were inside the house? Again, it is absurd to suppose that any sane man would carry out a deliberate crime under the very eyes, as it were, of a third person, who was sure to betray him. Lastly, supposing one man wished to dog another through London, what better means could he adopt than to turn cabdriver? All these considerations led me to the **irresistible**① conclusion that Jefferson Hope was to be found among the **jarveys**② of the Metropolis.

"If he had been one there was no reason to believe that he had ceased to be. On the contrary, from his point of view, any sudden chance would be likely to draw attention to himself. He would probably, for a time at least, continue to perform his duties. There was no reason to suppose that he was going under an assumed name. Why should he change his name in a country where no one knew his original one? I therefore organized my Street Arab detective corps, and sent them systematically to every cab proprietor in London until they **ferreted**③ out the man that I wanted. How well they succeeded, and how quickly I took advantage of it, are still fresh in your recollection. The murder of Stangerson was an incident which was entirely unexpected, but which could hardly in any case have been prevented. Through it, as you know, I came into possession of the pills, the existence of which I had already surmised. You see the whole thing is a chain of logical **sequences**④ without a break or **flaw**⑤."

"It is wonderful!" I cried. "Your merits should be publicly recognized. You should publish an account of the case. If you won't, I will for you."

"You may do what you like, Doctor," he answered. "See here!" he continued, handing a paper over to me, "look at this!"

It was the *Echo* for the day, and the **paragraph**⑥ to which he pointed was

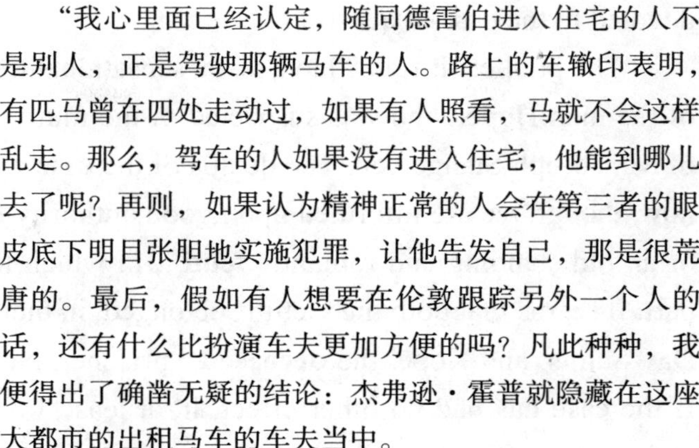

“我心里面已经认定，随同德雷伯进入住宅的人不是别人，正是驾驶那辆马车的人。路上的车辙印表明，有匹马曾在四处走动过，如果有人照看，马就不会这样乱走。那么，驾车的人如果没有进入住宅，他能到哪儿去了呢？再则，如果认为精神正常的人会在第三者的眼皮底下明目张胆地实施犯罪，让他告发自己，那是很荒唐的。最后，假如有人想要在伦敦跟踪另外一个人的话，还有什么比扮演车夫更加方便的吗？凡此种种，我便得出了确凿无疑的结论：杰弗逊·霍普就隐藏在这座大都市的出租马车的车夫当中。

“如果他充当了车夫的话，那就没有理由认为，他会改行不干了。恰恰相反，站在他的角度来看问题，突然变换工作反倒会引起人们的注意。因此，至少暂时，他会继续干他的营生。我们也没理由认为，他会改名换姓。他身处异国他乡，本来就没有任何人知道他原先的名字，他有何必要改名换姓呢？于是，我把那些流浪汉组织成街头侦察队，派他们全面调查伦敦的每家马车出租公司，直到找到了要找的人为止。他们干得有多么漂亮，我多么快捷地利用上了掌握到的信息，想必你记忆犹新吧。斯坦格森遇害的事情完全是个意外，出乎我的意料，但事情无法阻止。正如你知道的，通过这件事，我找到了那些药丸，其存在我早就已经预见到了。你看吧，整个事件就是一串逻辑因果的链条，环环相扣，中间没有任何断痕。”

“真是绝妙啊！”我大声说，“你的功劳应当得到公众的认可，你应当把案情叙述发表出来。如果你不发表，我来替你发表好啦。”

“你想要发表就发表吧，医生，”他回答说。“看这儿！”他接着说，递给我一张报纸，“看看这段文字。”

这是一份当天的《回声报》，他指给我看的那段正是有关本案的报道。其内容如下：

① irresistible [ˌiri'zistəbl] *a.* 不可抗拒的

② jarvey ['dʒɑ:vi] *n.* 二轮出租马车夫

③ ferret ['ferit] *v.* 搜索

④ sequence ['si:kwəns] *n.* 顺序

⑤ flaw [flɔ:] *n.* 裂缝

⑥ paragraph ['pærəgrɑ:f] *n.* 段落

devoted to the case in question.

"The public," it said, "have lost a sensational treat through the sudden death of the man Hope, who was suspected of the murder of Mr. Enoch Drebber and of Mr. Joseph Stangerson. The details of the case will probably be never known now, though we are informed upon good authority that the crime was the result of an old standing and romantic **feud**①, in which love and Mormonism bore a part. It seems that both the victims belonged, in their younger days, to the Latter Day Saints, and Hope, the **deceased**② prisoner, hails also from Salt Lake City. If the case has had no other effect, it, at least, brings out in the most striking manner the efficiency of our detective police force, and will serve as a lesson to all foreigners that they will do wisely to settle their feuds at home, and not to carry them on to British soil. It is an open secret that the credit of this smart capture belongs entirely to the well-known Scotland Yard officials, Messrs. Lestrade and Gregson. The man was **apprehended**③, it appears, in the rooms of a certain Mr. Sherlock Holmes, who has himself, as an amateur, shown some talent in the detective line and who, with such instructors, may hope in time to attain to some degree of their skill. It is expected that a **testimonial**④ of some sort will be presented to the two officers as a fitting recognition of their services."

"Didn't I tell you so when we started?" cried Sherlock Holmes with a laugh. "That's the result of all our Study in Scarlet: to get them a testimonial!"

"Never mind," I answered, "I have all the facts in my journal, and the public shall know them. In the meantime you must make yourself contented by the consciousness of success, like the Roman **miser**⑤—

"Populus me sibilat, at mihi plaudo
Ipse domi simul ac nummos contemplar in arca."

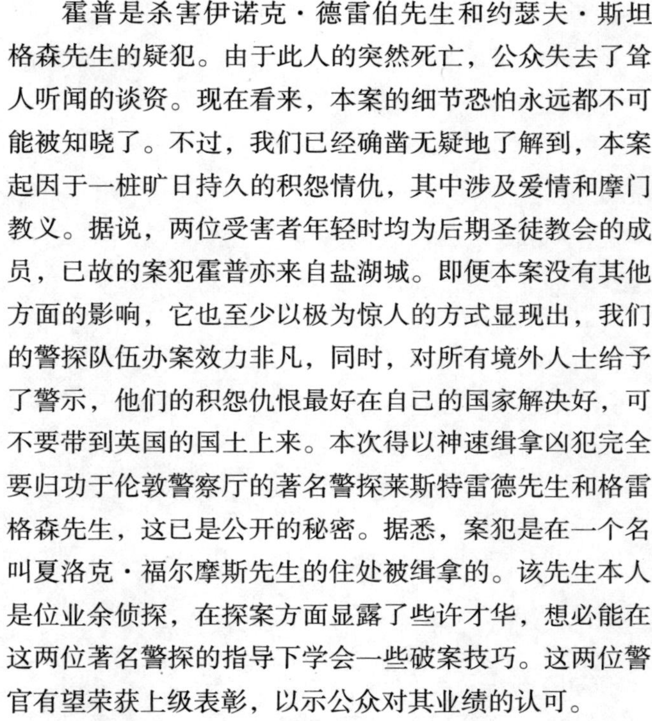

霍普是杀害伊诺克·德雷伯先生和约瑟夫·斯坦格森先生的疑犯。由于此人的突然死亡，公众失去了耸人听闻的谈资。现在看来，本案的细节恐怕永远都不可能被知晓了。不过，我们已经确凿无疑地了解到，本案起因于一桩旷日持久的积怨情仇，其中涉及爱情和摩门教义。据说，两位受害者年轻时均为后期圣徒教会的成员，已故的案犯霍普亦来自盐湖城。即便本案没有其他方面的影响，它也至少以极为惊人的方式显现出，我们的警探队伍办案效力非凡，同时，对所有境外人士给予了警示，他们的积怨仇恨最好在自己的国家解决好，可不要带到英国的国土上来。本次得以神速缉拿凶犯完全要归功于伦敦警察厅的著名警探莱斯特雷德先生和格雷格森先生，这已是公开的秘密。据悉，案犯是在一个名叫夏洛克·福尔摩斯先生的住处被缉拿的。该先生本人是位业余侦探，在探案方面显露了些许才华，想必能在这两位著名警探的指导下学会一些破案技巧。这两位警官有望荣获上级表彰，以示公众对其业绩的认可。

① feud [fju:d] *n.* 世仇

② deceased [di'si:st] *a.* 已故的

③ apprehend [ˌæpri'hend] *v.* 逮捕

④ testimonial [ˌtesti'məuniəl] *n.* 奖励

“我刚开始时不是对你说过了吗？”夏洛克·福尔摩斯说着，哈哈大笑了起来，“这就是我们研究血字的结果：为他们赢得表彰！”

“没有关系，”我回答说，“我把所有的事实都记录在日记里了，公众会知道真相的。在案件侦破过程中，成功的喜悦也一定会让你感到满足。就像那位古罗马的守财奴一样——

⑤ miser ['maizə] *n.* 吝啬鬼

任凭众人笑骂，我则充耳不闻。家有财宝万贯，自是了然于心。